'Poignant, passionate, deeply painful and profoundly inspiring in turn, it is a remarkable story by a remarkable person about remarkable moments in our history. I am challenged by it. The deepest and most searing aspects of the book are especially meaningful to those of us who went through the fires ourselves. Beyond Fear is a great gift, not just to Ebie's family, but to all humanity, with the magic of a fable and the hard brilliance of historical fact.'
ALBIE SACHS, ACCLAIMED AUTHOR AND FORMER JUSTICE OF THE FIRST CONSTITUTIONAL COURT OF SOUTH AFRICA, AND AUTHOR

'The serene voice of one of our most courageous and modest freedom fighters resonates beyond his last resting place, energising the living, decrying doubt, obliterating fear, jolting generations into action against all forms of racism, oppression and injustice. An inspirational memoir singing of survival against the odds and ultimate victory.'
RONNIE KASRILS, FORMER MINISTER OF INTELLIGENCE IN SOUTH AFRICA, AND MK VETERAN

'Beyond Fear is painfully honest and a beautiful historical account of the individuals who were willing to sacrifice insignificant comfort for our freedom. A true tribute to Ebrahim Ebrahim.'
JESSIE DUARTE, ACTING SECRETARY GENERAL OF THE AFRICAN NATIONAL CONGRESS

'There couldn't have been a more fitting title for this spell-binding account of Ebrahim Ebrahim's role in the South African struggle for freedom. His defiance of a ruthless political system whose stock in trade when dealing with resolute opponents was torture, beggars description.
'Incredibly, Ebrahim Ebrahim's extraordinary courage seems to have rendered him immune to the most sadistic methods of torture practised in apartheid prisons. Once he made up his mind that he was not going to betray anyone of his colleagues, that was it.

'Beyond Fear *is a must-read for anyone who wishes to learn about the commitment, sacrifices and exceptional courage the likes of Ebrahim Ebrahim made for South Africa to achieve freedom.*'
Mavuso Msimang, former member of the military high command of Umkhonto we Sizwe, and former Director-General in the South African Government

'*Ebrahim Ebrahim's biography takes us into this complex world of the liberation struggle and the actors who played a central role in shaping it. This 'quiet hero' began his own struggle history as a courageous 14-year-old, who refused to allow poverty and racial segregation to quell his spirit or take away his identity. Ebie, kidnapped, tortured and eventually detained on Robben Island during different periods, has never dwelled on his own pain and suffering at the hands of the apartheid state. Even when betrayed by close comrades, he asked the question "I wondered what kind of torture had led them to collapse and give way under detention and whether I had adequately prepared them for that very situation – this troubled me". Ebie's extraordinary story epitomizes the triumph of the human spirit, and his transcendence from torture to a state "beyond fear". It is a story of sacrifice, incredible humility and generosity and, above all, his absolute joy in finally being able to build a family with Shannon and his children. This book should be compulsory reading for students at high schools and university.*'
Yasmin Sooka, leading human rights lawyer, and former Executive Director of the Foundation for Human Rights

'*Ebrahim Ebrahim is a quintessential revolutionary. I shared a prison cell with him and other comrades on Robben Island for 10 of his 15 years of political imprisonment ... I also shared with him his brother and my fellow Africanist revolutionary Gora Ebrahim, one of the finest leaders of the Pan Africanist Congress of Azania.*

'*But as for Ebie, his every sinew, every moment and every thought for over 50 years was surrendered to the pursuit of equality and freedom. He was indeed beyond fear. His first stay on Robben Island should have deterred him but it did not. On his release from prison Ebie immediately rejoined the underground formations of Umkhonto we Sizwe. That led to his recapture in Swaziland, torture and another stint on Robben Island. Only brilliant lawyering and the pending death of apartheid brought respite to his life.*
'Beyond Fear *is an honest and gripping account of our history and of a*

remarkable revolutionary, who overcomes fear, displays endurance and rises to serve in our democratic transition and government. His gripping account culminates with Ebie finding love, a joyous marriage to Shannon and adorable children.'

Dikgang Moseneke, former Deputy Chief Justice of South Africa

'Comrade Ebie is a national hero to South Africa whose gentle nature, kind and benevolent in spirit, must be understood through the lens of his strength of conviction, his sacrifice, his pain and struggle in the quest for peace, freedom and prosperity for all. This forthright commitment is revealed in the pages of this intuitive book that at times reads like an epic novel of a compassionate giant and tells the many stories and sides of a true and honest activist. The book leaves one with a clear and deep appreciation of the greatest motivation for any action in life on earth, a commitment to humanity.

'Though the many years of torture and confinement on Robben Island, and even until his release, could have crushed any human soul, his was a roaring blaze of the struggle that ignited the will in many comrades across the globe to fight for justice and the end of apartheid. As a leader in exile, his trusted loyalty and calm demeanour acted as a source of power and a guiding light for many cadres through the grim shadows of battle.

'Admired and acknowledged for his noble qualities as a public servant, family man, community leader, mentor and loving friend, Comrade Ebie's courage to stay honest to himself for the sake of his country outlines a long string of outstanding achievements in all spheres of his life, and whom, beyond the limelight of power and politics, has made significant contributions to the growth and development of society. Comrade Ebie represents all of us, and he leaves us with an endowment of lessons that begs us to question our own duty, servitude and humility. His legacy continues to inspire us all and may this book be a guide to becoming gentle revolutionaries in our own communities.'

H.E. Kgalema Motlanthe, Former President of the Republic of South Africa, and former Secretary General of the African National Congress

'Commitment and Conviction do exist ... in Beyond Fear, Comrade Ebie says they reside in the political science of being, which even raging fire cannot extinguish ... they are of the human flesh, mind and spirit...'

Dr Mongane Wally Serote, National Poet Laureate in South Africa

Beyond Fear

Reflections of a Freedom Fighter

Ebrahim Ebrahim

First published by Jacana Media (Pty) Ltd in 2022

10 Orange Street
Sunnyside
Auckland Park 2092
South Africa
+2711 628 3200
www.jacana.co.za

© Ebrahim Ebrahim, 2022
© Cover photo: Liz Fish
Cover photo: Ebie on the ferry being released from Robben Island in 1991

All rights reserved.

ISBN 978-1-4314-3232-5

Also available as an ebook.

Cover design by publicide and Megan Mance
Editing by Russell Martin
Proofreading by Lara Jacob
Indexing by Megan Mance
Set in PSFournier Std 10/15pt
Printed by ABC Press, Cape Town
Job no. 003891

See a complete list of Jacana titles at www.jacana.co.za

*I dedicate this book to my beloved wife Shannon,
to my daughter Sarah, son Kadin, and elder daughter Cassia.*

Contents

Acknowledgements		xi
Foreword: The Quiet Hero		1
Prologue		7
1	The darkest of times	13
2	The confusing world of colour	17
3	Ma	23
4	The good doctors	27
5	The struggle became my life	35
6	Red Square	39
7	The regime panics	45
8	Lessons in politics	53
9	The walk on the bay	61
10	University for political purposes	69
11	A hiding place	73
12	The trouble begins	79
13	They always lie: The beginning of the Robben Island years	87
14	The despised	99
15	Beautiful Cassia	107
16	A story of sadness	109
17	University of Robben Island	119

18	The shock of what we did not know	127
19	Crossing the lines	135
20	Lenin and the blue Black Sea	147
21	Skylark in the bush	151
22	Life underground in Swaziland	161
23	Hélène Passtoors	167
24	Dutch support	183
25	Abduction by intelligence agents	187
26	Surviving torture in John Vorster Square	195
27	Trauma	205
28	On trial for treason	213
29	Statement from the dock	223
30	Second imprisonment on Robben Island	229
31	A landmark legal judgment	239
32	Forging the road to democracy	243
33	Lost opportunities	249
34	A great love story begins	257
35	Making a home	263
36	Revolutionaries never retire	267
37	Life starts at 70	273
38	Celebrating life at a time of loss	279
39	Closing the circle	283
Notes		287
Index		289

Acknowledgements

I WOULD LIKE TO SINCERELY thank Janet Smith for her many months spent editing and giving creative advice on this book. I will forever appreciate the selfless hours Janet spent turning my manuscript into a publishable book.

Foreword
The Quiet Hero

DURING THE SAME PERIOD in the early 1960s when Nelson Mandela was receiving military training from Algeria's FLN in Morocco, 'Rooi Rus' Swanepoel was receiving specialist training in psychological torture from French counterinsurgency experts in Algeria. Two and a half decades later these two trajectories were to clash in the body and mind of Ebrahim Ebrahim. How does one – as a kidnapped freedom fighter who has knowledge of the names and whereabouts of key combatants in the armed struggle against apartheid – survive the excruciating assaults on mind and body by the apartheid state's most notorious torturers? The answer? One gets *beyond* fear.

Beyond fear? What is fear? Should we even be beyond fear? These are questions I put to myself as I laid down this riveting memoir by my longtime friend and comrade, commonly known as Ebie. Chilling, passionate, painful and inspiring in turn, it is a remarkable story by a remarkable person about remarkable moments in our history. I am challenged by it. Isn't fear part of life; part of our inbuilt physiological defence system to alert us to real and imminent danger; part of acknowledging our humanity? But what happens when you get into a situation where all your body's alert systems are fully justified, the danger is real and overwhelming, and there is no way to escape the violence being physically enacted on your body and psyche?

Ebie writes: 'When I was abducted from the house I was staying in Pine Valley in Mbabane [in then Swaziland] in December 1986, I was not able to pack a single item – not a book, not a letter, not a toothbrush, not an extra pair of shoes. Two men had forced me into their car, as if through rendition. They had shot dead my courageous comrade Shadrack Maphumulo two days before that.' This was not the first time Ebie had been detained by the apartheid security forces. By that stage, he had already survived fifteen years of imprisonment on Robben Island, where he arrived just a few months before Nelson Mandela and from which he had eventually been released in 1979.

On the basis of his own hellish experiences of torture and his determination not to break, Ebie encourages us to get *beyond* fear. The security forces tried everything against him while he was detention. The information he had was vital. Had they wrenched it out of him, it would have destroyed the underground resistance. At one stage his torturer said to him, 'We are going to put you through something, and if you survive, I will be convinced that you are not human.' Still, he refused to answer questions about anything that had happened after his release from Robben Island in 1979. He 'refused to budge', and he remained the most human of human beings.

Where does this superhuman strength come from? One source was the intensity, implacability and richness of his idealism. Yet there is far more to it than that. He drew inspiration from the left-wing revolutionary struggle, and had the deep conviction that victory was on the horizon, and that the ANC's just cause was worth dying for. He regarded himself very much as an African who derived great strength from his Indian roots, and particularly absorbed himself in the ragas of Ravi Shankar's sitar. He recalls one occasion where, after years of hearing only prison sounds, the prisoners were allowed to broadcast music, and he managed to get hold of a Ravi Shankar record. When the warders heard it, they thought something had gone wrong with the sound system and called in an electrician!

The deepest and most searing aspects of the book are especially meaningful to those of us who went through the fires ourselves. However, for the general reader who, happily, hasn't known those fires, there is much, much more to this story. Ebie was born in Durban in 1937 – into 'a world of massive, obvious inequality'. Generations of people from South Africa's Indian community had gone to jail in passive resistance campaigns, as originally initiated by Mahatma Gandhi.

Ebie grew up knowing hunger and, as a child, brought in income for his family selling samoosas and popcorn made by his mother on Grey Street on Friday evenings. 'A samoosa or a bag of popcorn went for a penny each.' He paints a detailed and vital social history of a racially segregated Durban in the 1940s and 1950s, with an insider's view of Greyville and the characters and places that gave the suburb its particular, absurd, survivalist pulse. 'We went to movies at the magnificent 2,000-seater Shah Jehan movie house on Grey Street. That was owned by the Rajab brothers, who weren't gangsters but were very rich. There was also the Scala cinema, the Avalon, Raj and the Royal Picture Palace. It cost two shillings for the bioscope, and you could buy a Coke in a bottle for a tickey,' he writes.

> It was in those luxurious movie houses with their velvet seats, deluxe trimmings and air-conditioning that we fell in love with the Indian actors Bharat Bhushan and Meena Kumari, who were childhood sweethearts in *Baiju Bawra*. We laughed and cried as Raj Kapoor lost his heart to both Nargis and Nadira in *Shree 420*. Afterwards, we ate soft-serve ice cream. Those of us who didn't go to the matinees or dances at the Himalaya Hotel or the Bon Chance club had Milky Bar shakes, sweetmeats, curries, savoury snacks, cake and confectioneries at the Victory Lounge. Gangsters liked going there too, especially the ones who had a stake in the soccer clubs like Aces, which belonged to the Crimson League; Berea, which was owned by the Dutcheens; and Manning Rangers, which was linked to the Stiles gang.

Rich with real-life flavour, his descriptions are full of sensuous detail that transports the reader into the heart of the story *behind* the story – the choir festivals and gangster antics of an Indian community trying to make a go of life against the odds 'until the Group Areas axe fell on the backdrop to our lives'. This intensified the struggles of Indians in South Africa against the ferocious racism directed towards them. A disgusting Afrikaner nationalist rant at the time was 'K--- op you plek, C----- uit die land.'

Ebie mentions that the acceptance of armed struggle was far from easy for him. They started with homemade bombs using stolen explosives, attacking apartheid infrastructure, but with strong instructions not to endanger human life. Ebie went on to reconfigure the traits of the hero. Everything about his manner was mild. Softly spoken, he didn't impose himself in conversation. He was a great listener and offered his opinion when asked in a most modest, thoughtful way. I never heard him mobilising a crowd. He didn't have the posture, the strut or the voice of a hero. He saw himself as a servant of the people's struggle, rather than as a stirring leader. Yet the people he worked with loved and admired him for this very selflessness, for his courage, his intelligence and his sensitivity. Perhaps it was the very absence of masculinist frontage that made him especially attractive to those strong women comrades with whom he had intense love relationships.

Enthralling though the narrative is, from an emotional point of view this was not always an easy book for me to read. I don't know which was more challenging; remembering the taut brilliance of our idealism at the time, the intensity of the conviction of the best or recalling the constant dread that never went away even in the happiest of our moments, and the physical and mental distress inflicted upon us when we were captive.

Ever an optimist, Ebie recalled the spirit of Robben Island, where he and his fellow prisoners envisioned a 'new' South Africa. 'We were going to be the servants of the people. We were steadfastly against corruption, factionalism and ill-discipline. We condemned greed and the accumulation of wealth as we imbibed the values of comrades like Ahmed Kathrada, Harry Gwala, Stephen Dlamini, Zola Nqini, Reggie Vandeyar and others,' he writes. 'These values have become eroded, yes, but we must struggle to return to our core principles and the reasons why we took up the greatest fight of all.' He then quotes words by Nikolai Ostrovsky that inspired our generation: '[Every person's] dearest possession is life. It is given to [us] but once, and [we] must live it so as to feel no torturing regrets for wasted years, never know the burning shame of a mean and petty past; so that, dying, [we] might say: all my strength was given to the finest cause in all the world – the fight for the liberation of [hu]mankind.'

The intensity of our convictions was *us* – it was all around us. We lived by it. It bound us together. In Ebie's case it enabled him to withstand and survive the unendurable. I'm in love with its rapture and deeply mourn its passing. I'm saddened by the fact that it is not even understood or acknowledged by many in the present generation. And yet, and yet ... I'm terrified by the tyranny of its implacable beauty.

The book ends with Ebie embracing that implacable beauty. At the same time, he deeply welcomes the tenderness and generosity that came to him through a rich family life in his later years. Ebie's health in the more recent period had not been good. Though he never smoked a cigarette in all his life, he was operated on for lung cancer. The simple walks that he took with his children Sarah and Kadin became enormously meaningful to him. And he expressed his appreciation for the love, support and care that he received from them, as well as from his wife and great companion, Shannon, who brought him immeasurable personal happiness. 'You sit with me while I watch the news and try to finish this book, which is my gift to you and those who I will leave behind,' he writes. It is a great gift, and not just to them, but to all humanity, with the magic of a fable and the hard brilliance of historical fact.

Albie Sachs
Cape Town

Prologue

Dear Sarah and Kadin,

We've all packed a few boxes in our time, home being wherever those boxes are eventually unpacked. When you were three, Sarah, and you eighteen months, Kadin, we moved from our Silver Lakes home with its exuberant Mexican tiles to Bryntirion, the presidential estate in Pretoria. Every house there is a colonial mansion, each with its own history and eerie silence. I had been appointed deputy minister of foreign affairs.

You raced from one unknown end of our new garden to the other, preoccupied with whether I would let you get a rabbit at last. You were the only children on that graceful estate, riding your bicycles alongside the hedges and seeking out swings among the neighbours. You loved picking avocados and lemons off the trees and would picnic under the firs among the pine cones. The lawns would become lilac when the jacarandas bloomed in October.

Then there was the departure back to Silver Lakes, some twenty minutes away, when I retired. Packing up then was about finding some freedom, some noise. You probably remember the negotiations we had around what you could take and what we would let go. Our cats went with us. We left nothing behind.

Packing and moving were different experiences for me during my life before you were born. African American writer James Baldwin wrote in his acclaimed book *Giovanni's Room*: 'Perhaps home is not a place, but simply an irrevocable condition.' 'Home' had been a violent, uncertain situation of the mind for me for years, if not for decades. As you know, my first term of incarceration on Robben Island – where I arrived just a few months before Nelson Mandela – lasted for fifteen years. And even after I was released in 1979, I lived under a banning order. 'Home' was where the apartheid regime declared it would be, and it decided I could only stay in the Pinetown area of Durban. I couldn't be anywhere but in Reservoir Hills, an Indian suburb next to Westville, a predominantly white suburb.

Less than a year later, I left South Africa very suddenly in secret and thereafter I became accustomed to a suitcase, rather than a home, as a space sufficient to contain my identity and my needs. The African National Congress (ANC) had sent instructions that I was to proceed to Lusaka, Zambia, via neighbouring Swaziland and Mozambique. I did so. The few years that I later spent in the political underground in Swaziland required that I move from one safe house to another every six months to avoid detection and capture. Constantly changing locations meant 'home' was what I could pack.

In 1985, I slipped back into South Africa on a clandestine mission for the ANC, and then I began to live out of luggage undercover in Durban. I had to disappear during that time as I was being hunted by the security police. I even went into hiding in the basement of someone's house for a few months before I was smuggled back across the border to Swaziland again. I did not have the luxury of possessions during those precarious times. I mostly only had the clothes I was wearing. So any boxes of mine were smaller or fewer, or there were none, as I was constantly travelling around southern Africa until I returned to Swaziland in 1986.

When I was abducted from the house where I was staying in Pine Valley near Mbabane in December 1986, I was not able to pack a single item – not a book, not a letter, not a toothbrush, not an extra pair of shoes. Two men forced me into their car, to effect my rendition to Pretoria. They had shot dead my courageous comrade, Shadrack Maphumulo, two days previously. I was detained in Pretoria, where I was eventually charged with high treason in May and sentenced to twenty years' imprisonment in January 1989.

Would I really serve twenty years? Would we still be prisoners of war in the new century? I knew that was impossible as we were so close to victory. And, indeed, in early 1991 I was released after the courts found they had no jurisdiction to try me because I had been abducted from a foreign country. After two years of my second term of incarceration on Robben Island, a warder called me to the reception office one afternoon and told me I had won my case. He had been instructed to release me immediately.

As it was late in the afternoon, my first thought was, 'Where will I go when I get to Cape Town?' The boat was leaving in an hour, and I pleaded with the warder to let me remain until the morning, but he refused, as that was of course 'against the law'. I returned to what had been 'home' for two years – B Section, where Comrade Mandela and our political leadership had been imprisoned in single cells before being released or sent to other facilities some years earlier.

I had hardly enough strength to gather my few possessions, but I was as exhilarated as I was confused. Comrades put my lecture notes, my textbooks and a few other items in an apple box. Those apple boxes are familiar to all of us who were among the last political prisoners to be released. We were emotional as I said my farewells. The idea that there might be people I would never see again was on my mind as I embarked on the *Susan Kruger* ferry for the mainland. But unlike my first release from the Island, this time I knew it would be only a matter of months before many of my comrades still imprisoned there were also freed.

I looked back at that wretched prison as the icy Atlantic splashed against the sides of the old pleasure ferry once known as the *White Lady*. Diesel smoke poured into the vessel as we pushed away from Murray's Bay, helped along by a nippy south-easter. We gathered hardly any speed on the crossing, but this time I could watch the water and see both the island behind and the city ahead. A small group of us sat on the benches against the windows, while prisoners were kept below deck.

I had had my first sight of Cape Town in 1964 when I was on my way to the Island for the first time. People of Indian origin then weren't welcome to settle in the city and its surrounds, nor were Africans. The apartheid government had declared it a 'Coloured preference' area, but it was really a type of 'Coloured homeland', dotted with ghettos. Handcuffed and in leg irons, sixty-one of us ANC and PAC political prisoners were shoved roughly into the boat and down the stairs. We sat quietly in the recesses, not knowing what awaited us, but determined that our struggle would continue.

Waves pushing hard and irregularly against the boat had left us with terrible nausea on that first trip to Robben Island. I braced myself intensely for that awful sensation on my second trip from prison to the Cape Town mainland, and briefly wondered if I would ever experience it again. There are no guarantees in life. I thought about who would be there on the quay in Cape Town to greet me. Who would fetch me, and where was my home? The realisation suddenly grips you: you know your last ounce of energy is going to be needed to accept whatever and whoever is waiting for you on the other side. I fell quiet as the sea tossed around us, feeling somehow attached only to my cardboard box containing my most recent identity.

Then, a tumultuous cry surprised me. It rose above the rumble of the engines as we prepared to enter the harbour: 'Amandla! Viva, ANC!' Spread out in front of my eyes were scores of people on the quay. Their shouting and cheering, their fists in the air, their feet thumping on the stones, made my release instantly real. My imprisonment was over. It had ended. This was a new beginning.

There was a reception for me that day at Cowley House in Woodstock, which was a base for the families of political prisoners. When I saw again people I had known long before, it was as if our separation had merely been compressed between the walls of our various safe houses, jails and places of solitary confinement. We no longer had to hide or be afraid that we might expose one another.

After Comrade Tony Yengeni officially welcomed me on behalf of all those gathered there, I had one main thought to express during a brief media conference: my gratitude for the solidarity I had experienced. One of the reasons why that was important was to also extend an embrace from those I had left behind on the Island. We were now on our way to victory.

I stayed with my old friends, Omar and Naseema Badsha, in the suburb of Wynberg for a few days. This made it possible for many comrades – Steve Tshwete, Essop Pahad and Kader Asmal among them – to visit me and have tea. For the first time, I was able to walk about in public as I chose. Members of our family from Johannesburg flew down to Cape

Prologue

Town the day after I was released. So did my lawyer, Julie Mahomed, and she and I returned to the City of Gold together. I wish you could have seen the warm welcome from family and well-wishers at the airport there.

I have so much to tell you, yet you are my greatest teachers. I hope you will find something of value in my revolutionary stories.

Love now and always,
Dada

One
The darkest of times

IT WAS GETTING LATE, SO THEY ordered me back to my cell. When you're on the wrong side, the inside, of John Vorster Square, you can only tell it's dark outside by the empty sound from the street. It was midnight when a policeman arrived and said he had instructions to move me to another cell. Midnight feels like midnight, doesn't it? Your internal clock ticks you over into the next day, and when you're a political prisoner, that counts because it's one day less of remaining behind bars.

I ended up locked in cell number 221. That was probably the seventh or eighth cell I had been in over twenty-six years, and the third or fourth I'd been in alone. Dimensions widen or narrow when you're in isolation. It all depends on what's going on in your head.

I was drained that night. I had been questioned for hours on the tenth floor. I was asked about my background, which I readily gave; my childhood, joining the movement, my arrest, my trial, jail. But they already knew all of that, and I had nothing to hide in that respect. What I refused to answer was questions about anything that had happened after my release from Robben Island in 1979. I stayed committed to saying only one thing: complaining that I had been kidnapped from a foreign country. They made all sorts of threats, but I wouldn't budge. The torturer, Nicolas Deetlefs, got frustrated and then very angry. At one stage, he said,

'We are going to put you through something, and if you survive, I will be convinced that you are not human.' So, yes, I was drained of energy.

But the cell was odd. It was strangely placed and constructed on the second floor. When the grille banged shut, I knew the only way to accept that abnormality was to occupy it with my own presence. The other men in solitary confinement nearby were in hellholes where they were being tortured in terrible ways, left on their own to endure it, constantly tormented by policemen. I was aware that I had to immediately take control of my thoughts.

I had been separated completely. Why? When you're put in a cell like that, you must observe its smallest details. You must concentrate, as if you're breathing in to the count of three, and breathing out to the count of five. You might be exhausted, but you must look at every corner, starting at the bottom left and moving your eyes around with intent. This might be the last time you are so coherent; so use it.

Does the cell have windows? This one did: small, covered with thick perspex. Does it have a door with a grille? The grille was blocked. Was it possible to see outside? No way. And the lighting? This cell was very dimly lit. Looking up, I noticed the ceiling was covered with cardboard and plastic held together by wire mesh. There was a TV camera high up on one of the walls, but it seemed to be switched off. There was no red or green light flashing. There was no bed, no basin, no bucket, no chair. There was a mat and two blankets on the floor.

What was present, too, was piercing sounds. All sorts of sounds. They were concentrated and targeted at cell 221. I thought they came from prisoners on the upper floors of John Vorster, so I tried to ignore them. But the banging and clanging continued for the whole night.

As I said, you utilise whatever you have. I thought of my grandmother, Ma. When I was a child, she would lock up her grocery store in Effingham at the end of the day. The store was situated next to a quarry, and at the end of the day the rumbling of the huge 'golovans' full of stones finally stopped. But one's ears retained the rattling sound even when the drivers and diggers were singing at night. As I sat in my cell, I imagined the sound of the huge iron carts from the quarry amplified within the walls. And because there was no free-flowing air, I concentrated on the penetrating sounds that were like the knocking and creaking of buckets, rather than on the claustrophobic atmosphere. Then came other louder and more piercing sounds. They reminded me of the blackout drills in 1942 when we went into our house as soon as the air raid siren sounded. We would turn off the lights and shut the windows and draw the curtains. The first wails were the warning sounds – rising and falling, harder and softer. The second, a while later, was the all-clear – a single, continuing note. But this was not 1942 but 1987, and I was no longer a child during World War II but a fifty-year-old detainee probably facing the death sentence.

I was present, yes, and aware. Still, my brain soon felt fogged and my knees quickly began to feel weak. This continued the next day and the day after when the noise became more of an intermittent *boom!*: sharp and penetrating. Afterwards, it was as if someone was repeatedly throwing a folded wooden chair on the floor.

Two
The confusing world of colour

I HAD HAD LITTLE CONTACT with white people until 1949 when Ma moved to First Avenue in Greyville. This had been a white middle- and working-class area until the 1930s, when Indians moved in, rendering the suburb 'mixed' until it was declared a slum. After the Group Areas Act of 1950 was implemented, the area eventually became off limits to Indians.

I was a twelve-year-old boy of colour who was immediately thrown into a world of massive, obvious inequality. I was now living right inside a city where the parks and the beaches, the playgrounds, benches and eating places were 'reserved for whites only'. We couldn't use the same buses or go and see a movie with whites. The Post Office had separate entrances.

At times I would go to a tall building in the city to pay accounts for my uncle. The lifts were for whites only, although some of the owners let us use the goods lift at the back. I felt as a child that some human beings were behaving as if they were superior. I hated that. I couldn't understand it. I didn't want to have to exist like that.

Greyville was convenient, but it made our inferior opportunities glaringly obvious. We viewed whites from the periphery as we were not permitted to mingle with them. We often felt like taking off our shoes and running onto any beach we liked to feel the sand between our toes and the warm waters of the Indian Ocean. But, depending on the beach, that could have been illegal, and we could have been arrested. Only white children could frolic in any waves they fancied.

If Ma got tired while we walked to the beach, it was difficult to find somewhere for her to sit down. But history shows us that social interactions in Durban were racially segregated long before the formal introduction of apartheid in 1948. Bay Beach on the harbour side was developed in 1857, and then reserved for the use of white residents. And the more remote, rougher strand known as Back Beach only came into use after the turn of the twentieth century. Renamed Ocean Beach, the area was then transformed into a picture-postcard seaside with piers, boardwalks and a swimming enclosure – for white bathers.

Yet racial segregation of beaches was only officially introduced by Natal Provincial Notice 206 of 1930. A stretch of sheltered water at Vetch's Pier – a famous reef packed with mussels and other marine life – was in fact set aside for African bathers in 1929, although without any facilities or lifeguards. Not long afterwards, this pleasant lagoon was made exclusive to white snorkellers and surfers.

We knew where we didn't 'belong' right from the time of my earliest memories of living in Durban, even if the Reservation of Separate Amenities Act only came about in 1953. It was amended to include more beaches as late as 1960, followed by further regulations, with all the safest and most convenient spots reserved for whites. The famous 'African Bathing Beach' was relocated to the renamed Laguna Beach, and although there were efforts to 'relax' the racial restrictions during the late 1970s and 1980s, we were only truly 'allowed' on the beaches from as late as October 1990. All of these restrictions explain why I never learned how to swim.

White people called Greyville the 'coolie location'. It was a lower middle-class area, but also had a working-class section called the Magazine Barracks where thousands of Indian people had been housed in wood-and-iron homes after their indentures expired. Most worked as cheap government labour and would later be forcibly removed to Chatsworth. What whites probably didn't know was that Grey Street hosted Lakhani Chambers, where the ANC and a few trade unions and anti-colonial organisations had their offices. The Natal Indian Congress (NIC) was based in Saville Street, and not far from there was Red Square.

There was plenty more that whites did not know. We knew they would not have been able to deal with the ruthless Salot brothers and their sister Bebee. We spoke about the Salots, or the 'K' gang, in hushed voices. Old Man Salot (Moosa Ebrahim, or 'Bareen', which is Gujarati for 'bully'), 'Lighty', 'Dawood', 'Mascot' and 'Gloves' were thugs from Overport, an Indian area in a hilly part of Durban. Their various children were chauffeured to school in a Buick, a Lincoln or a Pontiac, depending on the day. The Salots, who were Gujarati and Muslim, ran a taxi business, among other things, and we had heard that Indian girls were not safe around their ranks.

Whites knew even less of the Crimson League, who had run the show in the Durban 'central Asiatic area' since the end of World War II. Their goal was to 'turn the streets Crimson', and if they had to do so in cahoots with white policemen, so be it. Everybody feared the leaders of the League – Big Daddy (a Hindu butcher and the crime king of the Casbah), Pine Mohammed (who owned a hardware store), Akie Vahed (a tailor) and Max Moola (who owned a snooker saloon). They ran an army of dozens, if not hundreds, of 'soldiers' on the streets, with a preference for Indians as they supported Indian nationalism. The Salot brothers had no such preference. They employed some Coloureds and a few Africans among the dozens of Indians who were their runners.

Our family knew the Crimson League a little more intimately as a relative of ours had married a gang member. But no matter whom you knew or how much protection money you coughed up, no place was safe when the League fought it out with the Salot brothers. They would take their battles to the casbah, which centred on the Grey Street business district and the west end of West Street, and we knew to keep our distance when the beatings, stabbings and shootings began.

Anglicised from the Arabic, our version of the 'qasba' was no citadel, but it was our playground. It was where we could be free for a while from the relentless oppression of South Africa. We went to movies at the magnificent 2,000-seater Shah Jehan movie house on Grey Street. It was owned by the Rajab brothers, who weren't gangsters but were very rich. There was also the Scala cinema, the Avalon, the Raj and the Royal Picture Palace. It cost two shillings for the bioscope, and you could buy a Coke in a bottle for a tickey. It was in those luxurious movie houses with their velvet seats, deluxe trimmings and air-conditioning that we fell in love with the Indian actors Bharat Bhushan and Meena Kumari, who were childhood sweethearts in *Baiju Bawra*. We laughed and cried as Raj Kapoor lost his heart to both Nargis and Nadira in *Shri 420*. Afterwards, we ate soft-serve ice cream.

Those of us who didn't go to the matinees or dances at the Himalaya Hotel or the Bon Chance club had Milky Bar shakes, sweetmeats, curries, savoury snacks, cake and confectioneries at the Victory Lounge. Gangsters liked going there too, especially the ones who had a stake in the soccer clubs like Aces, which belonged to the Crimson League; Berea, which was owned by the Dutcheens; and Manning Rangers, which was linked to the Stiles gang. The Dutcheens ran the dagga (marijuana) underground from Old Dutch Road, while the Stiles gang were bare-fisted fighters whose name came from the 1948 movie *The Street with No Name*. Its main character was a raincoat-wearing gang boss named Alec Stiles. There were also choir festivals at the Tamil Vedic Society, and music, music, music – our music.

One morning, 'Lighty' Salot took his second wife, Eunice, to see Mrs Habiba Khan, a dressmaker who operated from her house in Umgeni Road. 'Lighty' waited in the car outside. I lived in the area with my uncle and his family, and I was out in the streets when I heard a loud scream. I hadn't noticed two American cars pulling up, but there was 'Lighty' trying to get away from the hitmen by running into the house. Moments later, members of the Crimson League ran out and rushed into the cars. I found out later that they had battered 'Lighty' to death with an iron bar in Mrs Khan's house, but I didn't tell anyone what I had seen – not even my uncle. This all took place in 1954. The death of 'Lighty' was so sensational that it was even serialised as a crime story in *Drum* magazine at the time.

Members of the clan visited my uncle now and again, so I wasn't surprised when another Salot brother asked him, in my presence, whether he had any information about who could have been the killer. I kept dead quiet, because the Crimson League tended to be on the side of the Natal Indian Congress, whose activities I had started following as a teenager. We were also all afraid of the gangs. That was just how it was.

What was I going to do? I too had my secrets. I was glad I'd said nothing because, a few months later, a man by the name of Michael John was named as the killer. Michael John had been at Sastri, the same Indian boys' school I attended. He was killed with tomahawks, knives and iron bars by members of the Crimson League because he had started his own gang after the murder of 'Lighty'. He had fallen out with the League over money and tried to take over their turf. That was in 1955, and everybody knew what was happening when the trial took place. It was in the papers, it was on the radio. The seven accused got away without being convicted even though there were witnesses who were prepared to testify. It was unbelievable. Not many people would usually report or testify about what they saw, and neither did I.

The theory was that the gangsters were paying off Indian and white policemen and the judges, who were all whites. The thing was that there wasn't much crime prevention or detective work in our areas because the government was only committed to hunting down and prosecuting 'non-whites' who broke its apartheid laws. For the rest, it often turned a blind eye. If Indians wanted to beat each other up, have gunfights or extort money, we were more or less left alone to do so. And it suited the government if we didn't get along with the African or Coloured communities because it could then say that its Group Areas Act, which separated the 'race' groups from each other, was justified. That law had quickly followed the pogroms carried out by Africans against Indians in Durban in 1949. I remember those times with deep dread. Whites eagerly watched those riots unfold because they had no love for us: Indians were their competitors.

We were always struggling, not only politically. Our underworld was also about taking control of our own spaces and lives, however desperate or destructive the criminal activities might have been. I didn't venture into violence, but I did enjoy playing the popular betting game fah-fee, in which you backed numbers from 1 to 36 for 6d (sixpence) using a number with a special meaning to you. If your number was 'pulled' by the 'Chinaman', you would win 6s (six shillings), which was a fair bit of cash. The street lotto was controlled by the Crimson League, which was something everybody seemed to know, at least before Michael John started his own gang and muscled in. The story went that his strongmen forced the Indian waiters who worked in the hotels on the Durban beachfront to play so that his hoodlums would have a steady income.

My family would sometimes give me some cash on weekends to go to an agent in May Street to put money on 'umchina'. The lucky number I chose was drawn from my dreams. The 'mo-china', the runner, received the winning number from roving providers who operated the games and indicated with their hands which was the winning number. I mostly lost, though occasionally I was lucky.

Such was life in our Indian community – until the Group Areas axe fell on us.

Three
Ma

WE HAVE A BIT OF A mixed-up family history, and so I'll tell it to you traditionally, in layers. My earliest memory is of crossing a wooden bridge as we exited from the small railway station to get over the Umbilo River. Then my grandmother and I would walk over a hill to reach our property next to Effingham's quarry. The sound of motors humming and steam hissing on the tracks died away as we drew closer to home. I would watch our shadows – mine and Ma's – gliding on the sand.

Nature didn't recognise the Ghetto Act, which defined my childhood, because I remember miles of rich sugar plantations folding into the lush green bush all around our area. That law was designed to stop Indians from owning property in white areas, but the Durban vegetation didn't discriminate, and neither did the subtropical heat, which seemed to last almost throughout the year. Ma and I spent a lot of time together in that humid environment where there were still red and white mangroves and tall milkwood trees. There were monkeys, too, and colourful butterflies, crickets constantly clicking, frogs croaking, flycatchers, herons, battalions of ants and hedges of hibiscus.

We had a brick house while others had houses of corrugated iron. I was never alone as a child. Like many Indian families, we had a large, extended family set-up and I lived in the house with my Uncle Cassim and Aunty

Mary, and my cousins Zubeida and Goolam. We didn't speak English all the time at home; very few Indian people did. Most families living there spoke Bhojpuri, a beautiful dialect of the Bihar state in eastern India. We also spoke Urdu, which is now the official language of Pakistan.

I have a clear memory that my cousin Goolam disappeared when he grew up, and we all assumed he had died. To this day we don't know what happened to him, but his sister Zubeida would later raise a large family. Each of their histories became part of my story. Our family's cross-continental interlacing and looping through class and race sewed us all together.

I remember sitting around an 'imbawula', a four-gallon paraffin tin with holes into which we put coal to make a fire. The good company consisted of Ma, my cousins and our neighbours in Effingham. Daliet lived next door to us in Effingham. He introduced me to the history of Shaka Zulu around that 'imbawula', and I remember how I played hide-and-go-seek with his son, 'umfana Kanina'. Many of my friends at that time were African children because we lived in a rural area, and there weren't many Indians there. I wonder if 'umfana Kanina' and I would recognise each other now.

Ma would tell us about the terrors of the 1918 Spanish flu epidemic, which was brought to Durban by the ships. Only when Covid-19 arrived in 2020 did I properly understand what Ma had been through. Many Indian people were still travelling by ship at the time to make a new life in South Africa as British subjects. Our forebears, who were hoping to get away from the caste system which impoverished them, were enslaved through markets in Calcutta and Madras and sent to work on the sugar cane farms in Natal. That slavery took place over the course of fifty years, during which 150,000 people were brought from Madras, Agra, Bengal and Oudh to South Africa. They weren't the same as the 'passenger Indians', who were mainly from Gujarat and came to South Africa voluntarily, planning to start businesses using their own means.

I wish I knew more, but I do know that my dad was from Gujarat in north-west India, and he came here as part of a family in South Africa who registered him as their child. He was born Mohamed Adam Modan, but assumed the surname Ebrahim, as that was the surname of the family with whom he travelled to South Africa. Thus I also became an

Ebrahim. The unusual way in which I inherited my name forms part of the complicated stitching of our family history.

My grandfather was from the village of Chasa in the mainly Muslim region of Alipore in Gujarat. Alipore is the site of a great legend, and it is said to have been chosen by Ali, a relative of the Prophet who migrated there from Hadhramaut in south Arabia, or what is modern-day Yemen. Others then also migrated there to find spiritual comfort in Ali, who became a religious leader. In the 1880s, numbers of people from Alipore migrated to South Africa, most of them entering through Durban.

Ma's oldest daughter, Hafiza Bibi Khan, was my mother, but she was never 'mum' to me. I never knew Ma's husband, my grandfather, Abdul Majid Khan, who was said to be a disciplinarian. Maybe it's better that I never fell under his shadow.

My parents settled in Brits in what was then the Transvaal province of the Union of South Africa, and I was born there. My father ran a small shop but he went bankrupt – a serious liking for racehorses was the cause of that. My mother fell ill when I was just a few months old, and Ma agreed to take care of me in Durban. I was taken back to my parents in Brits when I was about two years old, but I refused to stay there because of my longing for my grandmother Sarah. I was so homesick for my grandmother who had raised me that I stopped eating. Sarah then had to fetch me and we went home to Effingham. That's why I called her Ma and grew up with her.

It barely mattered that we were the only Muslims among mainly Hindu families. We were invited to every local gathering, and my most striking memories of the community are of the weddings where Indian folk music was performed for the bride or the groom throughout the night. Whenever I hear the loud 'chak' rim beating on a dholak, the two-headed wooden hand drum, my mind is filled with images of that time. I catch a glimpse in my imagination of the open dance floor at the festive sangeet before a wedding. Those same musical triggers would give me comfort decades later when I was doing military training with Umkhonto we Sizwe (MK) in the Angolan bush, and was able to listen to Indian music on the radio.

We shared so much pleasure listening to the radio in my uncle's car on Sundays. There was half an hour of Indian music and half an hour of Zulu music, and I would lie on the back seat with the doors open, comatose with the love of it all. Sundays were the only time we were blessed to hear both forms of music on the radio.

Being denied our music on the other six days of the week was not the most important effect of apartheid on us. There was a battle to get me into school because there were very few places open for children of Indian origin. I remember that Ma took me to school at the beginning of the school year, every January from the age of six, only to be told there was 'no more place, try again next year'. It bothered her that I was ten years old when I finally got admission to the Hindu Tamil Institute, a government-aided school which worked on a 'pound-to-pound' principle: if the community raised £1, the government would also contribute £1. It was overcrowded and we had hardly any money for the ordinary things that a child would wish for. That was a source of sadness for me. That I could speak and read Urdu and English was the only benefit. Even textbooks and stationery would have been an additional burden for Ma and my parents.

My father didn't have any formal education, although he could read and write Gujarati. My mother had no education at all. History weighed heavily on us.

Four
The good doctors

THE 'GERMAN WAR', AS THE adults in my childhood called World War II, came between the time of my birth and my being admitted to school. I spent several years of my life anticipating sunset and the air-raid siren. It was like being in some sort of prison. It was as if we couldn't move. I was too young then to understand there were actual jail cells with no sight of the wide, dark sky or a homely ceiling.

General JBM Hertzog was no longer in power when the war began in 1939. By that time, he had already done plenty of damage. When I was born, he had shepherded through Parliament a number of 'Native Bills', which took away the vote from qualified African voters in the Cape, forbade Africans to buy land except where the government said they could, and restricted their ability to look for work besides that on white-owned farms or white-owned mines. Hertzog's National Party was determined to crush any signs of African, Coloured or Indian ascendance. It had long been clear, even before I was born, that white domination was the order of the day. Modern resistance to the oppression of black people in South Africa started to take shape in the 1930s when Dr AB Xuma – the first and at that time the only Western-trained African physician in Johannesburg – attracted international attention for his criticism of the government. (He later became president-general of the ANC.)

Then came the war. Our shadows moved around us as we bathed, ate supper and went to bed. It was an isolating sensation even when the house was full of people. When it got darker, before I fell asleep, I lay on my bed looking around me thinking about sweets, but there weren't any. Our greatest worries were about how to get rice and bread. Even after the war ended, we children stood in queues to buy rice. I remember feeling anxious while queuing because Ma was concerned about having enough to feed us. Families were allowed only one pound of rice each. I wonder if my attraction to communism and the Congress movement started then. We seemed to believe we only got rice because members of the Communist Party raided the warehouses of the rogue Indian merchants who were hoarding it to sell it at black market prices. The raiders would bring the rice out onto the pavements and sell it to us for 7d a pound. Meanwhile, bakeries around the country were ordered not to bake white bread because the government was exporting wheat to Britain and the Netherlands. This caused huge shortages for the South African people.

But these troubles – how to keep a little food on the table – were not the only subject of political conversation in our home. Not long after the war ended, the family would talk about the United Nations, which was founded in October 1945. Its posters were pasted around the city, showing people of many nations standing together as if there was a secret brotherhood out there beyond Durban. That is still vivid in my mind. I recall too that people were horrified by the reports of the Nazi concentration camps, and everybody celebrated the defeat of the Germans.

But I wonder if I retain the memory of any of these events as much as I do of the struggles of the people of India for independence. I was only eight at the time. Most Indian homes hung portraits of Mahatma Gandhi, Jawaharlal Nehru and Subhas Chandra Bose, and Muslim homes also had portraits of Maulana Kalam Azad and Muhammad Ali Jinnah. How we all hated British colonial rule. India had to be free! As a child, I was a vociferous Indian nationalist. But then came the partition of the country into the two dominions of India and Pakistan in 1947, dividing Hindus and Muslims and creating a massive migration on religious lines. The brutality shocked us. We heard stories of mass murder and general violence, and it felt as if it was happening to us too, as our extended families thousands of miles away in India, whom we hadn't met, were caught up in it.

In the beginning, it seemed so contrary to what we knew of India and believed in: 'satyagraha', a term I first heard in 1946. Gandhi introduced this form of non-violent resistance or civil resistance: 'satya' means 'truth' and 'āgraha' means 'insistence' or 'holding firmly to' in Sanskrit; thus 'satyagraha' means 'holding firmly to truth'. I gazed at resisters in Durban wearing the white Gandhi side-cap, which Britain had tried to ban in India. Gandhi wore it out of cultural pride, to show solidarity with India's masses. Nehru was also famous for wearing the cap. You may have noticed too that many people wearing Gandhi caps stood behind the African American civil rights leader Martin Luther King Jr when he gave his 'I Have a Dream' speech in 1963.

There were two names as big as Gandhi's in our community in the 1940s: Dr Yusuf Dadoo and Dr Monty Naicker, both of whom had a monumental influence on us. Dr Dadoo, who was Muslim, was chair of the South African Indian Congress (SAIC) and the Communist Party (CPSA), and a leader of the Defiance Campaign. Dr Naicker, who was Hindu, joined the trade union movement before he became president of the Natal Indian Congress (NIC). They promoted passive resistance, but, more importantly, when they took over and radicalised the SAIC in 1945, the unifying effect of one being Muslim and the other Hindu bolstered our common identity while the partition of India was happening. They focused us against the common enemy in our own country – white nationalism. Even today, Muslims and Hindus are not enemies in South Africa. Religion has never really been a problem for us. We are neighbours and, most of us, patriots.

The United Party government of Jan Smuts – which took the side of Britain in World War II – rejected nationhood in India, and it also didn't want Indians integrated into South African society. So they made it as difficult as possible for us to be Indian and South African at the same time. As for the opposition National Party, led by the Afrikaner church minister DF Malan, its 'Programme of Principles', while accepting Africans and Coloureds as 'permanent members of the country's population' who fell under the 'Christian trusteeship of the European races', declared that 'all groups' of the population had to be 'protected' from 'Asiatic immigration and competition ... by preventing further encroachment on their means of livelihood, and by an effective scheme of segregation and repatriation'.[1] This stance towards Indians intensified over the next ten years and created serious insecurity among our community. I didn't have the understanding at the age of eleven to comprehend that whites were 'citizens' and all the rest of us were 'non-citizens', but at least I knew we were standing together against the 'citizens'.

In 1948, in the lead-up to the general elections, there were huge posters of Malan and Smuts pasted all over the walls of the railway stations. Our parents couldn't vote, but we still had to see those faces. We – the Indians, Africans and Coloureds – didn't count as human beings of any substance. Although we played some role in the election as a symbol of what white racists feared, the actual process only benefited whites. All whites could go to the polls as well as a few Coloureds; but no one else.

For us, there was another underlying tension. The National Party of Malan had gone into an electoral alliance with the small Afrikaner Party of General Hertzog (after the latter was defeated by Smuts on the issue of participation in the war), and one of its policies was that we would be forced to 'go back' to India. The party proposed a scheme of 'voluntary repatriation', offering a sum of money to those who agreed to leave. The alternative – compulsory segregation – was designed to strangle our community. The National Party, which won the 1948 election by a small majority, was like the National Socialist German Workers' Party (the Nazis), which is why people called Malan 'Malanazi'.

After the National Party came into power, we weren't surprised – even if we were shocked and harmed – when 'riots' broke out in Durban in 1949 involving Africans and Indians. I was twelve. This was a pogrom in which two days of violence claimed dozens of lives and created tens of thousands of Indian refugees. The attack started in the Indian commercial centre around Victoria Street with assaults and the stoning of cars. But once that was contained, it spread to residential areas.

I was affected by the events all over again when I recently read Professor Donald L Horowitz's book *The Deadly Ethnic Riot* (2001), which examined dozens of 'intense, sudden, lethal attacks by civilian members of one ethnic group on another'. Indians and Africans had lived cheek-by-jowl in areas like Cato Manor; the Indians were employed mostly as shop owners and farmers. When the tide turned against us, our shops and homes were looted and burned. Indians had to flee to refugee centres. Even Ma and I had to change locations according to where we would be safest. I remember the hollowed-out feeling even as a child of something terrible going on, over which I had no control. I judge that awful sensation by the impact especially of the murders which took place during the riots. According to the historians Surendra Bhana and Bridglal Pachai, in their *Documentary History of Indian South Africans*, the 'loss of life and property was officially given as follows: deaths; 142 (87 Africans, 50 Indians, 1 white and 4 others whose identity could not be determined); injured; 1,087 (541 Africans, 503 Indians, 11 Coloureds and 32 whites; of the injured 58 died); buildings destroyed: 1 factory, 58 stores and 247 dwellings; buildings damaged: 2 factories, 652 stores and 1,285 dwellings)'.

We were frightened. Indian people were fleeing. There were suicides as families were separated and businesses destroyed. At the very least, Indians were subjected to insults and psychological trauma. It was known that some whites assisted Africans to commit violence against Indians until the South African Navy was called in to put an end to the riots. Their intervention then saw many African people killed – this time by the Navy. It took the leadership of the ANC and the NIC to restore some calm.

Few conversations at our home, with our neighbours and in the streets were not about the bloodshed. To some people, the riots were regarded as 'the Battle of Cato Manor'. Some people were honest about the fact that African people had suffered as the result of extortion by Indian slumlords, and we knew that not everyone had the interests of their fellow human beings at heart. Some of the Indian merchants were exploiting us by selling goods at high prices. But there was more to the events of 1949 than strife between Africans and Indians. Black people – African, Indian and Coloured – had been under siege since the time of Union in 1910. Our parents' and grandparents' generations had been through terrible battles just to stay alive.

To an extent, we could see that the government's aim was to push us out of our neighbourhoods, our cities and our country until most of us identified as 'Indian' were gone. But where to? To me, 'Indianness' lay in things like khandvi sprinkled with coriander and coconut. As a Muslim child, I was schooled in Islamic prayers and the reading of the Holy Quran. I had learned of the wars of jihad waged by the Holy Prophet of Islam. We grew up listening to the call of the muezzin from the minaret five times a day, declaring to the world the universality of humankind.

All of us who were not white experienced common oppression, but in an ordinary office building in Durban called Lakhani Chambers, unity against dispossession was being forged. The NIC executive committee spent the entire first night of the pogrom of 1949 in those offices to deal with the crisis. I found out later that it was their efforts which resulted in the refugee camps being set up to support the Indian community. Although I didn't know at the time about the 1947 pact between Drs Xuma, Dadoo and Naicker (known as the Doctors' Pact), the strength of that bond between Indian and African leaders was also honoured that night. The pogroms ended up bringing about a rethinking of African nationalism within the ANC Youth League, and an even closer relationship with Indian leaders in the 1950s.

I knew about workers power from a young age thanks to Ma, who told me about the Industrial and Commercial Workers' Union. She often spoke about it, and I was influenced by her.

In March 1950, when I was not yet thirteen, the ANC announced there would be a general strike on 1 May to challenge a host of unjust laws and increasing oppression by the National Party, which by then had been in power for almost two years. The ANC held a mass meeting in Johannesburg's Market Square to publicise the strike, and afterwards there was a Defend Free Speech Convention to protest against the prohibitions on prominent activists like Dr Dadoo and the Communist leader Sam Khan.

Some five hundred delegates, representing their various organisations – which, in turn, were estimated to have a combined membership of more than a million – attended that convention in Johannesburg. The ANC Youth League stood out because of the presence of its dazzling young leader, Nelson Mandela, who was then a firebrand of a lawyer.

I don't know if, at that stage, I fully grasped the occasion. What I do know is that our communities were under attack. Many people were frightened. And as 1950 went on and the Group Areas Act was promulgated, even we children could feel the impact of apartheid on our parents and grandparents. They were not free to come and go, and that damaged us too.

There were big issues at play in our movement, too. Behind the scenes, schisms were forming in the ANC. Dr Xuma would in fact resign from the National Executive Committee (NEC) of the ANC over the decision to stage actions like boycotts and strikes. Mandela would then take Xuma's place on the NEC. But Mandela was himself not resolved about the role of the Communist Party as a partner of the ANC. As a Christian, he was conflicted over communism, and he took a while to accept the Communist Party's 'multiracialism', coming as he did from a strong Africanist tradition.

During the May Day protests, the police opened fire and killed eighteen people, wounding thirty others. The regime then banned all public meetings. The country was like a pressure cooker.

Five
The struggle became my life

I AM PROUD TO SAY I WAS present at the start of the great Defiance Campaign on 26 June 1952. There was going to be another whites-only election in 1953, and the National Party was holding rallies around South Africa to mark three hundred years since the arrival of the Dutch colonialist Jan van Riebeeck at the Cape. Our movement staged its own large rallies in response, to protest against the unjust laws passed by the racist government after its victory in 1948. I was fourteen, and so impassioned by this rebellion that I decided to join the youth wing of the Natal Indian Congress. (We could not, of course, join the ANC until after the ANC's pivotal Morogoro conference in Tanzania in 1969.)

Yet as liberating as 1952 was for an impoverished boy with almost no prospects, it was also traumatic. That was the year Ma died. She had been everything to me. She was both a mother and a friend whom I loved dearly. I was grateful when she made sure I could continue living with her and my two uncles and their wives and children. We were a close family. As our lives were determined for us from the cradle to the grave by racists, there was not much pleasure in my childhood. My family was everything for me, as it is now.

But there had been a tug of war between my parents and Ma as to where and with whom I should live once I was at school, and that stress contributed to my developing a stutter.

Before Ma moved to Greyville, I had stayed with my parents in Durban, where they rented a two-room unit in Hatia Flats in the Indian part of Prince Edward Street. Being a resident of the Transvaal when he became bankrupt, my dad was in fact prohibited from living in Natal, so he stayed illegally in the city. I have memories of the police raiding our flat, arresting my father and deporting him to the Transvaal. But he always found a way of getting back to us, as he was asthmatic and couldn't find work there anyway.

We had a tiny kitchen with a fireplace and chimney. My parents couldn't afford a stove, and instead used two iron bars held up by some bricks under which we burned some wood. A fridge was unthinkable. We five children – Gora, who was two years older than me, our two younger sisters Fatima and Ayesha, and younger brother Essop – slept on mattresses on the floor. Our parents slept on the only bed we had.

My mother, an enterprising person, kept body and soul together by making earrings out of copper wire, which we sold from house to house. She also made carrier bags out of old sacks. Gora and I sold samoosas and popcorn that she made on Grey Street on Friday evenings. A samoosa or a bag of popcorn went for a penny each. Sometimes on a Saturday I would stand outside an Indian pub and sell her wares. The few shillings we made provided the money for food for the week.

I was aware of what living in poverty meant, and as I got older, I believed in the goals of communism: to create a classless society in which people share the benefits of everyone's labour. That's why Gora and I volunteered for revolutionary life at a young age. As we became teenagers under a fanatically anti-Soviet, anti-communist white regime – which had an intense hatred for India and Pakistan, the rest of Africa and any country dubbed 'third world' – we were increasingly drawn to communist theory. Like so many other countries, white South Africa used 'communist' as a synonym for 'evil' or 'radical': it spelled for whites the end of the world. Anybody who was anti-apartheid could be accused of being a communist and punished severely. Yet, were it not for the Communist Party, which organised African workers throughout the 1920s and from very early on called for black majority rule, we might not have had the kind of freedom we now enjoy.

After the government banned the Communist Party under the

Suppression of Communism Act and used it to stifle opposition, it took another ten years for the regime to ban the ANC and other liberation movements. This shows you how fearful the white supremacists were of 'communists'. Perhaps this was because the Communist Party was non-racial and was linked to freedom struggles around the world. Even my beloved ANC cannot make that claim for that stage in its development. It was not a non-racial organisation in 1950, and it was not very well known around the world yet. The ANC leadership was also not keen on communism, and it was facing divisions from within over that issue. But there was a common link between the two: the struggle against class and racial oppression.

It was only from the 1950s onwards that leading members of the ANC who were also communists came to occupy key positions in the ANC. It is important to remember that the Communist Party had during its long history also supported the Natal Indian Congress, the African People's Organisation (APO, the forerunner of the South African Coloured People's Organisation) and the All-African Convention of 1935. The communists always stood on the right side of history. As a teenager I was greatly inspired by speeches made in its name at mass meetings on Red Square. I waited expectantly for what was going to unfold.

In the digital world, mass meetings happen all the time on a large scale. Millions and millions of people watch the same events unfold in every country, yet you cannot feel another's handshake or see yourself reflected in their eyes even though you passionately share views and radical intentions. We could. We did. We and others like us had an ideological intention from a young age.

Six
Red Square

WHEN I FIRST SUBMITTED MY application for membership to the Natal Indian Congress (NIC), it was rejected because I was under sixteen. Its recruiters said I would be sentenced to lashes by the regime if I was caught, but I nevertheless continued with my volunteer activities in the movement.

It was at the end of April 1951, when the ANC called for ten thousand volunteers for the Defiance Campaign, that I knew what I wanted my life's mission to be. I didn't know what that decision to volunteer would bring me, and how class and racial divides dating back several generations would affect me as I drew closer into the ranks of the masses.

I would go to the NIC offices straight after school and would collect leaflets and hand them out at bus ranks. Sometimes I'd assist with printing posters on a cyclostyle machine, which was like a stencil copier, and then carry my own copies to the mass rallies which became an almost daily event. We also printed a news bulletin called *Flash* every other day.

Volunteers would gather at Red Square every weekend to see our heroes address us and we would sing freedom songs. To chants of 'Mayibuye iAfrika!' (Bring back Africa!), we would then march down West Street, the main thoroughfare in Durban, to Berea Road station. That became a site of radical activity, as 'non-white' volunteers would illegally occupy the white waiting rooms, knowing they would be arrested for defying apartheid laws. They would, as a matter of course, appear in court on the Monday, where they would be charged and fined. They would refuse to pay the fine and then serve their sentence as an act of defiance. This was in line with the NIC and ANC policy of passive resistance.

The first batch of volunteers was led by Dr Naicker and Stalwart Simelane, but many more would follow and go to prison. This inspired me. I became chairperson of my own NIC branch, and we held weekly meetings in a madrasa classroom in May Street. I was only seventeen. Ismail Gangat, a well-known travelling salesman in Durban, a communist and a senior leader in the area, was a mentor to me, and held us together as a fledgling unit. The august Ismail Meer and Fatima Meer conducted regular political classes for us during our meetings, teaching us about colonial exploitation and how common struggles had led to the formation of the NIC and the ANC. The Meers' lessons described my destiny.

A turning point came when the prominent academic and ANC veteran ZK Matthews told our comrades in leadership that he thought that a 'congress of the people' should be organised to draw up a Freedom Charter. He envisaged that it would document the ideas, desires and dreams of all South Africans. We were ready to agitate for broad public participation in developing the Freedom Charter. This would involve an important alliance between our various organisations, which would alleviate frustration around the lack of clear direction.

I attended the first meeting to set the congress in motion. It was held in Durban at the AI Kajee Hall, and put us young revolutionaries in contact even with older white people outside the political community. Prominent among them was Ken Hill of the newly formed Liberal Party, one of whose founders was the acclaimed South African novelist Alan Paton, who wrote *Cry, the Beloved Country*. The Liberal Party was a non-racial political organisation, yet its 'non-white' membership consisted of only a few African and Indian intellectuals. While not opposed to the concept of a Freedom Charter, it mostly expressed reservations about the proposed 'mass character' of the campaign and distanced itself from it. Later, in 1968, the Liberal Party, to its credit, decided to dissolve rather than bow down to a new law passed by the National Party that banned multiracial political parties.

The Congress of the People campaign needed wide interaction to find out what was meant by 'freedom'. What type of society did people long for? What was their truth? Comrade Gangat turned us into a form of leadership, a role which many of us have carried out for decades. He was not only a long-time activist but had the skills of being a former teacher and salesman who would travel all over Natal to market goods for Indian-based merchants in Durban. A likeable person and the joy of any party, he was the perfect coordinator.

We printed questionnaires which listed grievances and demands. I took mine from door to door, evening after evening, weekend after weekend, handing them over and collecting them on a subsequent visit. The completed questionnaires were then submitted to our head office. Not everyone was ready for us, which wasn't surprising considering that the white-controlled media mentioned little, if anything, about the campaign. We had to explain to many people what the Congress of the People was all about. Positive responses bolstered our tireless canvassing.

The campaign gained considerable momentum by 1954, and a mass assembly to adopt the Freedom Charter in Kliptown, Soweto, was planned for 25 and 26 June 1955. The ANC's paid-up membership was estimated to be as much as 100,000 at the time.[2] The date of 26 June was of significance to the Congress movement because that's when the Defiance Campaign had been launched in 1952.

I was excited to be elected to represent my area at the Congress of the People. For a young Indian person who had never travelled outside Durban, going to Johannesburg was like a dream unfolding. But such were the barriers that it was also like going to another country. Indians were prohibited from inter-provincial travel without acquiring a six-week permit. And, even then, Indians were not allowed to visit, or stay in, the Orange Free State. So this was a trip of some magnitude in terms of defying racist laws.

The chances of my getting a permit to go to Johannesburg were nil. Dawood Seedat – the editor of the progressive newspaper *New Age*, and a communist whom I admired – tried to persuade me not to go without one. Comrade Gangat ventured a more brazen approach. He knew of the tireless work I had done in collecting the demands of the people and wanted me to travel to Kliptown with him. A *New Age* poster read, 'All

Roads Lead to Kliptown'. But the security police were intent on making those routes as impassable as they could to prevent delegates from attending. Fortunately, we had a middle-aged Coloured comrade travelling with us in Comrade Gangat's car, and it was decided that my cover would be that I was that comrade's nephew, as Coloureds didn't have to carry a travel permit. I was briefed on my cover in the event we were stopped and questioned by the police. Yet we were of little interest to the cops, as they were concentrating their attention on the buses headed to Kliptown. As a result many people were delayed and some couldn't get there at all. For me, my first sight of Johannesburg was of a true city of gold with its shimmering mine dumps.

We were welcomed by Essop Jassat, a medical student at Wits who became a prominent leader of the Transvaal Indian Congress. He arranged for some of us to stay at the musafir khana, a Muslim travellers' inn. The intensity of being in that crowd of thousands has never left my mind. A platform had been erected for the speakers, and the rest of us were ushered into rows of wooden benches set close to the ground. Not that people simply sat. Most rose up to sing and dance, experiencing each other's power in the richness of the moment, coming as we did from all walks of life – the cities and the countryside, the mining compounds and factories, the farms, where most earned slave wages, and (for a few) the white suburbs. There were young and old; Christians, Muslims, Hindus and Jews. Many of the women were dressed in the ANC's black, green and gold. Banners demanded freedom for all. Even the ruling National Party was invited to this people's assembly, but it refused to attend – a fact not lost on us some fifty years later when it adopted the ethos of the Freedom Charter in its negotiations for a new constitution with the ANC and other parties in the early 1990s.

The chairmanship of the Congress movement used to rotate between the ANC, the South African Indian Congress, the South African Coloured People's Organisation and the Congress of Democrats, a radical left-wing white organisation. That's why there was a resonance in the Charter's opening words: 'South Africa belongs to all who live in it.' But the government would not let the adoption of the Freedom Charter happen without intimidation. The police were stationed at tables at the entrance to the Congress venue, which was surrounded by a fence, and demanded that everyone submit their names, addresses and identity documents. Reggie Vandeyar, who befriended me at the assembly, told me to give the police a fictitious name and address, which he provided. They asked me for residency papers such as those which Indians living in the Transvaal had to have, but I said I did not have them with me, and I got away with it.

Police also raided the Congress on horseback. But this only spurred the delegates on to sing louder, and the adoption of each clause was greeted by a revolutionary song. As we left the conference site, people sang and danced as if the birth of a 'new South Africa' was at hand. There was a mood of defiance as our determination to struggle until we achieved the aims of the Freedom Charter took hold and grew in complexity. We resolved to resist, even unto death.

Seven
The regime panics

AFTER KLIPTOWN, STARTING IN 1956, I began working in earnest for the weekly newspaper *Advance*, and then for its successor, *New Age*. First entitled *The Guardian* and soon the mouthpiece of the Congress movement, it was banned in the early 1950s. Its name was then changed to *The People's World*, but not everyone appreciated that choice and it then became *Advance*. When it was banned again, it re-emerged as *New Age*.

I first sold copies of *Advance* for 3d and later for 6d at the Durban bus rank near the popular Victoria Street bridge on Friday afternoons after school as well as at rallies and meeting places on Saturdays and Sundays. I got a bit of commission – say, a penny for each copy sold. That was my only way of earning any money at all during that time. The gregarious editor, MP Naicker – who took over from Dawood Seedat – saw an advantage in selling it from door to door, so I did the rounds. I also distributed copies of the Freedom Charter from house to house. At the same time I became more and more politically confident in the process.

In 1959, I was in my final year at Sastri College, the first Indian high school and teacher training college in South Africa. Opened in 1929 and mostly funded by the Indian community, it got its name from the Honourable VS Srinivasa Sastri, who had been the Indian government's representative in South Africa. The school is architecturally beautiful, a design of Gandhi's friend Hermann Kallenbach, who created some of South Africa's most celebrated buildings. But I was not the most devoted pupil. My mind was on what was happening beyond its walls.

For instance, there was no way I could ignore one of the largest mass rallies ever, held at the Curries Fountain sports ground in Durban to announce the potato boycott. This came after the investigative journalist and communist, Ruth First, exposed the horrendous treatment of labourers on potato farms in the Bethal district of the Transvaal. The months-long boycott, one of the most successful of the time, started in that small town, which is about ninety minutes' drive away from Johannesburg. Here slave labour was commonplace. In some cases, African teenagers were trafficked there, taken to farms as 'punishment' for alleged pass law offences. They were forced to wear sacks as clothing and thrown into appalling living conditions. They had no choice but to use their hands to dig for potatoes on farms while being regularly beaten. Many died and were buried in the fields. Comrade Ruth's investigation and the subsequent boycott led to the regime appointing a commission of inquiry, after which conditions for the labourers improved somewhat.

Our people's refusal to buy potatoes encouraged us to do the same with other goods produced by or sold to companies aligned with the government. Boycotts gave us a spirited advantage and were true to the passive resistance principles of our movement. But that tactic could not go on forever. Within a few months of the potato boycott, the ANC was looking at other ways to fight the enemy. But it would have to do so without some of its members, who joined the breakaway Pan Africanist Congress (PAC) that year. Even before they hived off, the Africanists, a relatively small group within the ANC, had gradually begun to unsettle our gatherings, through excessive debate or sheer obstinacy, sometimes even challenging our leadership. Then came the breakaway in 1959, which had a profound effect on us and on the ANC.

The PAC was founded partly out of the suspicion that the ANC intended to include Indians and whites as members. At that time, the ANC only allowed Africans as members and the PAC intended to follow that position. The ANC also had the backing of the South African Communist Party (SACP), while the PAC was avowedly anti-Communist. Those who shared that position perceived the PAC as a political home

The regime panics

for nationalists and Christians, although the ANC was also a home for Christians. The problem was that the ANC and the PAC still had many of the same political, if not ideological, objectives, and their resistance campaigns were based mostly on the same issues. At the PAC's inaugural congress, Robert Sobukwe was unanimously elected as the party's first president.

* * *

The divisions between the ANC and PAC also had implications on the wider African continent, where sentiments in favour of independence were at that time at fever pitch. By the early 1960s more than thirty countries had gained independence and therefore became members of the Organisation of African Unity (OAU) on its founding. But the OAU would also recognise liberation movements in countries not yet independent which had the backing of the oppressed people. Which would it be in South Africa's case: the PAC or the ANC?

Mandela wanted to persuade the newly independent African countries to support the ANC, and so set off on a tour of several African countries in 1962. When he returned, he travelled around South Africa in secret to report back. MP Naicker, editor of the *New Age* newspaper, where I worked, asked me to attend a clandestine gathering of young cadres selected to meet Mandela. This would happen in the home of an Indian family who was hiding Mandela in Durban. On the way we had to change cars twice for security reasons, but once our small group got there, the strapping Mandela warmly welcomed us. He recounted his discussions with African leaders and their perceptions about our movement, and told us about the false information the PAC was spreading about the ANC. The PAC projected itself as the 'only true African nationalist movement' in the country, and said the ANC was dominated by whites, Indians, Coloureds and communists. That angered us. Mandela had taken his trip into Africa to stem the isolation of the ANC, but it was clear that we too required an 'African image'. His words triggered a deep change in our strategy and tactics.

The split between the ANC and PAC also had a personal dimension for me: my brother Gora, who had also been a close political ally of mine, in time joined the PAC. Ultimately we took different forks in the political road. To some extent, our separation was crafted by an ANC comrade, AB Ngcobo, whose political tendency, like that of a few others, was long visible in our movement before it grew into the PAC. Gora and I spent many late nights with Ngcobo, who was only a few years older than us, arguing about the policies of Africanists in the ANC, who became very vocal after the adoption of the Freedom Charter. Ngcobo advocated pure black nationalist politics. In fact, he and others, such as Gora later, rejected the ANC's arguments about the value of white participation in the struggle. Some even deplored the participation of communists in our ranks. These positions which they adopted weakened their links with us and would later lead to a complete break.

The years 1959 and 1960 witnessed intense mass action. In Durban, ANC volunteers wearing khaki uniforms and carrying the iconic black, green and gold flag marched through the city and surrounding townships. The flag comprises three equal horizontal stripes, the black symbolising the indigenous people, green the land, and gold the mineral and other natural wealth. This flag would also be unveiled as the MK battle flag in 1961.

I was grateful to be able to work at *New Age* because it took me so close to what was happening. Comrade MP sent me on all sorts of assignments, one of the most remarkable being to the north coast, to the municipality now known as KwaDukuza (named after Shaka's royal residence), which incorporates the town of Stanger and Groutville. I had to collect opinions from Chief Albert Luthuli. The regime had 'offered' him a 'choice': give up his membership of the ANC or be removed as the elected traditional leader of the AbaseMakolweni. 'Chief' would not renounce the movement, and so he was stripped of his traditional powers. When he became president of the ANC in 1955, he was placed under a banning order which was renewed every few years until he died under suspicious circumstances in 1967.

We most often met in the house of an Indian lawyer, where I received the statements from Luthuli, which were always handwritten in a school exercise book. 'Chief' was highly talkative. He referred to the white regime as 'a dictatorship'. On one occasion a group of us from Durban and some comrades from Johannesburg went to meet him in a stationary bus. He addressed us in that unusual space because of his banning order, taking the opportunity to relate a story of a village where young people were disillusioned with the older generation. The youth decided to rebel and send the elders into exile, but, having done that, they became confused and disorganised as they had little knowledge of how to conduct affairs. Then a bright boy began to emerge with solutions, and soon the others completely relied on him. Without him, they would have been in chaos. When they asked the boy for the source of his wisdom, he told them: 'When you exiled your parents, I did not do the same. I hid mine there, in a cave.'

I was grateful for the simplicity of Chief's message. I hadn't had the kind of parents who could necessarily provide that wisdom, but I did acknowledge the influence of Ma. As I deepened into the revolutionary movement, I realised that one's own brothers could be one's elders, and our leaders, our parents. In my case, Phyllis Naidoo took me as her revolutionary son, and I accepted that honour. That's how it was for us.

Our leadership informed us that 31 March 1960 would be the starting day for the campaign against the pass laws. Africans would be called upon to burn their passes and face the consequences. But the PAC pre-empted the ANC's action by calling on its supporters to leave their passes at home and report to the local police station on 21 March. AB Ngcobo, who had had many conversations with Gora and me, led fewer than a dozen people to assemble that day outside the Smith Street police station in Durban. I doubt the police took any notice of them. But in the township of Sharpeville, south of Johannesburg, police action led to a massacre which marked the moment when the apartheid regime declared war on African people. This state-sponsored terrorism not only shocked all in South Africa, but it also had a huge impact on the international community and as a result some governments and the United Nations began to change their diplomatic policies towards South Africa.

Chief Luthuli called for three days of mourning and a national strike in outrage at the slaughter. He argued that Africans had been shot dead, and, as the ANC was the primary organisation of the African people, it needed to take a leading role in the protest. The reply of the people would remain one of passive resistance. There was incalculable sadness among our people. Certainly, we were fearful of police raids, but we still worked through the night printing leaflets in support of the strike for distribution the next day. The event indeed took place on the Monday and was the most victorious of its kind.

I took part in the heroic marches and demonstrations in the days which followed. Chief Luthuli, Walter Sisulu and other ANC leaders, together with trade unionists like Moses Mabhida, took the lead in burning their passes. But the regime was determined to stay one deadly step ahead and declared a State of Emergency. Many of our leaders were arrested in the early hours of 31 March.

That evening I attended a habeas corpus hearing in which lawyers for the ANC argued that the detentions were illegal as the state could not produce a copy of the relevant Government Gazette. The state argued the gazette was in Cape Town and on its way to Durban, but Judge Edgar Henochsberg demanded it be produced in court immediately or all detainees would have to be released straight away. Four comrades in court that day – Joe Matthews, Dr GM Naicker, Jaydew Nasib Singh and Rowley Arenstein – were free to go, and quickly disappeared underground. Others were released and then rearrested within hours. The government rapidly announced legislation to ban the ANC and the PAC.

The levels of mass protest that followed are hard to imagine today. These took place even as the regime suspended all arrests for failure to produce passes. None of our meetings could be advertised for fear of not accommodating all the people who wanted to be there. But every venue would be overcrowded anyway once volunteers had spread the word. A few of us worked through the night again producing more flyers, this time calling on people to march through the city to the prison to demand the release of all the detainees. Then we met in the darkest hours, in secret, with some of our leaders who were on the run, among them Kay Moonsamy, who had been a revolutionary from a young age just as I was, and Rowley Arenstein.

The financial markets meanwhile responded negatively to the State of Emergency, and the government was forced to lift it, but the liberation movements remained banned. That presented a serious challenge to us. Some argued the ANC should continue its work under a different name. Similar organisations had had to do this in other African countries. Others were determined that the ANC, given its history, should remain underground. Soon our leadership issued a statement: the ANC would continue to exist as it was.

Nelson Mandela, whose banning order had recently expired, then addressed a consultative conference in Pietermaritzburg. Comrade MP and I attended, and while I sold *New Age* and other publications like *Fighting Talk*, MP covered the meeting. I was never more inspired than when I listened to Comrade Mandela at that rally. I sensed that things were changing and that a new phase of struggle was on the horizon. Yet, as a reminder of how brutal the state was, he was later arrested since Africans weren't allowed to be in town after certain hours at night. After calling for a three-day national strike, he would go underground to direct our movement.

More and more volunteers were willing to defy unjust laws and accept imprisonment. But as the regime panicked and passed increasingly draconian laws, our efforts became more dangerous and, eventually, almost impossible. Although the ANC and the SAIC had led our movement, there were other discussion forums and organisations that attracted some attention. Among these was the Non-European Unity Movement (NEUM, or Unity Movement), a Trotskyite group which argued against the campaign. My brother Gora was also a member of the NEUM at the time. The NEUM described the campaign as 'adventurous' and questioned how committed Marxists could associate with Gandhian-style passive resistance. Mystifyingly, they argued that a mass campaign of this type would lead to the 'demoralisation' of the masses.

I couldn't understand the logic of this, as I felt that a campaign of this nature was far from demoralising. It inspired me and many others to become activists in the struggle for freedom. Another major result of the campaign was the transformation of the ANC itself from a relatively small organisation into a mass movement, which heightened the political consciousness of the oppressed and, I believe, cemented unity in the country. This historic moment propelled us into the next era.

Eight
Lessons in politics

MD NAICKER ASKED ME to join the SACP in 1961 after he had been requested by the party's Durban district committee to recruit me. Like many others, I was quite taken aback – but not by his request. We thought the communists were organisationally dormant. Yet the leaders had been more strategic than we had thought, pre-empting the crackdown of 1950, when the Suppression of Communism Act was passed, by dissolving the party in 1948 and then secretly resurrecting it in the early 1950s without making any public announcements.

Comrade MD was an interesting and complicated man who had his own battles with the South African Indian Congress (SAIC). He discussed with us the reasons why the SACP had in fact been 'officially' reconstituted years before, in 1953. We came to know more about how some of the 'old' party members had taken serious strain, coming under intense police scrutiny and harassment. As the political situation began changing rapidly, the party decided to deal directly with the people again, and resurrected itself.

Months before the Sharpeville massacre, I had received a cyclostyled copy of *African Communist*, a Marxist publication whose possession would have meant immediate imprisonment if I had been found out. This was the first publication of the new SACP, and I read it with enthusiasm.

Political education was what gave me energy at the time, and still does today. When I was somewhat more attuned to what its aims were in our current period of activism, the SACP earned my allegiance, and I became active in a cell in Durban.

The atmosphere had changed dramatically after Sharpeville, the declaration of the State of Emergency and the banning of the liberation movements. I believed it was fitting that the SACP should step up and declare itself publicly, despite still being an illegal entity. Leaflets were then distributed in the name of the SACP, calling on opposition to the apartheid government and support for the ANC.

There were four of us in our initial unit. Comrade MD was the convener and chaired it. The other members were Comrade Dawood, who was not only an activist but a World War II veteran, who liked calling the British Empire the 'British Vampire'; and Poomoney Moodley, who had been dismissed from her job as a nurse. We usually met at her flat in Carlisle Street in central Durban.

Comrade MD made it clear that the party required iron discipline. We were not allowed to miss a meeting, no matter what excuse we had. Time-keeping was important and it was not acceptable to be slightly late or even early at a meeting. We had to call each other by code names and carry out assignments with the utmost sense of duty. The plan was that we meet once a week, when we would read through the directives of the central committee and the district committee. Sometimes we would go out in the evening to distribute leaflets.

Comrade Dawood felt he had to get his criticism of the party's unexpected announcement of its existence off his chest. He believed it was a mistake and hazardous to imagine the revolution was 'just around the corner'. MD did not share his opinion, and we understood their positions would have to hold.

There was soon a change in the composition of our unit, and we were joined by Eleanor Kasrils; Kalakhi Sello, a Lesotho national who was studying law at the University of Natal; and my struggle 'mom', Phyllis Naidoo, who was practically a full-time, unpaid functionary in the movement. She not only kept my spirits up from when I was about sixteen, but she also kept me fed. This was especially true when I was a student at college. Phyllis was married to Comrade MD at that time, although they later got divorced. This was an extraordinary moment for me, to work closely with two such brave women as Phyllis and Eleanor.

The security police had threatened to kill Eleanor if she did not lead them to Ronnie Kasrils, her partner, who was in hiding and who was wanted on suspicion of involvement in sabotage. This was of course something I knew plenty about since Ronnie and I were involved in some of that sabotage together. Eleanor, who had a day job at Griggs Bookstore in Durban, was already working underground for the ANC and supported many cadres. She went on to show real daring and courage.

Comrade Phyllis had a huge personality to match her unassailable loyalty to the liberation of South Africa. But the way her actual engagement with our unit began was rather unconventional. She had become suspicious of Comrade MD's weekly absence from home, and this led to marital problems. He couldn't say what he was doing, for security reasons, but when women in the neighbourhood informed Phyllis that they saw MD at Poomoney's flat every Monday evening, the truth had to be told. We recommended to the district committee that Phyllis be recruited. That may well have been one of the best decisions we made, as Phyllis became a mother to all the cadres, including me. She was extraordinarily fearless and dedicated. Often our main thought was hunger, and I was indebted to my beloved struggle 'Mom' who gave us late night meals in her tiny flat in Durban, even though she was earning a meagre salary as a teacher.

As part of our activism, our unit went on a slogan-painting spree one evening. A dozen of us gathered at Eleanor's flat to collect pots of black paint and paintbrushes. Ronnie and I were paired to go into the central part of Durban. He had borrowed a Morris Minor car from a Congress movement supporter in Cato Manor, an area then better known as Umkhumbane, where forced removals had recently destroyed the existing community of Indian and African people.

As we were driving along Umgeni Road, we saw a freshly painted wall at a bakery factory and stopped the car. We were already on the scene when a security guard posted on the opposite side of the street spotted us and started running in our direction. We bundled ourselves back into the Morris Minor and, in the rush, I spilled some of the paint on the car floor and on my jeans. Fortunately we got away, and once we returned to base, we quickly got rid of our graffiti tools. But the jeans I had been wearing were still splattered with black paint.

It wasn't long after I reached home in Greyville – where I was still living with my uncle and other family members – when there was a loud knock on the front door. It was the police. I was in bed. My uncle protested, insisting I was not at home, and this gave me a chance to throw my wet jeans outside the window and try to hide. But he soon had to open the door, and the police rushed in, looking for me. Since the light bulb in my room was not working, the police could not immediately see me in the dark underneath a pile of washing. They were about to leave our house when they went into the yard and found the jeans outside. That was it. They then found me and arrested me.

I was locked up in the police station and appeared in court the following day when I got bail. Those of us who had been held had to prepare our defence without betraying our comrades. The owner of the Morris Minor made an unsworn statement that I had borrowed the car for a night, saying I needed it to carry out some work. He said that when I returned the car late at night, he noticed paint in it, and said I had claimed this was from the work I had been doing and that I had promised to clean it the next day. The owner was found not guilty. His was a reasonable explanation. I was, however, sentenced to a period of imprisonment. But when the matter was taken on appeal, on the grounds that I had been convicted on someone's unsworn statement, I won.

Nevertheless, I was in a state of considerable anxiety. I realised that the regime was drawing closer, and that the security police had now identified certain cadres, including me, as suspects. Thus, whenever a bomb went off, a policeman from the nearest station would come to my home to see if I was there. I was questioned many times about my movements prior to the explosions. It was a tense time. As our campaign intensified, the security police were more obviously on our trail.

The re-emergence of the Communist Party as well as the formation of MK created a vibrant political climate and led to more significant tactical discussions about the way forward. Sabotage continued throughout the country while community organisations were established in the townships to develop protest actions and make demands about housing and other local issues.

Meanwhile, the comrades grappled with theory. We were aligned either to the Communist Party of the Soviet Union (CPSU) or the Chinese Communist Party (CCP). We were Leninist or we were Maoist, and thus we directly experienced the split between the People's Republic of China and the USSR over doctrine and the way each had implemented Marxist-Leninism during the Cold War. The Soviets' tendency towards peaceful coexistence with the West stood in stark contrast with Chairman Mao's belligerence, as he regarded the USSR policy as 'revisionist'. Comrade Rowley, who conducted Marxism classes with some of us, was critical of the Soviet Union's stance towards the West, and was strongly committed to the revolutionary Chinese line of thought.

In 1963, there was to be an election in the newly self-governing bantustan of Transkei, which the apartheid regime set up as a homeland for Xhosa-speaking people. The intention of the homeland policy was to deny African people their South African citizenship by making them 'citizens' of territories like the Transkei. Comrade Rowley opposed the decision of the ANC to boycott the elections there, arguing that Lenin had advocated the participation of revolutionaries even in reactionary institutions like the Duma in Tsarist Russia. When he persisted in this argument, there was a verbal battle with Moses Kotane, general secretary of the SACP, during a clandestine meeting. Kotane bellowed that Rowley had little understanding of bantustan politics and should rather 'shut up'. Rowley was defiant. He was against the armed struggle, to the point that he went on to help set up a political party in the Transkei under Leonard Mdingi to contest the elections. Rowley then submitted his resignation to the SACP, but the district committee refused to accept it. It instead decided to expel him.

I was a bit puzzled, and wanted to know why his resignation could not be accepted. Comrade MD gave me a theoretical explanation: the party was not a bourgeois organisation, and one could not just simply *choose* to leave. We were then asked for our opinion, and I expressed my disquiet. I felt that before such a decision could be taken, all aspects had to be considered. Eleanor supported my view. Sello was also against the expulsion. Nonetheless, it was difficult to defend Comrade Rowley specifically, and not because he held different views. He had sought to undermine the entire organisation. At the time, we were under immense pressure, and we needed to show unity.

Rowley had also advocated the formation of community bodies that took up ordinary people's grievances and organised local rallies and marches. This somehow worried the ANC head office in Johannesburg as it insisted on being projected as the dominant protagonist of the struggle, leading from the underground. It would be problematic if local community organisations 'replaced' the ANC in the mass imagination. Yet there was no doubt that those grassroots organisations were useful and helped define the relationship between the rulers and the oppressed. Those bodies were precisely how people experienced solidarity against the apartheid system. So while we may not have been able to stand with an individual – in this case, Comrade Rowley – we could see that without cultivating the grass roots, political consciousness would suffer. And this was also where the rise of militancy was happening. Sector-based organisations became an essential part of our struggle.

To a certain extent, I felt a sadness that Comrade Rowley eventually left the Congress movement and joined the Inkatha Freedom Party to support Chief Mangosuthu Buthelezi, with whom he had been associated from the time Buthelezi was his articled clerk in the 1950s. At that time, Buthelezi was a member of the ANC and associated with Mandela and Sisulu. Later he took a conservative turn and accepted the largesse of the apartheid government as chief minister of KwaZulu.

Rowley's departure was an emotional matter for many comrades. He endured thirty-three years of being banned by the apartheid regime, which was the longest period of banning in South African history, as well as the longest house arrest of eighteen years. His wife Jacqueline Arenstein, a journalist and a family member of Ronnie Kasrils's, was also under house arrest for six years, and banned for nineteen years. She had been a defendant in the 1956 Treason Trial while Rowley, a lawyer, defended our comrades accused of political offences at all times.

Yet, despite our feelings about the Arensteins, we had to defer to the SACP, and although there were many among us who saw it as authoritarian, we either had to be of one mind or we would split apart. We could not risk the latter. A battle over Marxist-Leninism has always existed in the ranks of our freedom movement. I have grappled with this my whole life.

Although many cadres remained communists and stayed that way, the ANC's leadership chose to set aside our movement's inherent socialism in the early 1990s during negotiations towards democracy with the apartheid government. That decision was as strategic as it was ideologically controversial. We understood it was designed as a means of attaining a 'higher stage' of capitalism to eventually open the way to socialism. This is why the ANC says it is still engaged in a National Democratic Revolution (NDR). But while it assures us the NDR remains under way, not everyone believes it. This is why you'll sometimes hear people describe the ANC as communist. Some think that is a good thing, while others regard it as the ultimate evil.

Nine
The walk on the bay

WITH THE DECLARATION OF the State of Emergency and the banning of the ANC and PAC, we all had a sense that the era of non-violent struggle was coming to an end. Just before the State of Emergency was announced, OR Tambo and Dr Yusuf Dadoo were instructed to leave the country and set up a Congress mission in exile. When Comrade Mandela 'disappeared' so as to enable him to travel around the country – the media became fond of referring to him as the 'Black Pimpernel'– we became more aware than ever of what we needed to do.

While there was much expectation among cadres and many of our people about a new phase in the struggle, there was also continuous discussion about the feasibility and correctness of armed action. Some leaders in the Indian Congress who were wedded to the Gandhian philosophy opposed it. There were others on the left who questioned the absence of a suitable environment. They urged us to acknowledge that South Africa lacked the terrain for guerrilla warfare and there were no friendly countries across the borders from which attacks could take place, and to which combatants could retreat.

We debated the issues until late into the night with comrades like Ronnie Kasrils, Curnick Ndlovu and Stephen Dlamini. What about Algeria and the absence of jungles there? The Algerian National Liberation Front had nevertheless used guerrilla warfare to ultimately defeat the French colonial power and win independence. Moreover, the issue of 'terrain' was changing as more people moved into cities, and guerrillas all over the world were having to adapt their movements. This was especially true in Latin America during our time. Many liberation movements found that cities offered more cover and protection than bush, jungles or mountaintops. And what about Cuba, whose revolutionaries faced the same problem as we did of not having any friendly neighbouring countries at the time?

Rowley Arenstein and others believed that sabotage might divert the people from mass action and lead to terrorism. Some produced Lenin's texts *What Is To Be Done?* (1911), his 1917 classic, *The State and Revolution*, and even his 1918 work *'Left-Wing' Childishness and the Petty-Bourgeois Mentality*. They quoted Marxist condemnation of using terror as a tool. The leadership was adamant that it did not intend to harm innocent civilians, but I too was among those who initially expressed scepticism. Over some time MD Naicker and others led us towards an acceptance of armed struggle. In their view, there was little room for legal political activity. The SAIC wasn't prohibited but it could not function, as all its officials were banned. Government harassment had made protest impossible. I was finally somehow convinced.

Mandela too needed to push the idea of an armed struggle within the movement. In those days he was a fiery leader, who spoke with vocal aggression and was uncompromising in his views. But other ANC leaders – including its president, Albert Luthuli, who was dedicated to passive resistance – were not convinced that armed struggle was the way forward. Mandela, however, was determined. Reflecting on this clash with Luthuli in his 1994 autobiography *Long Walk to Freedom*, Mandela wrote that 'the state had given us no alternative to violence ... Violence would begin whether we initiated it or not. Would it not be better to guide this violence ourselves, according to principles where we saved lives by attacking symbols of oppression, and not people? ... The chief [Luthuli] initially resisted my arguments. For him, non-violence was not simply a tactic. But I think that in his heart he realised we were right. He ultimately agreed that a military campaign was inevitable.'

We had to fight back. There was no other option.

The first MK bombs aimed at government buildings and infrastructure exploded all around South Africa on 16 December 1961. This day had been specifically chosen to coincide with a public holiday, the Day of the Covenant, which marked the day when the Voortrekkers defeated a Zulu army under King Dingane at Blood River in 1838. For its part, the PAC had its own armed wing, Poqo (meaning 'pure' or 'alone'), which carried out violent attacks in the Cape at the same time as MK. It was a time of numerous acts of sabotage. Because MK operations were happening everywhere, while Poqo focused more narrowly on the Cape, MK earned a national character, which we believed was essential to counter sectarian class bias and narrow Africanist tendencies.

In 1962, I was working in the *New Age* office when Ronnie Kasrils, who was a year younger than I was, popped in and suggested we go for a walk. He was a frequent visitor there, though we seldom took strolls together. Ronnie had been radicalised by the Sharpeville massacre. He was much admired because he was also a founding member of MK. The timeline is of course important here because the ANC had been banned in 1960, eighteen days after Sharpeville – and not only the ANC, but also the SACP, of which Ronnie and a number of other comrades were members. This meant it was dangerous and illegal to talk about these things in the open in 1962. So if we wanted to discuss something confidential, we usually went outside.

Ronnie and I made our way down the main streets until we got to the bay area. We couldn't sit down on any of the whites-only benches together in case we attracted attention. Always very security-minded, Ronnie was calm but careful, and I had a feeling from the time we left the office that what he was going to say would change my situation.

As we were walking, he told me the MK regional high command wanted me to join. It also wanted me to establish and lead an MK unit in Durban. I suppose this was not unexpected, but I felt a huge sense of responsibility in the way I should reply. I was committed to the struggle, but I wasn't in favour of violent resistance. It was complicated to move from years of peaceful resistance into armed opposition. I was also young – twenty-five years old – although I had already been in revolutionary circles for ten years. My comrades were like family; our common fight was the context of my life. There was no turning round and living some other life.

There was also a realisation among us that the scope for non-violent resistance was narrowing because of the brutal determination of the regime. What would waging an armed struggle mean if I said yes? I would have to agree to organise and participate in sabotage, to hit back at the regime using explosive devices targeting government infrastructure. The instruction from the leadership was to avoid the loss of innocent lives at all costs. Most of us didn't have the luxury of time to really think the issue through. We were certainly not able to discuss it far and wide, particularly not with our closest family members. Our decision had to be made largely on our own conscience. So I agreed.

My first task was to identify comrades in the Durban central area who I thought would be loyal cadres. We weren't looking for many. We needed a tight group. Ronnie would then convey their names to the regional command, which fell under a national high command, for approval. As it happened, the first of them came to me. Sunny Singh, who joined the resistance movement in the early 1960s, arrived at the *New Age* office one morning and expressed a keenness to sign up for the NIC Youth Congress. He had read about the Sharpeville shootings and the subsequent mass demonstrations.

Natvarlal 'Natoo' Babenia, a Gandhian who had been involved in the struggle in India, was another willing soldier recommended by MD Naidoo, who knew Babenia through his volunteer work. Babenia was quite a bit older than I was, having been born in 1924. His family had moved to India in the 1930s because of economic hardship in South Africa, and there he joined the Indian Congress movement in Gujarat. He was even jailed for his activism in India. So Babenia was an experienced young revolutionary when he came home to Durban in 1949, took up membership of the NIC Youth Congress, and became an organiser for the NIC itself. He had a rudimentary knowledge of chemicals and explosives.

I also recommended Siva Pillay, a BSc student, who was later jailed on Robben Island like many of us. He could play the guitar, and in prison we found that very comforting in the evenings after lock-up, although if his strumming was audible to the warders, he could be charged with 'making a noise' and 'refusing to sleep'. David Perumal, a factory worker, also joined us, and the five of us constituted MK's Durban Central Unit. Babenia quickly progressed to becoming a member of the technical committee of MK.

But there were challenges. None of us had any training in bomb-making or the handling of explosives. Our only 'weapon' at first was chilli powder, which we sprinkled on the ground to put off tracker dogs. We decided to steal dynamite from a government construction site at night. There was a shed there with equipment inside and we went armed with a carrier bag, not knowing how big the dynamite was or how it really looked, only to find out it was contained in big boxes. It's hard to believe that we threw away the detonators, as we had no clue of the function of the 'little metal pieces'. Someone from ANC headquarters had to come and show Ronnie and me the correct way to use and store the dynamite. We found out that night how to pack it in tightly sealed plastic containers. Once we knew how to do that, we stole so much dynamite that we had enough to supply MK in other provinces as well.

It was challenging not to have proper factory-made timing devices, though. We thus had to solve the problem of how to ignite the fuse without blowing ourselves up. We understood from our basic lessons that if you pour a certain chemical onto sulphuric powder, you get fire, but of course we had to delay the liquid from contacting the powder. We found that if we put it in a small capsule, it took about half an hour to eat through, in turn igniting the powder. To prolong the delay to about an hour, we put the small capsule into a bigger one. From beginning to end, our operations lasted about two hours each, including being picked up and getting home. Throughout, we had to follow the most stringent instruction: injuries were to be avoided at all costs.

We sought out isolated places on the outskirts of Durban where we would dig a hole and bury the containers of dynamite. Ronnie and I memorably buried one in the Bluff region overlooking the sea on a sand dune. Thereafter, whenever we needed dynamite for an operation, I would take a bus to the suburb of Merebank on that headland, bearing a paper bag. I earned near to nothing in wages at *New Age*, and paid my own costs to fetch the explosives. I would walk up the hill to the viewpoint where we had sunk the container, and would dig around in the soft sand with my bare hands until I felt it. I would then remove the necessary explosives, put these into the bag, close the lid and once again hide the container. I then carried the dynamite back with me in the bus to meet Ronnie and hand over the packet.

We also kept explosives in Natoo Babenia's May Street home in Durban where we held meetings. Although we took all the necessary security measures, they were inadequate and dangerous. The thing was that we lacked sufficient resources and had no transport of our own. This meant our operations were, on the face of it, rather amateurish, and when I look back, it's with a slight shudder. What drove us was our determination to free ourselves of racial oppression.

Our unit successfully carried out several acts of sabotage, targeting the offices of the provincial National Party newspaper, *Die Nataller*, railway lines and government buildings, although our first attempt nearly went tragically wrong. We had prepared a bomb, intending to attack the merchant AS (Kohsaan) Kajee's offices early one evening. Kajee was a stooge who accepted concessions from the apartheid government through the Natal Indian Organisation, which he had founded. Friendly with Prime Minister Jan Smuts, Kajee had been a member of the NIC, which I supported, but he disliked the swing to the left that the Congress made in the late 1940s. He felt it had been taken over by 'communists'. We 'communists' were disgusted when Kajee proudly took the salute in Pretoria at an official Republic Day celebration, occupying a separate 'Indian' display stand where he hoisted the apartheid flag. (South Africa had become a republic, led by a white supremacist government, in 1961.) There was a photograph of Kajee at those celebrations in his office, which was at the end of a narrow passage in Alice Street, near a musafir khana, a Muslim travellers' inn.

When we got there, there were people upstairs, so that made things tricky. Our plan was to break in. We began our work by sealing his office window with adhesive bandages but were disturbed by the shadow of a security guard. He shouted, believing we were thieves, and we ran into the darkness. We would have to do fresh reconnaissance, and the next time we would have to move more quickly.

On the second occasion we put the explosives next to the door while one in our unit kept watch for the guard. We hadn't been able to use a timer because we were concerned the nightwatchman might spot it. After placing the charge, we made a run for it, disappearing into the busy night streets of Durban. Not five minutes later, there was a very loud explosion, with extensive damage to Kajee's office.

But not every attempt was successful. Once we devised a plan to blow up a telephone cable by placing a pipe-bomb inside it. But three days later, the pipe-bomb was still there, not having exploded. Nobody had even noticed it. We also decided to attack goods trains with Molotov cocktails, by standing on top of a bridge and throwing the petrol bombs down on the passing wagons. This was fruitless, though, as the goods were covered with thick canvas, and the damage we caused was very minor.

Then came a major operation. This one involved a special unit which included Ronnie Kasrils, Billy Nair and Kisten Moonsamy. Billy was a trade unionist and a leader of both the NIC and the South African Congress of Trade Unions (SACTU). Kisten was also a unionist and a political commissar in the NIC. The plan was to target the city of Durban itself, and the most obvious way was to blow up a pylon which supplied power from generating stations to bulk stations. Interestingly, the word 'pylon' comes from the Greek word meaning 'gateway', and indeed this successful act of sabotage was for us a kind of portal into our next phase as freedom fighters.

Ronnie and I first did reconnaissance, going by car to the Clairwood area where the transmission towers were situated, and looking at the dimensions and distances between the pylons to understand which was the most valuable structure in terms of our plan. The best one loomed maybe twenty metres high. We had to plan our retreat and escape routes very carefully, working together with Billy and Kisten to ensure we had support, back-up and a getaway driver.

We planted the dynamite on the steel trusses of the pylon with a timed delay of about two hours. This operation was seriously labour-intensive. We secured the device with tape, put in the fuse, and then, on the spot, filled the capsule with acid. Making sure our skin never came into contact with the acid was not an easy task. Billy then picked us up, and dropped me off at my uncle's place. Within two hours, all the lights went out in Durban.

The next day when I went to work, I suggested to Comrade MP, editor of *New Age*, that I go to the area where the explosion happened and take some pictures for our paper. He didn't expressly know I was involved, but I suspect he had an idea that I might know more than I was letting on. I went to Clairwood by bus with my camera, and made enquiries from people living in the area, who directed me to the spot where workmen were already trying to carry out repairs. Our next edition of *New Age* was full of this story.

It was revealing to us that the media and the government blamed foreign nationals – especially Cubans and Russians – for these acts of sabotage. But this didn't dampen the expectation of the people, who believed that the ANC now had a military wing which was taking action against the oppressors. That mattered to us.

We continued to prepare explosives at Natoo Babenia's flat, and carried out our most successful operation when we worked in two teams as pairs. Perumal and Sunny placed explosives on railway tracks along Brook Street where the historic 'God's Acre' cemetery, with its numerous settler headstones, is situated. There is also a Parsee section there, and land for Muslims, which includes the tomb of Badsha Peer, one of two Islamic saints who lived in Durban and was said to have performed many miracles.

Babenia and I meanwhile worked on cables on the Victoria Street Bridge near the 'non-white' bus rank, which was a vivid site in my childhood memories. There was an open-air vegetable market there and the traders would sleep on the road overnight so as to start work in the early morning hours. Our target was the main South Coast line that ran from Durban to Rossburgh. We studied the timetable for the trains as we had no intention of endangering lives, and so we couldn't risk destroying the line while a train was passing or approaching. We also had to make sure we knew the movements of the watchmen and the railway police. At that time, police dogs were used to patrol the railways, which is why our chilli powder came in handy. Dogs were marvellous at tracking.

We succeeded in our operation. An explosion followed, so enormous that I could hear it more than three kilometres away, where I lived. The attack damaged the signalling gear, and when I walked past the area the next morning, hundreds of people were gathering to see the damaged lines. Trains were delayed for many hours as a result of our work.

Ten
University for political purposes

I ENROLLED AS A STUDENT at the new Indian University College on Salisbury Island in Durban Bay in 1963, three years after I completed high school. I attended secondary school from standard eight (Grade 10) at Clairwood Indian High School and then completed matric (Grade 12) at Sastri College.

The Indian University College was the institution which the apartheid government opened in 1961 strictly for people of Indian origin, in keeping with its apartheid plan. The regime passed the Extension of University Education Act in 1959 under which the Indian College and three other 'ethnic' universities were set up: the University of the Western Cape in Bellville for Coloureds; Turfloop in the northern Transvaal for Sesotho and Setswana speakers, and Ngoye in Zululand for Zulu speakers. Fort Hare University College, which had opened in 1916, was now to be exclusively for Xhosa speakers. Its alumni included Mandela, OR Tambo, Robert Sobukwe, Chris Hani, Julius Nyerere, Robert Mugabe and Seretse Khama. This meant that predominantly white universities such as the University of Cape Town, the University of the Witwatersrand and the University of Natal were no longer allowed to accept students who were not white unless they had specific government permission.

Let me be clear that we were all strongly opposed to 'tribal' universities, and that was our public stance, but some of us were instructed to register at these institutions for political purposes. Certainly, this also gave me a cover when it came to avoiding the security police, but the strategy behind my enrolment was that a group of us would mobilise students on campus.

The Indian University College was no ordinary campus. It was like Alcatraz – difficult to reach, unless you were white and then you could take a free ferry. For the rest of us, the route there was commonly on foot by way of a nasty causeway, unless we could afford to pay for a ticket on the ferry. Student numbers were not very high because of the Congress movement's rejection of apartheid institutions, but we still had to ensure that those students who enrolled could be politicised. We nevertheless boycotted all administrative structures like the Student Representative Council.

We established an underground body called the Island Students Association (ISA) and created a system of cells. One of our main tasks was to print and distribute leaflets supporting the freedom struggle and condemning victimisation by the university authorities. ISA became so popular that whenever the rector, Professor SP Olivier, addressed the students, a hissing noise created out of the acronym ISA could be heard during the assembly. This was much to the annoyance of the university's administrators, especially Olivier, who wanted to show that his 'ethnic college' could achieve outstanding results by luring the brightest (and most conservative) scholars from Indian schools. He was, like other Afrikaner heads of 'tribal' colleges, a member of the secret Afrikaner organisation, the Broederbond.

The National Union of South African Students (NUSAS), a white-dominated and sometimes progressive body, was very keen on establishing links with us on Salisbury Island. Adrian Leftwich, who was its president at the time, contacted me to set up a meeting with the ISA committee. ISA strongly opposed exposing our members to NUSAS, which had a chequered history of involvement in liberation politics and relations with our movement, but agreed that I could meet him alone. We all had concerns about informers, which would become more intense as the years of struggle continued.

Leftwich offered to give us financial assistance through NUSAS's Loan Fund, which later became the Political Freedom Fund. NUSAS also arranged scholarships for activist students who wanted to study abroad, especially if they had to flee the country because of political pressures. NUSAS fundraised by approaching overseas institutions and sympathetic international student movements. I refused this offer. Leftwich was as persuasive as possible in trying to gain access to some of our activists at the university. I learned subsequently that he was keen to recruit also for the National Committee of Liberation, later the African Resistance Movement (ARM), a clandestine organisation which white dissenters in the Liberal Party had established as their own 'companion' body to MK. Its saboteurs targeted government installations and services from September 1963 to July 1964, bombing power lines, railway tracks and rolling stock, roads and bridges, plotting to turn other whites against the regime and so promote a collapse of confidence in the country and its economy.

But after John Harris, one of its members, planted a bomb in the whites-only waiting room at Johannesburg's Park Station, killing a commuter and injuring many others, everything changed. Harris was hanged and Leftwich ultimately collaborated with the security police under threat of torture after he was captured. That resulted in the brutal interrogation and imprisonment of other members of the ARM. Leftwich turned state witness in two trials, before being allowed to go into permanent exile in the UK. Reconnecting with those he had betrayed became a lifelong quest for him. Some, such as the writer and former student activist Hugh Lewin, who spent seven years in prison as a result of Leftwich's testimony, found it in their hearts to forgive him.

I was grateful that my instincts had enabled me to make the right political decision, although it's doubtful whether any of our members would have taken part in the ARM's activities. In any case, I was only able to remain on Salisbury Island for two or three months before it became essential to go into hiding. The police were looking for me.

Eleven
A hiding place

IN 1963 THERE WERE arrests nationwide after the promulgation of an amendment to the General Law Amendment Act, known as the '90-day law' in 1963, which allowed the police to detain without warrant a person suspected of a politically motivated crime for up to ninety days without access to a lawyer. We heard daily of beatings and torture in detention cells, and the deaths of comrades at the hands of the police. Then came the biggest blow of all — the capture of our national leadership at Lilliesleaf farm in Rivonia, Johannesburg, on 11 July. Acting on a tip-off, the police raided the farm, which was then the headquarters of the SACP and a safe house for ANC activists.

In the trial that followed, Mandela, who was already serving a prison sentence at the time of the raid, was accused number 1. He and other leaders were charged with sabotage and high treason for 'recruiting persons for training in the preparation and use of explosives and in guerrilla warfare for the purpose of violent revolution and committing acts of sabotage', 'conspiring to commit the aforementioned acts, and to aid foreign military units when they invaded the Republic', 'acting in these ways to further the objectives of Communism' and 'soliciting and receiving money for these purposes from sympathisers in Uganda, Algeria, Ethiopia, Liberia, Nigeria, Tunisia and elsewhere'.

The final indictment listed ten accused. These were Comrade Mandela (who was to spend twenty-seven years and eight months on Robben Island, in Pollsmoor Prison and in Victor Verster Prison), Walter Sisulu (who would serve twenty-six years on Robben Island and in Pollsmoor Prison), Lionel 'Rusty' Bernstein (who was found not guilty and discharged, then immediately rearrested and released on bail before he went into exile), Denis Goldberg (who spent twenty-two years in Pretoria Central Prison, as Robben Island was only for black prisoners), Bob Hepple (against whom charges were withdrawn before he went into exile), Ahmed Kathrada (who served twenty-six years on Robben Island and in Pollsmoor Prison), Govan Mbeki (who served twenty-four years on Robben Island), Raymond Mhlaba (who served twenty-six years on Robben Island and in Pollsmoor Prison), Andrew Mlangeni (who served twenty-six years on Robben Island and in Pollsmoor Prison) and Elias Motsoaledi (who served twenty-six years on Robben Island and in Pollsmoor Prison).

During the 1963 raids, Ronnie Kasrils and I escaped the first raft of arrests, which had included comrades Curnick Ndlovu and Billy Nair, but we quickly received an instruction that we should go into hiding. On the night of the Rivonia arrests, I moved from my home to a safe house: that was fortunate as the police raided my uncle's home. I was instructed to become part of a new Natal High Command together with Ronnie, and fellow saboteurs Bruno Mtolo and Steven Mtshali, but there was no preparation for us to operate from the underground.

The police were surveilling the homes of our family and friends. I had no transport or money to move around. Every day I had to find a new place to sleep and means to feed myself. This was confusing. We had an organisation, a movement, behind us. Had we been abandoned? Ronnie then suggested we briefly move to Kloof, a predominantly white area about twenty minutes' drive from Durban, where Eleanor's mother had a two-room out-building surrounded by trees, which was not easily visible from the road. There was a water tap outside but no toilet. We had to go to the nearby railway station to relieve ourselves, and even that was a source of concern for us.

Bruno Mtolo soon joined us at Kloof. The three of us were in hiding there for about two weeks. This was rather a long time considering how often we usually moved around. At that time, Bruno was a trusted member of our unit. We had no reason to doubt his loyalty, and so we held our cell meetings there with comrades David Ndawonde and Bafana Duma, whom I had worked with at *New Age*. We mainly received reports of arrests and the state of readiness of other MK units. As for ourselves, we had to assess the safety of our equipment and the possibility of future sabotage actions.

Our head office in Johannesburg had divided the province of Natal into ten regions. We had to identify cadres in each region who could form a nucleus for MK activities, in line with Mandela's M-Plan. Umkhonto was organised like a web linking cadres to contact persons on a vertical basis. There was a regional high command in Durban and four subregional commands in the rest of the province. The latter were responsible for a number of cells under the control of an area organiser who reported to the regional command. The thing was that the ANC and MK in Natal were rather divided on the issue of armed struggle. Since the SACP funded the ANC to some extent, the relationship between the two had to be strong to be effective.

I argued that we had to have a retreat strategy to preserve and consolidate our forces. We couldn't be effective in what at times felt like a vacuum. For Ronnie, Bruno and I, living in those out-buildings in Kloof could not be sustained, so we had to make a decision to move. Ronnie contacted an estate agent to find different accommodation. This was a house up on a hill about three kilometres from central Kloof. We got some basic furniture to reduce the echo in the empty dwelling. It had many rooms and bathrooms with bathtubs. All my life I had bathed in a drum of water, so this was a new experience for me at the age of twenty-five. We also had to learn how to make our own dinners as we had little experience of cooking. Our rice, for instance, resembled mielie pap.

But those weren't major worries. Because of the nature of apartheid South Africa, blacks and whites living together in a house would tend to arouse suspicion and give rise to gossip in the area. That meant Ronnie had to pretend to be the owner of the house, Bruno the gardener, and I the painter. Eleanor was our contact person and she brought us food and other necessities.

Then came Saturday, 8 August 1963. Bruno left the house to link up with Comrade Steven at our old Kloof hideout. Steven wanted to join us in the house on the hill but did not know where to find us, so Bruno was going to direct him. We expected him back by lunch, but he did not arrive. By late afternoon we were becoming anxious, and by early evening, when Bruno had not yet come back, we were seriously stressed. Bruno was not the most disciplined of cadres, and he had a tendency to disappear from time to time, mostly to visit girlfriends. But that evening Ronnie and I sat around in a sombre mood, speculating about what could have happened. Perhaps Bruno had not found Steven and then decided to visit a friend. Or, perhaps not. Of course, if he had been caught, he could well reveal our hiding place.

We were uneasy that night and the next day. We then agreed I should go back to the out-buildings in Kloof on foot, as we did not have transport. I surveyed the area from a distance, and saw signs of people having been there. When I got back to the house, I found an anxious Ronnie concealed among the foliage and shrubbery in the garden. At about six o'clock, Eleanor rushed up the driveway in her car, and instructed us to leave the premises and wait down the hill in the bushes for someone to pick us up. It seemed the police had discovered the old Kloof hideout and were questioning her mother about it. Bruno had meanwhile been arrested, and so too had the other members of our unit. We hurriedly grabbed some of our belongings and waited in the dark before being picked up by Pedro, a Portuguese comrade, who drove us to his house in Pietermaritzburg, where we discussed what to do next.

Ronnie suggested that I go to David Ndawonde, who was due to meet us in Kloof the next morning. It was decided that I would meet him at the Kloof railway station, and then take him back with me to Pietermaritzburg and join up with Ronnie there. I was given R5 to take a train the next morning and pay for our tickets back. Pedro dropped me at the station. When I got to the platform, the train had just left. I knew that David would arrive in Kloof at one. It was then about ten in the morning. I had to get to him so he would not be arrested.

I saw a bus destined for Durban, bought a ticket, and boarded. Much to my frustration the bus made a brief stop in central Pietermaritzburg to pick up more passengers, but what was even more discouraging was that the bus stopped en route at the scenic Valley of a Thousand Hills for about an hour. It finally entered Kloof at exactly 1 pm. I got off at Kloof

A hiding place

station and immediately spotted a notorious security policeman, Grobler, who was known to have tortured many detainees. I was hoping he hadn't seen me, but it was soon clear that the place was crawling with the enemy. I was wearing overalls for the purposes of blending in with the locals. I bent down to take a drink from a water fountain, thinking I would then make my exit, but Grobler was on to me instantly. He pointed a gun at me, later telling me he wished I had tried to run away as it would have been 'his pleasure' to shoot me dead.

I was then put into the back seat of a waiting car with security policemen Prins and Steenkamp. As the car moved off, they began beating me. 'Where is that Jew, Ronnie?' they shouted. I remembered what Comrade MD had repeatedly told us in our unit: you only need to give the police your name and address. Do not answer questions even if they seem harmless or innocent. So I remained determined not to answer, come what may. Steenkamp was especially violent. The police then drove me to the Midmar Dam, shouting: 'Coolie, where is Ronnie?' They then pushed me under the water as if to drown me. I lost consciousness and then regained it: this went on and on for what felt like an eternity.

When they tired of their torture, they threw me back into the car and drove me to the house in Kloof which we had vacated the night before. It then became clear that Bruno had led them there. They had raided it mere hours after we had left. What affected me more was that David Ndawonde had also been arrested at Kloof station, where we were planning to meet that day. In the security police's enthusiasm to arrest him, they knocked him around hard enough for a packet of dynamite he was carrying to fall to the floor. Some cleaners discovered it later. It was very fortunate that the police never noticed it.

I was detained in a police station that night, bruised and in great pain. The police said they would 'come back for me' later that night. Meanwhile, I was to 'think hard about Ronnie'. They wanted information about MK. I looked at them in disgust.

The iron grille of the cell slammed shut with a loud bang and I heard the keys turn in the lock. I sat on the cement floor trying to go through everything that had happened during the day. Having got out of bed a 'free person' in the morning, I found myself a prisoner in the evening. I tried to nurse my injuries and come to terms with what could happen next. All I knew was that I should not succumb to the interrogation. Some of the people in whom we had placed so much confidence did break and betray us. I did not want to be one of them. I refused throughout my interrogation to answer any questions.

When the '90-day law' was passed, we had wondered what the consequences of detention and isolation would be. That area of psychology and psychiatry is today very well researched. We now know that prolonged isolation is a form of torture; it's permanently destabilising. Perhaps we did not know as much about the long-term effects then as we do now. What I do know is what torture has left me with for the past six decades. Holocaust survivor and philosopher Jean Amery studied and explained torture in his 1966 book, *At the Mind's Limits*. He said: 'Whoever was tortured stays tortured. Torture is ineradicably burned into him, even when no clinically objective traces can be detected.' He also concerned himself with what happens when people are not able to handle torture and disclose information. 'Whoever has succumbed to torture can no longer feel at home in the world. The shame of destruction cannot be erased. Trust in the world, which already collapsed in part at the first blow, but in the end, under torture, fully, will not be regained.'[3]

I was, however, optimistic that most of our comrades would go through interrogation and survive it – and many did. Bruno and another comrade, Solomon Mbanjwa, who both occupied leading positions in the movement, did not. Both turned state witness, and Bruno went on to be 'Witness X' at the Rivonia Trial and at what was dubbed the Little Rivonia Trial, at which I was accused number 1.

Twelve
The trouble begins

I HAD NEITHER A MAT nor a blanket in my cell. I no longer had my overalls. All I was wearing was a pair of wet trousers. Later, when it was completely dark, a policeman opened the grille and a fellow prisoner threw in a sisal mat and two old, smelly blankets, along with a plate of soft pap. I left the porridge on the floor. I was in pain and had no appetite.

I took off my damp clothing, wrapped myself in a blanket and lay on the mat, exhausted, and then fell asleep. I have no idea what time it was when someone kicked me hard, and I jumped up in sheer fright. There was not a sliver of light inside the cell, but by the shape of the shadows looming over me, I could make out about three security policemen. They continued to kick and punch me. 'Bruno told us you and Ronnie were living at the house in Kloof,' they shouted. 'Where is he, you bastard coolie?'

They kept kicking, slapping and punching me. At one stage they banged my head against the wall. They passed me from one to the other. I was in serious pain but stayed silent. My absolute concentration on remaining silent was somehow diverting. I believed that if I could get through the first bout of physical aggression, I could use the same technique again.

After a while they said something in Afrikaans and left the cell. I lay on my mat again, this time unable to sleep until the break of dawn. In the morning a policeman opened my cell and I was given more pap. By this time, I was very hungry and ate it. I also complained about my wet clothing and was brought some prison garb.

That afternoon I was transported to the Bluff area of Durban, to security police headquarters. I was taken into a room where many policemen were seated. I was asked to sit down, and then they shouted: 'Are you prepared to co-operate with us?' I shook my head.

Grobler was present. He showed me a piece of paper with a prayer written on it. I recognised my comrade David Perumal's handwriting. Grobler informed me that 'all the members' of my unit had been arrested and I 'could help them very much' by co-operating with the police. They threatened that if I failed to do so, I would be 'sentenced to death'. I replied that I was prepared to stand firm and face the consequences. They then said there had been 'another person who was an important leader' who also 'refused' to speak and he 'only lasted twenty-seven days. We shall see if you can beat his record,' Grobler announced.

I was then beaten up again. Eleanor, who had by that time been detained herself at the security police headquarters, saw me, bloodied and unconscious, being dragged down the stairs. I was then taken back to the police station. They made a few more attempts to interrogate me, without success. It was obvious that people like Bruno, who had been a member of MK's Natal High Command from its inception, had indeed revealed the names of people in various units, including my own. I wondered what kind of torture had led them to collapse and give way under detention and whether I had adequately prepared them for that very situation. This troubled me.

After about a month, I was transferred to the Durban Point Prison and put into a tiny, isolated cell. Only a sleeping mat and a water bottle could fit in there, with little space left over. Such cells were shut by a steel door with a tiny peephole through which a prison warder could look in at me. This was after comrades Mosie Moolla, Abdulhay Jassat, Harold Wolpe and Arthur Goldreich, who were all linked to the Rivonia Trial, had escaped from police cells in Johannesburg.

I want to share part of a letter written by Phyllis Naidoo, about how she brought me food and clothes during this difficult time.

In 1963, when the mass arrests took place, we were convinced that

Ebie had escaped the dragnet. My ex-husband was detained and so weekly we called on the-then 'visiting Magistrate of detainees' to check if our fellas had not been killed in detention.

Babla [Saloojee] and Looksmart [Ngudle] were already killed in detention! And while the magistrate was bound not to divulge his findings, we managed to get him to confirm that they were alive.

One day I had a call from Mr Smith, the-then 'visiting Magistrate'. I had to borrow money from my neighbours to get to Berea (in the white part of town).

He confirmed Ebie's detention some three weeks earlier. My boy was in a cell 3-by-3 – he could not stretch.

How do you find clothes on a Sunday? How do you buy food when you are broke? How do you travel to Point prison when you have no bus fare? That will fill pages. But I did, after getting family/friends to take care of [my sons] Sha (1 year) and Sadhan (2 years).

I earned motherhood, and claim it now without any reservations, whatsoever. I learned of the torture that had been applied to [Ebie's] malnourished body that would fill pages, not least was his hands being handcuffed behind his back and leg irons on his feet and being kicked into Midmar Dam.

Only when he gulped for breath did they surface him. They wanted him to disclose the whereabouts of our comrades.

He betrayed no one.

Phyllis's family was to experience tragedy after tragedy. Sadhan was assassinated in 1989 by an apartheid hitman who had infiltrated the ANC's Chongella Farm where families lived in exile in Zambia. He was a manager there. Sha died after complications from surgery for a long illness soon after returning from exile in 1990.

I discovered that others I knew were in jail with me: Billy Nair, Stephen Dlamini, George Mbele and Kisten Moonsamy. This meant that in the evenings after lock-up we could communicate and even hold political discussions. We would decide on the nature of the discussion and would take turns to lead debates on topics like the history of the liberation movement in South Africa, the trade union movement, and Stalin's 1913 work, *Marxism and the National Question*. Our discussions were held in this way: one person stood close to the door and either put their mouth or their ear to the small peephole in it, depending on whether they were talking or listening.

During this period of detention, the authorities gave the Bible to those who requested it. I asked for a copy to keep my mind occupied during the months of isolation. I ended up reading the Bible from cover to cover, and when I contemplate this now, I think it quite ironic that I was reading the Bible by day and participating in discussions on Marxism by night!

We were eventually charged under the Sabotage Act and brought to trial. The specific charges against me were:

1. Sabotage: Fire bomb placed in 3rd-class coach of passenger train between Durban and Verulam. Night. Safety of public endangered.
2. Sabotage: Dynamite placed and detonated next to high-tension pylon. Night. Adjacent to white residential area. Electricity power supply interrupted. Safety of public endangered.
3. Sabotage: Dynamite placed and detonated against office door of Indian man. Indian business and residential area, city centre. Night. Safety of public endangered.
4. Sabotage: Pipe bomb attached to communication cables of South African Railways and Harbours alongside railway line adjacent to city centre residential area. Trains delayed. Safety of public endangered.
5. Sabotage: Dynamite charge placed and detonated against the rails of main line. Night. Trains delayed. Safety of public endangered.
6. Sabotage: Dynamite charges placed and detonated against signal control box of South African Railways and Harbours. Rural area. Night. Trains delayed. Safety of public endangered.

All counts would be treated as one for the purposes of sentencing.

We first appeared in the magistrate's court to be remanded. That was when our families found out what had happened to us. When we were all brought together, there was great excitement to see our fellow comrades after the long period of detention. We were anxious to see who was not among the accused, as this gave us an indication of who would likely be state witnesses in our trial. Nineteen of us were charged, including comrades Billy and Curnick, who were members of the Natal MK High Command. As Bruno and Solomon were not among the accused, it seemed obvious that they would be used by the state against us.

On the first day we were able to consult our lawyers, Rowley Arenstein and Thumba Pillay, but our case was adjourned when Rowley was banned and not allowed to travel to Pietermaritzburg to represent us. We objected to this and went on hunger strike to demonstrate our dissatisfaction. But we were increasingly being presented as a danger to society; we were people who 'wanted to kill the whites'. We were portrayed to the international community as 'seeking to establish a Communist state by means of a violent revolution'. As this was the time of the Cold War, we were therefore very much 'the enemy'. Our trial was held at the same time as the Rivonia Trial, and it lasted for about four months.

It's demanding on one's emotions to explain how it felt to see people with whom you had worked so closely give damaging evidence against you in a courtroom. Were we not all comrades in the struggle, singing freedom songs together, swearing solidarity, dedicated to defeating the oppressors, come what may? Were we not all oppressed by apartheid and committed to attaining freedom for ourselves and our people? I could understand why some comrades made statements but refused to become state witnesses. But what about those who did?

Many people could not stand the beatings, torture and prolonged isolation in solitary confinement. So I understood why they disclosed information for tactical reasons. Some even felt this was correct politically. But turning state witness could only have been about the fear of going to prison and the desire to save one's own life at the expense of other freedom fighters. That, I could not stomach.

Solomon Mbanjwa had recruited Matthews Meyiwa and Joshua Zulu from rural Hammarsdale in Natal. These two had had faith in Solomon and held him in high esteem, but he would stand in the witness box and, apparently without shame or guilt, testify against these two soldiers. I wondered how Mandela and other leaders of our movement felt when some of their respected comrades turned against them in the Rivonia Trial.

Once we got past the first ninety days' detention, we demanded the limited rights accorded to awaiting trial prisoners, namely that family members, friends and partners could visit us and bring us food and civilian clothing. We demanded reading material too. My family only found out what had happened to me when I was charged in court and our names appeared in the newspapers. They thought I was still in hiding, as the police had raided their homes looking for me. The government was under no obligation to inform the families or the public about detainees.

Soon after my first appearance in court, my mother and father visited me in prison. They were concerned, as rumour had it that we would all be sentenced to death. Like all parents, they had great anxiety about their children. What were we doing? All of us had to assure our families that our struggle was not directed at taking innocent lives, but at attacking and destroying government property.

Some of our co-accused were breadwinners who had children to support and send to school. Others had older parents to look after. Many families wondered how they were going to survive if we were jailed. At times when we were locked up in our cells during the night, I could hear the sounds of soft prayers and even quiet sobbing. Many were battling with fear for families left behind to fend for themselves. I think if I had had children back then, I too would have sunk into despair. Yet even this did not affect our revolutionary morale and our militancy during the trial. I remembered the words of Chief Albert Luthuli: 'Our African revolution, to our credit, is proving to be orderly, quick and comparatively bloodless. We must let courage rise with danger.'

Our trial was held in Pietermaritzburg, about a hundred kilometres from Durban – a far distance for most of our families to travel. During December, we insisted on being transferred to the Durban Central Prison to be closer to them. At first, the authorities agreed and took us there. But a few days later, we were told we were moving back. This was sheer vindictiveness, so we refused and had running battles with the warders in the prison yard until they forced us into the police trucks.

When I first appeared in court, there were nineteen of us, but only eighteen were sentenced. This was the first time that I had appeared in the Supreme Court, and it was intimidating. We were constantly in contact with our lawyers, who wanted statements from us. The prosecution was very hostile. They brought evidence against us, hoping we would get the maximum penalty: death. They led evidence from people who betrayed us.

Perhaps all we could rely upon was daily routine. After court, we would go back to our cells and discuss among ourselves the evidence against us and who had said what. The next morning, we would be back in the police van to be taken to court. This went on for many months. It was depressing, but it did not affect our spirit. We maintained a high morale. We stood up to say that we were members of MK and we were fighting an

Ebie in primary school in Durban, 1947. Ebie is in the second row from the back, and the fifth from the left.

LEFT *Ebie and his family at his parents' home in Candella Rd, Durban in 1955. Ebie is on the far left, his brother Gora on the far right, and his father and mother are to the right of him.*

RIGHT *Ebie as a young man in Durban in his early twenties.*

BOTTOM-LEFT *Ebie cuts the cake at the celebration of 25 years of the* New Age *newspaper in 1962 in Durban. To the left of him is Ronnie Kasrils.*

LEFT *Ebie's father Mohamed Modan and mother Hafiza in tears outside the Pietermaritzburg Supreme Court on 28 February 1964, after Ebie was sentenced to 15 years on Robben Island*

RIGHT *Ebie walking in the streets of Durban on Eid day in 1979 after his release after 15 years on Robben Island*

Ebie with his brother Essop, mother Hafiza, and sister-in-law Fatima in Reservoir Hills, Durban after Ebie was released from Robben Island in 1979

Ebie with his brothers Essop (left) and Gora (middle) at his underground house in Swaziland in 1983

A sketch of Ebrahim in heavy disguise while underground in Durban in 1985, drawn by Jansie Niehaus and given to Hélène Passtoors as a birthday gift while they were both in Pretoria prison

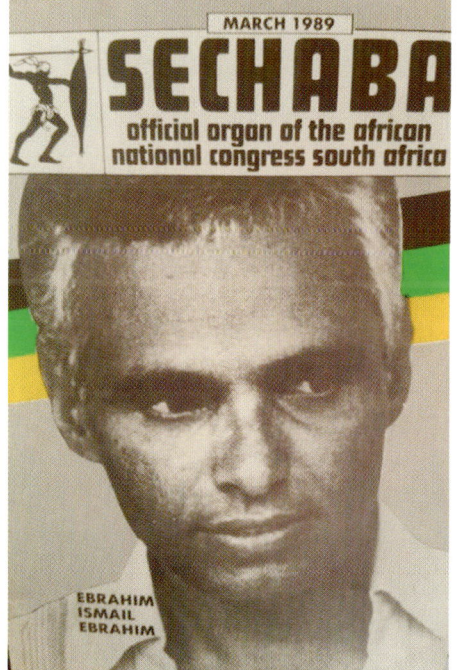

Ebrahim on the cover of the ANC's March 1989 publication of Sechaba. *The publication carries his statement in mitigation of sentence during his treason trial in 1989.*

ANC newsletter of July 1989 dedicated to freeing political prisoners. Ebie features in the bottom row, second from the right.

Ebie on the ferry on his release from Robben Island in 1991 (Liz Fish)

Ebie arriving at the Cape Town docks after being released from Robben Island on 26 February 1991 (Liz Fish)

Ebie waving to well wishers on his release from Robben Island (Liz Fish)

LEFT *Ebie with Nelson Mandela after his release from Robben Island in 1991*

RIGHT *Ebie at a lunch with Nelson Mandela, Walter Sisulu, Rica Hodgson and others at the home of Amina Cachalia after his release from Robben Island in 1991*

Ebie at an ANC rally with Terror Lekota, Harry Gwala, Nelson Mandela and Chris Hani

Ebie and President Nelson Mandela at a function post-1994

Ebie on Human Rights Day after being presented with a medal from the ANC for his contribution to the fight for human rights in South Africa

Ebie as a member of parliament in 1997

LEFT *Ebie and his brother Gora at a meeting of the Patriotic Front in 1991*

RIGHT *Ebie and Shannon at the Taj Mahal 2001*

Ebie on a camel safari in the Great Thar desert in Jaisalmer, India in December 2001

Ebie and Shannon on the sand dunes in the Great Thar desert, 2001

Ebie and Shannon on their first visit to Jerusalem in July 2001. Behind them is the old city.

Shannon and Ebie meeting with Yasser Arafat in his compound in Palestine in July 2001

Ebie and his mother-in-law Susan Walker on a visit to the stone quarry on Robben Island in 2003 where Ebie broke stones from 1964–1979. In the background is the dyke which the prisoners built.

unjust system. Two of our leaders – Billy and Curnick – took the witness stand to address the court specifically on the oppression that we suffered. It was a grim process.

To an extent, we were bolstered by the Rivonia trialists, and by other trials going on around the country. In Cape Town Neville Alexander and ten other members of the National Liberation Front (NLF) went on trial in 1963 for distributing literature about guerrilla strategy. Neville had been affiliated to the Unity Movement before forming the Yu Chin Chan Club (referring to 'guerrilla warfare', as executed by Mao) – later known as the NLF – with revolutionaries Dulcie September and others. Neville would be convicted of conspiracy to commit sabotage in 1964 and jailed on Robben Island.

At the end of our trial, one of our co-accused was found not guilty and discharged as there was insufficient evidence against him. The rest of us did not deny our involvement in sabotage, nor did we plead guilty. I was sentenced to fifteen years' imprisonment, and Billy and Curnick to twenty years each. Comrade Babenia was sentenced to sixteen years.

My mum and dad cried in court when the sentence was passed, and so did the parents and wives of others among us. Yet the relief that we did not get the death sentence was supreme, although the long prison terms and the thought of what kind of conditions we would have to suffer while incarcerated affected them very deeply.

The lieutenant in charge of the matter wrote in his report to the Prison Board about me:

> Accused was a regional committee member for a sabotage group called Spear of the Nation which committed sabotage in Natal in an attempt to intimidate the government and members of the public in preparation for a general guerrilla war against the white population and the violent taking over of the government of the Republic of South Africa.
>
> The prisoner was a member of the Natal Indian Youth Congress from about 1946.
>
> His associations are with political fanatics and the general impression the prisoner made on the investigating officer is that he is communistically inclined.
>
> He is a well-known agitator.

I was comfortable about accepting all of the above.

My personal history register stated that I was fit for hard labour. It noted that I had no physical defects and that I was of above-average intelligence. It described my parents as 'well-behaved people and law-abiding citizens'. But the summary noted: 'Prisoner is a dangerous, unscrupulous blaggard totally lacking in respect for the government and opposed to its policy. He is very cunning and would not hesitate to resort to violence to achieve his freedom. It is recommended that this prisoner be detained in a maximum security prison for the bulk of his sentence and that he be placed on Robben Island as speedily as possible.'

Once again, I was comfortable about accepting that description.

Thirteen
They always lie: The beginning of the Robben Island years

WHEN WE GOT BACK to prison, the attitude of the prison warders had changed. Previously, they would greet us; some would even smile. Now we were convicted prisoners and they wanted us to feel it. They spoke to us in harsh tones, and ordered us to remove our civilian clothing and hand over our books and few possessions. In return, we got oversized prison trousers and shirts. That was it. For George Naicker, who was of small build, the trouser length was shoulder-high and the waist double his size. It sounds wrong, but we couldn't help laughing – at the clothing and the attitude of the warders. Soon we were separated, each of us put into our own cell. That meant there was silence after lock-up.

I had a sense at the time that none of us thought we would actually serve even a portion of our sentences. After all, the Organisation of African Unity had already been established, to liberate the continent from colonialism and racial oppression. A spirit of militant African nationalism was sweeping through Africa. Even the British prime minister Harold Macmillan had warned of 'the winds of change' in a speech at the South African Parliament in Cape Town. Moreover, the General Assembly of the United Nations passed a resolution in 1963 by a record 106 votes to 1 (apartheid South Africa) demanding the release of political prisoners in South Africa.

But the truth was that many of our leaders had in fact left the country to continue the struggle from abroad. Ronnie Kasrils would join other ANC members undergoing training in Odessa in the Soviet Union in 1964. By 1965, the ANC had recruits based at MK camps in Kongwa and Morogoro in Tanzania. Others were undergoing training courses in Czechoslovakia and China. Yet we know the numbers were comparatively small. There is no evidence of any major exodus of anti-apartheid militants between 1965 and 1970. By 1966, South Africa's liberation movements had been all but quelled. It would be fair to say there was an apparent quiescence among the people in the country. Attempts by Bram Fischer and Griffiths Mxenge, among others, to gather and mobilise the remnants of the ANC and SACP inside South Africa were summarily put down by the security police, making large-scale recruitment for guerrilla training unlikely.

Thus, when the sun went down outside and we were still in our cells, night after night, the silence became more and more pronounced. Only Joshua Zulu's chants broke the stillness. He was a dedicated Christian and always prayed for us, and we would all shout 'Amen' at the end before we lapsed back into our private thoughts. Comrades' mental health quickly took a decline, as they became increasingly stressed about their loved ones, especially their children, who were now effectively fatherless. Now that I am a father, and benefit every day from being with my children, I can understand how those men felt about that gulf growing between them and their sons and daughters.

Of course, the months of isolation, interrogation and torture affected us all rather badly. There was no psychological treatment; none of us was able to properly comfort or counsel others. We were all alone with ourselves and our violent dreams.

It is true that the police had little respect for those who had betrayed us. Some of the police admitted after the trial that they admired us for standing by our principles and surviving their torture. They would tell us, 'Look at So-and-so ... give him a "klap" [a smack], he told us everything.' They said the traitors were weak while we were men of substance. They always lie.

The day after our sentencing was a Saturday and we expected visits from family and friends in the morning. The warders instead told our families to collect our belongings. We were woken up at five and instructed to line up in the prison yard, where we were given pap to eat as usual. After that, we were made to stand in pairs, handcuffed and leg-ironed together. We were shuffled roughly into a huge prison truck and escorted by police vehicles out of Pietermaritzburg. Thus began my long journey of fifteen years. When I left, I had little hope of ever being a parent, ever being married and having a family. How could I envisage that? The handcuffs and leg irons hurt, and the heat of the sun and lack of air inside the truck made us perspire.

It was late afternoon when we arrived at Leeuwkop Prison in Johannesburg. The next morning was 'reception' day, when all our particulars were taken, and we were fingerprinted and given a prison number. After that, we had to visit the sick bay and assemble in the hospital yard where we had to strip naked and squat in a row on the cement floor. This practice was actually illegal in terms of prison regulations. When we got to the yard, there were already a few rows of common law prisoners lined up naked, but at a distance from us. We were considered too dangerous to mix with them.

To our surprise, a doctor walked through the ranks of the common law prisoners as if he were inspecting men on a parade, and declared them all fit. There was no medical examination. This, we later found out, was the procedure in most of the prisons. But not for us. We were examined individually by a doctor who appeared friendly and listened to our medical complaints. Then, while we were still naked, we were instructed to turn to face the wall in the prison yard. We then had to bend over and touch our feet. I noticed from the corner of my eye that a warder was putting on a pair of gloves before he picked up a container. Comrade Billy whispered that they were probably going to give us an injection. But that was not so. The warder was, rather, inserting his finger into each prisoner's anus to check whether any of us was hiding a weapon. This very painful and humiliating experience turned out to be a common procedure in apartheid prisons.

We then had to dress in prison clothing, consisting of a pair of short khaki pants and a khaki shirt; we were not given shoes. After that, another regular prisoner appeared in the yard with a sheep-shearing machine and proceeded to move from one man to the next and shave off all our hair. A warder instructed us that we were required to shave and he then sharpened a blade on a piece of stone. He gave us each a blob of liquid soap and we had to shave with the blunt blade.

Another blob was all we were given to wash our bodies in a cold shower under what felt like a few seconds of water. The warder said there were no towels available, and we would have to run in the yard to get dry. Warders were stationed in various spots around us bearing batons, and we had to run fast to escape their assaults. This went on for about half an hour before we were herded into our cell, wet with perspiration and completely exhausted. All political prisoners were housed in one section, walled off with a long triangular yard. All eighteen of us were put into one cell.

The running and the beatings were carried out twice a day to fulfil prison regulations that allowed prisoners 'exercise'. This was punishment, accompanied by food deprivation with the excuse that we 'did not run fast enough' when collecting our rations. This hell continued for a week before we were finally transported to Robben Island as a group of sixty-one prisoners, handcuffed and leg-ironed in pairs and crowded and squeezed into huge police trucks. Most of us sat on the floor of the truck with the leg irons bruising our ankles. When one of us wanted to relieve himself, it became a nightmare. There was a bucket for that purpose in the truck. This indignity was only one aspect of the torturous road trip from Johannesburg to Cape Town.

We travelled the whole day until we reached Colesberg, where we were held at the local prison overnight with our leg irons on. I happened to be shackled to Dennis Brutus, a visionary comrade who fought for apartheid South Africa to be boycotted from international sporting events. He told me that my brother Gora had left the country. I knew of course that the police had been looking for him, but the last time I had seen him was when he was a student at Wits University, living in Johannesburg, in 1962. When I was on trial, he went into hiding from the security police. Dennis worked closely with Gora to ensure South Africa did not take part in the Olympic Games, and Gora took over his role at the South African Non-Racial Olympic Committee (SANROC) when Dennis was jailed. They coined the slogan 'No normal sport in an abnormal society', and succeeded in preventing the country's sporting bodies from participating in sporting events and competitions overseas until 1992. It was a huge achievement for human rights and made a remarkable contribution to the other sanctions applied against the regime.

Jacob Zuma was also in our truck. He could speak a bit of English, but at times Shadrack Maphumulo would translate some words for him. I had known of Comrade Zuma casually in Durban as he was in the trade union movement and an activist, but I had never really spoken to him before. All of my fellow Pietermaritzburg trialists – including Billy, Curnick and Sunny – were with me, and the sixty-one of us in that truck would end up in the same cell on Robben Island.

The following afternoon we arrived in Cape Town. For most of us it was our first sight of Table Mountain. I had wondered about that majestic sight for many years. For the next fifteen years, I would be looking at it almost every day, depending on whether I was working in the quarry, on the seashore or being punished. Sometimes when my family and I travel to Cape Town on holiday, I get a shiver of recognition. I connect that picture to my imprisonment. I connect my imprisonment to every postcard I see of the mountain.

When we arrived in Cape Town we were shackled and handcuffed together in pairs and had to shuffle our way onto the *Susan Kruger* ferry. We were not allowed to choose where to sit, or talk, and were all but thrown into the deck below. It was difficult to make our way down the stairs joined together, but we somehow managed.

It was late summer, March, but the calm Cape weather had no good effect on the sea. It was rough as the boat bobbed up and down on the waves. Some prisoners were physically ill as they had never been on the ocean before.

When we disembarked from the ferry at Robben Island's Murray Bay dock, a group of white warders armed with guns and batons were waiting for us. There were no black guards, apparently out of fear that they might sympathise with our cause. We didn't know much about the place then, but it had a heavy and ominous air. We could see the remains of structures close to the shore and, over time, became aware of the hundreds of people unjustly held there before us, many of them buried in graves of those after succumbing on its inhospitable ground.

During the 19th century, most had died from the chronic infectious disease leprosy, after being stripped of their civil rights and banished to the island. The Cape government passed the Leprosy Repression Act in 1891, which mainly affected African people until 1931, when the Leprosarium on Robben Island was finally closed. There were four cemeteries, yet more and more bones were found scattered around. To this day people claim that the island is haunted by the spirits of the dead.

We were to be jailed in the 'old prison' where Comrade Mandela was held. We noticed that parts of the prison were incomplete, and it seemed we would have to construct our own 'new' jail ourselves.

The warders told us that planes flying overhead could 'bomb us'.

'You see these planes, they are our planes, and we can bomb you,' the warders said.

We had to hand back our Leeuwkop Prison garb the moment we arrived and cover ourselves with dirty blankets before we were given pants, a shirt and a pair of shoes or sandals each – the Robben Island uniform. It took many years before we were given any underwear. Indian and Coloured prisoners were given long trousers, but in terms of the apartheid regulations Africans got short pants only. Indians and Coloureds were given shoes, but Africans were only given sandals.

Our details were recorded and fingerprints taken, and we were then marched to the main prison in twos to the sound of a warder shouting 'stap'. Not understanding Afrikaans, I thought this meant we had to 'stap it', so, being in the front of the line, I stopped. The warder swore at me and beat me on the head until someone explained that 'stap' meant 'move'.

When we got to the prison yard, a lieutenant addressed us. 'This is not a five-star hotel or a holiday resort,' he bellowed. Warders rarely spoke: they always shouted. One warder roared at us, saying that our time would be spent working and obeying instructions. I looked at the grim surroundings – a quarry in which the walls of stone were so intense in the sunlight that the surfaces appeared blue – and I knew we were in for a worse time than we had imagined.

In 1964, Robben Island's prison population was about 1,500. South African anti-apartheid campaigner and author Mary Benson reported in *The Guardian* in August 1964 that 'about 500 [prisoners on the Island had been] convicted of crimes such as murder, robbery, rape, assault, fraud, housebreaking and theft. The remaining 1,000 [were] political prisoners. Three hundred have been convicted of sabotage, a political crime which imposes heavier penalties than the common law crime of treason, and places the onus of proving innocence on the accused. The remainder [were] convicted of offences in terms of the Suppression of Communism Act (1950), the Public Safety Act of 1953, the 1953 Criminal Law Amendment Act outlawing passive resistance, the Riotous Assemblies Act (1956) and the 1960 Unlawful Organisations Act outlawing the ANC, the PAC and, later, the Congress of Democrats.'[4]

It might seem strange, as Robben Island is now embedded in our history, but in 1964 we had very little information about it, as it had only functioned as a maximum security prison since 1961. We came to know it like the inside of our minds. It felt as if there were other people's awful histories and memories of hate and subjugation everywhere, even though it hadn't been a prison for so long. Later, in 1969, a kramat was erected on the Island – a Muslim shrine which memorialised our brothers and sisters from the East Indies who had resisted the Dutch colonisers and who had been exiled to the Cape in the 1600s and 1700s. Some were princes and imams. We Muslim prisoners were not allowed to visit the kramat after it was built, although we knew there was a holy site on the Island. It's now one of more than twenty sites forming 'the Holy Circle of Islam' surrounding Cape Town. Some common law prisoners built that kramat, which is similar to the humble building with the green dome on Signal Hill near Lion's Head, that now gazes down on the endless blue sea.

We political prisoners were put to work breaking stones in the blinding quarry. Here we were joined by another 'span' (a group of prisoners who did hard labour), led by Andrew Masondo. In 1963 Masondo was the leader of an MK sabotage unit based at Fort Hare who sawed down an electricity pole leaving large parts of the town of Alice and the university in darkness. Like so many of us, he was fearless and therefore a target for the warders. His group refused to obey an instruction at the quarry and were brought to the prison yard to be punished by having to pick up heavy boulders and run and throw them down into the foundations being dug for the new prison building. Warders with batons beat the prisoners on their heads and backs as they ran. To demonstrate to us that we were not 'on holiday', the warders made us join this torture. I could scarcely carry some of the boulders.

On our first night we got pap to eat as usual. We were also given sisal mats that scratched us and offered little to no protection from the cold cement floor. If our political movement had placed some of us higher on account of our seniority, none of that mattered in terms of the living conditions within the prison system. It was common to be in an overcrowded cell, crammed with more than eighty people instead of the intended twenty-five. I tried to stay as near as I could to comrades George Naicker, Steve Tshwete, Douglas Sparks and a few others. We were only about ten ANC comrades there and we occupied a corner next to the entrance. Eighty unrolled mats would never have been able to fit into the cell, so every three prisoners would sleep across two mats and share their threadbare blankets. We only got beds after the mid-1970s. What made sleeping also difficult was that the prison authorities insisted on keeping the fluorescent lights shining in the cells all through the night.

Earlier that evening, we laughingly showed each other the assault marks on our bodies. We laughed because, despite the torment, we knew we were better than the warders and the government which paid them, and that their brutality and fear of us would never stop our freedom from coming. But the physical assaults on our first day in prison became routine, as did being sworn at and brought to near starvation. Many warders delighted in this entertainment. It killed the boredom of their existence. By the late 1960s, it seemed many had joined the prison service to escape conscription into the army, yet the prison system was itself militarised and all personnel had some kind of military training.

A bell rang at six in the morning and we had to get up at once or be punished. On waking, we had to fold our blankets into a pile and place them on top of the mat, which then had to be rolled up. The sixty-one of us had to clean ourselves in a small washroom which had only two toilets without surrounding cubicles: there was no privacy. There were three showers which we had to take turns to use. Hard, brackish, cold water spat onto us, and there was no chance of it washing the soap out of your hair.

We then had to get dressed and be ready when the warders opened the cell and shouted 'Val in!' (fall in line). We had to stand in twos to be counted. Warders would be posted on either side of the doorway to hit us with their batons as we stepped out of the cell. Since we always had to leave our shoes and sandals outside in the open, we simply grabbed any two we could lay our hands on as we went out. As a result the shoes we wore all day were often of different sizes, and sometimes meant for the same foot. On the way to the prison kitchen, inmates were able to make a quick exchange.

We queued for breakfast. This consisted of a plate of soft mielie porridge and a teaspoon of brown sugar handed to us as we passed the kitchen. We would then collect a metal mug to scoop black coffee out of a huge pot, and squat in rows to eat. Seagulls would hover, motionless, above us throughout the meal, and their droppings sometimes fell into our food. We were given wooden spoons when we arrived, and after eating, we had to lick the spoon and put it into our pocket. That spoon would remain with us at all times.

Then would come the call for 'hospital'. A medical warder would call out 'fuba', meaning 'chest'. All those who had a cold, cough or problems with their respiratory system would stand in a queue. The warder would not enquire as to your ailment but simply proceed to administer to everyone in the queue the same medication from a tiny glass, drawing on a huge bottle. We all used the same glass. This procedure would be repeated for 'maag' (stomach). Whatever your gut issues, you were given the same medicine as everyone in the queue. On one occasion, the notorious commanding officer of the prison, Major PA Kellerman, was present when the medication was being administered, and he instructed that all those in the 'maag' queue be given castor oil – a kind of laxative. I don't wish to tell you what the result of that was: and we had only two toilets.

There were also queues for 'kopseer' (headache) and 'pyne' (general aches and pains). The warder wasn't interested in the nature of our ailments, and the chances of seeing an actual doctor were slim. We were in fact discouraged from seeing the doctor who visited Robben Island twice a week, on Tuesdays and Thursdays. One just prayed not to fall ill.

Then came the call to go to the stone quarry along the seashore. Mandela and the Rivonia trialists, who arrived on the Island some months after us, worked, on the other hand, in the lime quarry where they dug out lime used to repair the prison roads. They were kept in individual cells in the isolation section of the prison. We had very little physical contact with them, although we were able to correspond with them by using clandestine methods to smuggle messages.

As we got to the quarry, the warders called out to all the 'coolies' and 'amper basies' ('almost-bosses', referring to the Coloureds – the diminutive form makes it even more insulting) to stand to one side. We had to take barrows, which had iron instead of rubber wheels, making it much more difficult to push because the iron sinks into soft sand. I would struggle to push the barrow up an incline, and a warder would beat me relentlessly with a baton. 'You coolie,' he shouted, using other insults and swearwords. 'You want to rule my country but you can't even push a wheelbarrow!'

Lunch was cold, boiled mielies. Indians were given cold, hard mielie rice, which was even worse as it had been stripped of any nutrition whatsoever. We also got a mug of very weak, diluted 'phuzamandla', a kind of powdered soup.

We returned to the prison building in formations of four, and then had to undergo a strip search. We often waited in line completely naked for more than twenty minutes. Young and old, father and son, brother and uncle, all had to go through this violation of our dignity and, often, impairment of our health. We were exposed to unbearably freezing conditions. The warders seemed to enjoy this. One by one we had to go to a waiting warder and hand over our clothing one item at a time to be searched. We then had to open our mouths and show our backsides to prove that we were not hiding anything.

Years later, we acquired an abridged copy of the prison regulations, which clearly stated that if a prisoner was to be strip-searched, it had to be done privately: 'A prisoner must not be asked to strip in the presence of another prisoner.' Once we knew that, we refused to be searched in that manner again. The warder had to see us each separately, in an office, a procedure which took up a lot of time. We would undress slowly and then take ample time while getting dressed again. The authorities soon tired of this and resorted to frisking us.

Our hearts would sink when the bell rang in the morning. Many of us would fear what the day might bring. We worried whether we would escape punishment. The arbitrary sanction of 'drie maaltye' (three meals) was used extensively by the prison. A warder would take your prison card for no apparent reason and have you deprived of three meals over a weekend. Your last meal would thus be served on a Saturday at about two, and then you would be locked up in a separate cell until Monday morning, when you would have breakfast and go to work in the quarry. If you escaped 'drie maaltye' during the day, you considered yourself lucky. I starved over many, many weekends.

In any case the food given to us was always insufficient. This meant food smuggling was a constant problem on the Island, often emanating from the store. Warders and common law prisoners would steal from our supplies as soon as these were delivered to the prison, leaving us with less than we should have had – and it was not much, or nourishing, to begin with. As prisoners we were perpetually hungry.

I was also spiritually hungry. For fifteen years, I was not permitted to see a Muslim cleric and was not even allowed a copy of the Holy Quran.

Cruelty towards us on the island was routine, and many prisoners fell desperately ill. When we first arrived on the Island, there was no toilet paper and we had to tear off pieces of cement bags. These were lying around from the construction work. This added considerably to our discomfort, but after a year, the prison authorities realised that the paper from the cement bags were blocking the sewage pipes, and they finally decided to give us toilet paper.

The other thing we desperately needed was a handkerchief to blow our noses during the lengthy days at the quarry. Many prisoners had ongoing colds and flu. Every Sunday during inspection, we would demand handkerchiefs and, finally, much to our surprise, we were all issued with pieces of red cloth for this purpose. At weekends, we would wash the cloths in the bathroom basins and hang them out to dry by tying them to the cell window grilles. One weekend, Captain Naude saw the red handkerchiefs all tied up and started shouting and performing, claiming we were 'flying the red flag'. He demanded that all the communist cloths be confiscated immediately.

Fourteen
The despised

I'M NOT SURE WHICH OF ONE'S many trials in life affect one the most. I try not to count and place everything in a ledger. Instead, when I used to balance the books (as it were) during the anti-apartheid struggle, the fact that the ANC would win the war of liberation had to dominate one's thoughts. Yet even that prospect was challenging to imagine at times on Robben Island. As I have mentioned already, we were expected to push a wheelbarrow full of sand up a soft sandy incline and were beaten by the warders if we failed. That just about describes the general psychological state that we endured during imprisonment. Not long after we arrived on the Island, I resolved not to endure that gruelling punishment. I made the decision to refuse to do our torturous manual labour one morning as we marched to the quarry. I was given an iron wheelbarrow and a common law prisoner tipped a mountain of sand into it. As I tilted the barrow to level it, a warder watching me swore at me as he instructed the other prisoner to fill it higher. I again tilted the barrow and the warder again instructed that more sand be shovelled in. He then assaulted me. He went on to do this three times and finally demanded my prison card.

In terms of the regulations, a warder had to tell a prisoner to do something three times, and be ignored three times before the convict could be charged with insubordination, which is considered a serious crime in prison. This warder, a notoriously aggressive individual who went by the name of Kleynhans, marched me back to the prison, swearing at me all the way. Fortunately I did not understand Afrikaans, and the only word I knew was the derogative 'coolie'. He took me to the head of the prison, who said I would be charged, but first he insisted I be taken to the prison hospital to ascertain that I wasn't ill.

The doctor happened to be there on that day. He checked my pulse and requested I do some exercises, then he examined me, during which time I explained the situation of the prisoners. Finally, he wrote in his file that I should not be made to push wheelbarrows any longer and instead be given 'suitable labour'. The warder was fuming as he took me back to the head of the prison, who shrugged his shoulders and said there was nothing he could do about it.

I wrote a letter to the commanding officer a week later.

Dear Sir,

On Monday, I was severely assaulted by a warder while at work at the 'new' quarry.

I reported the assault to the chief warder on the same day and also showed him the injuries. He thereupon promised to investigate the matter. I was also examined by a doctor on the following day.

I deeply appreciate the fact that the prison authorities had undertaken to investigate the matter, and as such I do wish to leave the matter in your hands.

I surely hope that a repetition of this nature will not occur.

Thanking you,
Yours faithfully,
Ebrahim Ismail

The next day I was not sent to the quarry but given a cloth and Brasso to shine the pipes in the prison. I was kept in the yard for a few days doing this, mainly in the temporary corrugated iron building set up for common law prisoners, who were used as builders for the stone jail. But after that, I was sent back to the quarry, which remained a site of struggle. Prison life was a continuous struggle for survival and an uninterrupted fight against mistreatment.

Once when I was working, an infamous warder, Sergeant Du Plessis, ordered me to remove my shoes and step into a pool of stagnant water to dig out small sharp stones with my spade. Vindictive as he was, he knew my feet would get cut. He repeated his order three times, and I refused three times. Du Plessis then took my prison card and marched me to the office, where the officer in charge decided I would be charged with insubordination. I immediately asked for a 'letter privilege' to write to Rowley Arenstein in Durban. He was my lawyer. In terms of the 'letter privilege', political prisoners in category D (the lowest category of all) could receive only one letter each six months.

The next day, Du Plessis ordered Indres Naidoo to get into the stagnant pool and do the same as I had been asked. He also refused and wrote to his lawyer in Johannesburg. While we waited for our cases to be heard, Indres was taken to the isolation cells and cut off from all contact with us. We found out later that he had appeared in court without a legal representative and Major Kellerman had presided over his case which lasted well into the night. Indres was sentenced to four strokes on his backside with a whip. It appears that when his lawyer phoned the prison administration, he was dissuaded from appearing by being told it was 'a small matter' and that Indres would not be punished for it.

The next day, I was informed I would be appearing in court that day. I was asked to identify my witnesses and made to stand before the administration office for about two hours while 'thinking of my defence'. Eventually I spotted a boat arriving from the mainland and was glad to see I had been provided with a lawyer. But when he and I met to discuss my case, I wasn't aware Indres had been punished. This would have created a precedent, and I could also have been sentenced for the same offence.

When my trial began, Du Plessis gave evidence that I had refused an instruction. The next witness for the state was a common law prisoner – someone I had not seen before. He testified that I was instructed by the 'baas' to get into the water to remove the stones. But when the prosecutor asked him what happened next, the prisoner said I stepped into the pool and removed all the stones. My attorney from Cape Town, whom Comrade Rowley had instructed to represent me, immediately asked for a discharge on the grounds that the witnesses gave conflicting evidence. The presiding lieutenant agreed and discharged me, but I was puzzled at the outcome of the case.

It wasn't until I got back to the cells and found out that Indres had been unlawfully sentenced that I realised what had happened. If I had been found guilty, the court would have had to decide what my sentence would be. That is why the common law prisoner was told to contradict Du Plessis so that I could be found not guilty on their own evidence. Of course the prisoner was rewarded by being promoted to work in the kitchen, where he could help himself to our food.

Warders were generally afraid of lawyers and the law. At times when a warder took your card to punish you, and you threatened him with a lawyer, he would return it. One day in the quarry I refused to overfill a wheelbarrow pushed by another prisoner, and a warder nicknamed 'Boxer' – for good reason – took my card and promised to discipline me for not working properly. Accompanied by another warder, he marched me to the administration office, but all along the route he assaulted me, calling me a 'cheeky coolie'. They beat me until my nose was bleeding and my lips were cut.

I reported the matter to the chief warder, who instructed that I be taken to the hospital where a doctor was available. The doctor examined me and wrote a report. The next day, I demanded to see my lawyer so that I could lay charges, but the authorities said I could charge 'Boxer' without legal assistance. A hostile police detective from Cape Town arrived on the Island and took a statement from me, my witness and the warder. The detective couldn't understand why a prisoner should have the audacity to press charges against a white warder, and repeated the question: was I certain that I wanted to do this? My case nonetheless went before a magistrate in Cape Town, where the warder was found guilty and sentenced to a fine. After the case, 'Boxer' was a completely changed person. He became my friend, and a friend to all the prisoners until he was removed from the Island. That showed us that ordinary warders could be prosecuted if they followed officials' instructions to mete out brutality.

So as prisoners we developed a policy that we would overwhelm whoever toured the Island, including prison officials who came for inspection on Sundays, with our complaints. We would surround the visitors and protest relentlessly. The PAC prisoners soon followed suit. When the MP Helen Suzman visited the Island, we spoke out about the

The despised

beatings, the foul language directed at us and the punishments. She was accompanied by the national commissioner of prisons, who turned to the commanding officer of the prison for an explanation.

Most of our battles were not fought in that way, though. They were fought in the heartlessness of the quarry where we drilled huge slabs of stone day after day to make them crack apart and then pulled them out of the deep holes to the surface.

A group of us would 'dress' big slabs of stone for the building of the prison while others would break up stones into smaller pieces for use in concrete. This labour destroyed one's mind as much as it was physically agonising. We went through hell having to break a certain quantity of stones every day and then pile them into a pyramid. At the end of the working day, a warder would come around to each of us with a measure, and if the stone chips did not fill it up, we would be punished with 'drie maaltye'. It was almost impossible to meet the quota, especially for older prisoners, whom the rest of us would try to assist and thereby protect from additional punishment. This practice continued for many years.

Eventually we defied the authorities one day by refusing to fulfil the quota, and we were duly charged for disobedience, but this time we were not punished by 'drie maaltye'. Instead, we had to appear before a prison court presided over by a prison official. This entitled us to be represented by a lawyer, so we wrote to a law firm in Cape Town to take advantage of our situation and use it as a test case. And indeed, the case was cut and dried. There was nothing stipulated in prison regulations or the law about meeting 'quotas', much to the dissatisfaction of the presiding officer. After that, we worked only as much as we could, even though the warders continued to harass us. This ultimately resulted in the hated quarry being closed a few years later.

Another battle that we fought in the context of the quarry – that hostile echo chamber of spades and hammers – also produced a positive outcome for us prisoners. The quarry on the Island was exposed to the cold Cape winds whipping off the icy ocean, and although we had a canvas jacket in the summer, and a jersey and thicker jacket in the winter, these provided little protection against the gales. It felt as if the wind was biting into us and penetrating our bones. Many prisoners suffered rheumatic illnesses, and there was never appropriate medicine or means to treat them. Some died as a result. To try to shield ourselves, we often put up shoulder-high shelters of corrugated iron or plastic. We also used plastic bags or cut up our sacks to create windproof vests to keep slightly warmer.

One afternoon as the icy air billowed in and froze our joints, Captain Naude skidded into the quarry in a government car and shouted at the warder in charge, demanding we be made to break down our ramshackle shelters and throw off our meagre coverings. The only option we had once 'Naude' left was to take our stones for breaking and sit along the dyke or embankment next to the quarry, which at least slightly held off the wind. The warder in charge did not object.

The following day, Naude came again and was furious that we were occupying a moderately warmer place to break our stones. He screamed that we were 'not in a township'; we were prisoners and had to bear the chilly wind. He instructed the warder to move us, but we all refused. The atmosphere was tense. It was Friday and we were to be taken back to the prison much earlier. As we left the quarry, a truck packed with common law prisoners arrived. They were to move our stones from along the wall and place them again on the open ground.

By now, our mood was defiant. There was plenty of singing in the ANC cells over that weekend and we in the leadership had to give some direction as to what the prisoners should do on the Monday at the quarry. We told all our members not to move from our position on the dyke.

Early on the Monday, the warders, led by the head of the prison, Major Kellerman, raided the cells with dogs to intimidate us. At that time there was a separate section for prisoners who had permission to study. Only that section was opened for prisoners to go to work in the quarry. I was one of them. As usual we were supplied with hammers, a rubber holder and wire-mesh protection for our eyes. We collected our seats for breaking stones and proceeded to the dyke with our rocks. Immediately, a warder pointed his rifle at us, and demanded we stop moving. We ignored his instruction.

Soon, truckloads of armed warders led by Kellerman descended on the quarry. A volatile situation quickly developed. Many of the warders waved their rubber batons, itching to beat us up. We were prepared to defend ourselves. Kellerman shouted at his warders to remain still. Then, unexpectedly, he began to plead with us to obey his order to break the stones out in the open and, furthermore, raise our complaints with him. Zola Nqini, who spoke on our behalf, made it clear that we were not prepared to be victim to the weather's ravages any longer. He told Kellerman we would die right there, on that day, rather than perish slowly from exposure. We would not surrender.

Kellerman panicked. He had to restrain his men, who were eager to assault us. He then ordered that we march back to the prison. We were put in separate cells after that, and all privileges were revoked, including the right to study – for a year. Nonetheless, the comrades continued to defy the order to break stones in the open, and eventually we were all allowed to sit next to the dyke. This was an important victory and demonstrated unity in action even under the enemy's overall control. As for Kellerman, he was removed from Robben Island. That was a moment of triumph for us.

From time to time, we were sent to collect seaweed from the ocean. This was the everyday task of the 'bamboo span', a specific team of prisoners. We had to pile the seaweed up on the shore to dry. The warders would arrive in trucks to collect it and take it to a workshop to be ground into a kind of compost for export to France and Japan, and for use in shampoos and other cosmetic products. The labour involved in working with the seaweed left our uniforms very slimy and dirty, and we were forced to wear the same clothing the next day and the next. It was only at the weekend that we were given newly washed uniforms. Whether we worked in the dusty quarry or on the shoreline, we always wore filthy clothes.

On my first day in the 'bamboo span', I was told about the mussels we could collect off the rocks with our spades. At first, my friend Reggie Vandeyar, whom I had met in Kliptown at the launch of the Freedom Charter in 1955, would wash them and we'd eat them raw. Although they were quite tasty, they needed to be cooked. So during our lunch break, we would find a tin container that had drifted onto the shore, fill it with seawater, make a fire and boil the mussels. Most of the time, the warders didn't object. We thoroughly enjoyed the change of taste, given our spartan diet.

Some warders could be 'civilised'. They saw that if they treated us rudely and roughly, we would respond rudely and roughly. If they spoke to us in a more normal tone, we would respond in the same way. Some realised that the only way they could get our co-operation was to co-operate with us. In fact, with the co-operation of some of these 'civilised' warders on the beach, we would sometimes eat so many mussels that we weren't hungry for the dreadful prison dinner served once we got back to the yard.

On very few occasions, we were able to catch crayfish by going deeper in among the rocks. This was forbidden by the authorities, but if we had a friendly warder, he would allow us to do so – if we gave him a crayfish as well. We would boil the crayfish during lunchtime and share them among ourselves. They always tasted delicious cooked in saltwater.

Sometimes we even became conservationists for a day. When there was an oil spill off the Island, resident penguins would become saturated with oil from the slick and be unable to swim and catch fish. This was life-threatening to the birds. Some of us would be formed into a smaller 'span' to catch the penguins on the beach and rocks, and place them in baskets with covers. Chasing them was one thing, but actually catching them took some doing. It was more than a respite from the unpleasant work: it was even fun. It gave us comic relief watching the other men hurtling around after the penguins. The warders would take the captured penguins to the mainland where they would be washed before being released back on to the Island.

One day while I was working in the 'bamboo span', we found oranges and cartons of milk on the shoreline. A passing ship had lost some of its load, and this treasure miraculously reached us. The oranges were very welcome, as we were never given fruit in the early years. We all battled with vitamin C deficiency. The milk was fresh and we gulped it down.

Some prisoners would trap guinea fowl along the fence in the stone quarry. There was a shed in the vicinity, and Jeff Masemola, who worked as a prisoner blacksmith, always had a fire going, so he would cook the fowl for us. One morning, the prisoners found they had accidentally caught a peacock, which was quite rare as there were only a handful of these beautiful creatures on the Island. Knowing they would be severely punished if the authorities got to hear about it, they quickly skinned it, got rid of the feathers and had it cooked. The consensus was that it was very tasty. For days afterwards, the warders spent time looking for the missing peacock but never found it. This was a private joke among us for a long time.

Fifteen
Beautiful Cassia

I OFTEN WONDERED WHEN I was on Robben Island whether I would ever have children. I calculated that I would be forty-two when released, so it would still be possible that I could meet someone and start a family. But I had my doubts that I would ever be able to settle down. I knew I would remain committed to the struggle, and that would mean continuing my activism until the very moment of victory. This wasn't conducive to a 'normal' life.

When I was living under banning orders in Durban after my incarceration on Robben Island, I was introduced by some comrades to an American woman, Julie Wells, who wanted to interview me about my struggle history. She was doing graduate studies at Columbia University in New York. I got the sense that she was interested in me as a person too. We got to know each other over a few weeks before she returned to the US.

We lost touch for four years until she returned to southern Africa to visit some friends in Durban. On that visit she travelled with a friend to Swaziland. It turned out they were both looking for me, as they had heard I was based there. As luck would have it, I bumped into Julie at a market in Mbabane. We were both very happy to reconnect, and she decided to stay with me for a few days before going back to South Africa. We had fun, which was something so unusual for me, and we went out to restaurants and explored the countryside outside Manzini. She then returned to South Africa as planned.

A few weeks later I got a surprise visit from her. She had come to tell me that she was pregnant, and that she very much wanted to keep the baby. The news was stunning, to say the least, but Julie knew that I was living a complicated and dangerous life in the underground, and we couldn't be together in what one would consider a 'normal' relationship. I saw some of my comrades being good parents under extreme pressure, and some who had been separated from their children. Many were broken by that. I saw some who did not want to have relationships and responsibilities because they were so fearful. Everything was happening to us so quickly and under such hazardous conditions. We are still unable to judge each other fairly around these issues. I suppose we may never be able to do so, but that the kind of life we led affected our children is undeniable.

My first thought when Julie brought me the news was that Swaziland was not a safe place for her to stay. She returned as planned to her established life in New York and kept in touch with me long distance. In Swaziland there was always a struggle to just stay alive, and I thought if I could do that, that was about as much certainty as I could create.

When I first saw a photograph of Cassia, taken the day she was born on 12 December 1983, I was overcome with emotion. I had never anticipated becoming a father, and I loved her immediately.

Could Julie have brought her to me in the intervening years? How do I explain all of this in a way that is not painful to either her or me? For it is painful.

Julie's life continued in New York, and it would be five years before I first saw Cassia in person. That was in 1988 when I was being tried for treason in Pretoria. I have a clear image in my mind of that day. I wondered how a young child could understand that this person, surrounded by so much noise and drama, was her dad.

Sixteen
A story of sadness

I WAS CONSTANTLY MINDFUL of how difficult my imprisonment was for my family, especially my parents. It was not easy for them to visit me in prison during those years, as they were living in Durban, and the trip was expensive for them to undertake. I remember that my sister Ayesha had taken what money she had and made a three-day journey to visit me on the Island. She was absolutely heartbroken when she arrived at the Cape Town docks and was refused permission to see me. She literally had to turn round and make the journey back home. There was simply no humanity in the way the authorities treated our families. She tried again a year or two later and brought my mum with her. On that occasion the two of them succeeded in talking to me through a glass partition, having come all that way for only a half-hour visit. It was very emotional seeing them, and I could discern the real concern for my well being in their faces. That was the last time I saw them while on the Island as I discouraged them from visiting again in view of the expense.

Letters from home were like gold, but sometimes they affected us on a deep level – especially knowing that our loved ones were also going through their own troubles, and there was nothing we could do to assist. Some letters, like those from my niece Shaenaaz, Ayesha's daughter, gave me a poignant glimpse of the outside world.

Darling Uncle Ebrahim

Sorry for not writing earlier. I was a bit occupied. I hope you are fine. Did you receive the birthday card I made for you? Sorry if you received it late.

Grandma is in Durban. They came on the 2nd, the day of the July Handicap. She came to our place on Thursday and left on Saturday.

On the 4th (Monday), mum, dad and their friends went to the Mehmood Junior show at City Hall. They saw comedian (Tun Tun). We will be going to the fun fare soon.

Amina's wedding is on the 23rd July. We got an invitation but will not be going to the wedding. I suppose it's because we are casted as third class and poor. Mum says we rather stay at home instead of going and disgracing their rich and white families. We are known to be black. Mum's heart is broken.

Maybe you will understand when you come out. I am anxiously awaiting that big day.

Anyway, Iqbal received his birthday card. We had a small party for him. Inshaalah next year we will have a big one.

Did Uncle Kisten [Moonsamy] receive my letter? I haven't received a reply. Pass him my regards.

Bye for now. Please reply. Sorry for mistakes. Forgive.

Your loving,
Shaenaaz

This letter was a reflection of her world with its intra-community issues that brought their own harm. I could identify with what she wrote: I too had known that world while growing up, where some Indian people would be 'acceptable', but others not. I enjoyed the reminder of the July Handicap horserace, which is held annually in Durban. I could also imagine the excitement of my family seeing Naeem Sayyed, better known as Mehmood Junior, the film actor and singer from the 'real' India, and Tun Tun – the stage name of singer and comic Uma Devi Khatri, who was also from the subcontinent – live at the City Hall. A part of me longed to be there with my family. That spark was still inside me; that enjoyment of our popular culture, of the escape that movies and music brought us, which enabled one to forget the hard times.

But letters and messages could also bring deep pain. On the evening of 19 July 1968, I was called out of the supper period by the commanding officer. I had to go to his office, where he gave me a message: my dad had passed away. The message arrived in the form of a handwritten telegram sent from Pine Street Post Office, Durban, and addressed to me at R. Eiland Prison, Cape.

It read: 'Father died this morning will bury 7.30pm. Essop.'

The absence of emotion in the message hit my heart like a cannonball. It had arrived at the prison the previous day at 10.30am – I could see that from the date stamp at the top of the telegram – but I only received it thirty-three hours later – after my dad had been buried according to Muslim rites. I recognised my younger brother Essop's handwriting and his signature on the telegram. Next to his signature was that of the prison superintendent, who noted on the form that permission had been granted to show me the telegram. The officer said I could write a letter to my mother.

This was undoubtedly one of my saddest moments in prison. I went back to the prison yard and squatted next to George Naicker, who tried to comfort me. George was one of our most beloved comrades, and I believe we all relied on him in different ways. On that night, he recognised the pain of a prisoner losing a parent, having himself lost his mother while he was on the Island. But I felt terribly alone, despite the comfort George offered. It was an emptiness of a kind only a prisoner may know, because on most other issues we were able to share our feelings with one another. But when it came to the death of a loved one, there was no way of properly understanding another's emotions. We could only offer our condolences and commiserate with their loss. We were essentially left to deal with our grief inside ourselves.

I wrote to my mother the next day. I found it a difficult letter to write. I had last seen my dad crying in court when I was sentenced. That had been complicated enough as I had never had a relationship with him, because I grew up mostly with my grandmother. I think my dad resented this and felt rejected. He sometimes expressed his resentment physically. In my letter, I reminded my mother of how we respected her for bringing up a family virtually on her own.

As I mentioned earlier, we were permitted to write and receive only one letter every six months. Moreover, letters were censored, and as a result we could never describe prison conditions or refer to anything the authorities would consider 'political'. That meant the pain of the heart was censored too.

Our families tried to help us by sending us money. This was difficult for my parents as they had no money to speak of. There was no accrued wealth in our family. Every cent mattered for them. Money, and the little it could buy, were important for us on the Island. We were certainly not provided with everything we needed. We had to pay for many, if not most, things we required.

In February 1966, I wrote a letter to the commanding officer enquiring about money from home which had never been acknowledged.

Dear Sir,

Last month I received a visit from my aunt from Durban and she informed me that my parents have sent me some money for my use here in prison.

She also informed me that my parents have been sending me regular money.

However, I have no knowledge of how much money I have received and whether I have received the money at all.

When I approached the lieutenant about enquiring how much money I have, I was told to put my enquiries in writing. Hence, I am doing so now.

I hope, sir, you would inform me as to how much money I have in my property so that I could inform my parents the same.

Sir, it is necessary for me to acknowledge receipt of all moneys so that my parents could be satisfied that I have received the money.

Thanking you,
Yours faithfully,
Ebrahim Ismail

Our families continued to scrape together every rand they could to support us. They wanted to help us build some kind of a life – and an education was central to this. Even prison regulations encouraged further education, and an intellectual routine was necessary for developing some emotional stability. The authorities would relent after a while, but they made our academic path as challenging as possible. The University of

South Africa (Unisa) was identified as the institution to which we could apply for post-matric studies, while Rapid Results College was used by those requiring a primary or secondary education. These were strictly correspondence institutions, and we relied on the postal system and the warders for obtaining books and submitting our essays and exams.

I was fortunate to be among the first five prisoners, along with Comrade Mandela, to register for a Bachelor of Arts degree, since we were not permitted to take law degrees. The other three were 'Kathy' Kathrada, Siva Pillay and Jeff Masemola, who cooked the guinea fowl for us in the blacksmith's shed. Comrade Mandela was doing a BA Honours, Comrade Kathy a BA, Comrade Siva a national diploma, and Comrade Jeff a BA. I approached the captain in charge of studies in the prison in 1965 to show my interest in registering at Unisa. He took my details and, to my surprise, decided to enter me for the university. My lawyers in Durban – Phyllis Naidoo and Thumba Pillay – sent me money to cover my studies. The funds came from the Anti-Apartheid Movement overseas and were channelled mostly through the Defence and Aid Fund. Phyllis was truly compassionate: she even sent me dark glasses for when I worked in the quarry. In those days, we received concessions on university fees and paid only R10 per subject. That was still a fair amount of money, though after a few years the concessions were cancelled.

If we were allowed to study, we weren't allocated specific study time and could only work after lock up in the evening. One advantage was being placed in the special 'study cell' with about thirty other prisoners. We could then agree among ourselves that we would have study time from 5 pm to 7 pm, and thereafter do whatever we wanted until 8 pm, when we had to go to bed. If the warders found you awake after that time, you would be punished, although university students could apply to be given extra time to study until 11 pm, as I did. The lights were in any event never switched off in the cells.

Prescribed material was also often denied if it had a political-sounding title. For example, if a title included a reference to the Russian or French revolutions, or the independence struggles in the colonies, it would be banned. I wrote a letter to the commanding officer in 1969 regarding a book I needed for my history course. At the time it felt like a futile fight, but we had to keep it up.

Dear Sir,

Sometime early this year, I received some prescribed textbooks for History III from Van Schaiks Book Shop. To my surprise, Mr Steenkamp, who is in charge of the study office, refused to let me have the books.

I then complained to you both verbally and in writing.

As a result, I saw the captain and showed him where the books were prescribed, and he then agreed that I could have the books. But Mr Steenkamp informed the captain that he had sent the books back to the book shop. The captain then informed Mr Steenkamp to get the books back for me.

A few weeks later, Mr Steenkamp informed me that the captain had changed his mind about letting me have the books. He went on further to state that I could only have my prescribed books for one week!

This, you would agree with me, is ridiculous.

Since then, I have made 28 complaints both to you and other junior officers, but all my complaints have so far been ignored.

I wish you to note and place on record that there has been complete indifference on the part of the prison authorities to all my complaints regarding the above matter, and that the lack of prescribed books has seriously hampered my studies, and I am unable to write or pass this year. Even if I was to write my exams, there is no possibility of my passing without the prescribed textbooks.

I had sent for a number of books from the university library and I did not receive a single one of them. All the books have been returned without even informing me.

I am also told that I have to pay for all the books sent to the university library by registered post. Therefore, I have been paying for the postage of books that I do not even know of. The books which Mr Steenkamp says he returned to the book shop seem to be lost for I have not received a refund from the book shop.

Even an ordinary English novel of mine is held by the study office.

I paid R130 at the beginning of this year for registration with the university only to find the study office has made it very difficult for me to carry on with my studies. I wish therefore to apply to the Commissioner of Prisons for a refund of R130 which I spent for registration this year. I also wish to get a refund for the books which seem to me to be lost by the study office.

Finally, I hope you grant me permission to contact my attorney and also inform my parents, who are responsible for my fees, to take up the matter with the Commissioner of Prisons.

I hope you would treat the above matters as urgent.

Yours faithfully,
Ebrahim Ismail

The missing textbooks included *The Bolshevik Revolution*, *Soviet Foreign Policy* and *Psychology Book on Sex*.

I had earlier written to the commanding officer to complain that I was not allowed to read outside the prescribed list even though 'as a university student, I am required by the university to read as widely as possible on the subject I am doing'. I said: 'No university student in the world is restricted to a few prescribed or, for that matter, a few recommended books. One is expected to read as many books on a particular subject as one could find. So one is quite often expected to search for the best book for oneself.'

At a certain stage, there was a rule that we were not allowed to share the books we received, which was absurd as we all stayed in one cell. If a book assigned to you was found with another prisoner, you could be punished by having your privileges withdrawn. But we supported one another. Some prisoners who wanted to complete primary school but were not registered would borrow books, and we'd assist them to study under their blankets away from the watchful eyes of the warders.

At times, even returning our Unisa assignments was delayed by the prison as these had to be posted to the Pretoria campus. They could, and did, take their time in posting them to Pretoria for us, and this had repercussions for our marks. During exam time, we would be locked up in the single cells near where our leadership was incarcerated, and given our papers to write.

I chose to study history, psychology and English in the beginning, and later added Special Latin and French, as Latin had been absent from my matric certificate. Latin was later excluded from 'Bantu education' as it was a prerequisite for legal studies, and the apartheid government did not want 'non-whites' to become lawyers. It took me four or five years to complete my BA, which was no small feat considering the constraints.

When I completed my BA, I registered for a BComm degree and took accounting, economics and business economics. I managed to complete that degree too before leaving the Island in 1979. Gaining a proper education was also a way of preparing ourselves for life beyond prison.

I recollect that Dikgang Moseneke was among our highest achievers. Ten years younger than I was, he had joined the PAC at the age of fourteen. The following year, still a child, he was arrested, detained and convicted of participating in anti-apartheid activity, and spent ten years, most of those as the youngest prisoner, on Robben Island. While imprisoned, he obtained a BA in English and political science and a BIuris degree, and would later complete a Bachelor of Laws, all from Unisa. That remarkable young prisoner went on to become the deputy chief justice of South Africa.

Studying was a vital aspect of my life when I had no control over the rest of my daily existence. It was like that for all of us who took up that option, but sometimes we had to embark on more extreme acts. The hunger strike was thus an important weapon in prison. In theory, it has limited aims and should be of short duration. In reality, it is agonising. When the only form of power you have is over your own body, you exercise it.

Our first hunger strike began in the quarry in 1966, when a warder discovered there was a shortage of food for lunch and instructed common law prisoners to remove some from each of the plates of the political prisoners. This brought about one of the first major acts of resistance by us against the brutality of apartheid's prison colony. Spontaneously, we refused to accept anything to eat at all, and thus the strike began. That first hunger strike lasted about a week and proved taxing. We were already malnourished, and the strike severely weakened us. We were desperately hungry, yet we still had to work.

A small group of PAC members led by Selby Ngendane would not join us. Ngendane was vociferously anti-ANC and anti-communist. He proclaimed he was not prepared to be led by us and seemed to regard the hunger strike as some sort of 'Red' plot. But a majority of PAC members stood united with the ANC on this stand, and the result went in our favour if one can even say that about such a miserable situation.

Suddenly, the food with which we were presented at meals was made to look a little more appetising, and the lieutenant in charge tried by all means to persuade us to eat. The prison authorities were undoubtedly concerned. On about the seventh day, the head of the prison came to the quarry to address us and take our complaints. We welcomed this as we knew it had to be our choice to eat again. Although we were suffering, after the first couple of days the physical anguish strangely subsided even as the psychological effects began to hurt us more and more. Many of the older comrades were collapsing. Yet the officer's show of care was brief.

Even if this was the first time we had used a hunger strike as a means to receive better treatment, we knew the pattern of official behaviour from other rebellions. The prison officials reacted when we displayed radical behaviour, and then reverted to the evil kind of 'normal' to which we were constantly subjected. They wrote down all our complaints but ultimately did little to address them.

Seventeen
University of Robben Island

When I arrived on the Island, most prisoners were from the PAC. The leader of the PAC, Robert Sobukwe, had been imprisoned on Robben Island in 1963 and was kept in solitary confinement in living quarters that were separate from the main prison. He had no contact with other prisoners and was allowed books and to wear civilian clothes. Parliament had enacted a General Law Amendment Act that included what was termed the 'Sobukwe clause', which empowered the Minister of Justice to prolong the detention of any political prisoner indefinitely. Sobukwe was incarcerated on the Island for six years.

Among the ranks of the political prisoners on the Island there were some prominent ANC comrades who provided us with support. These included Reggie September, Indres Naidoo and Shirish Nanabhai, whom I also knew from the Indian Congress. There were many comrades from the Eastern Cape, an ANC stronghold, and a number of leading African activists, including Andrew Masondo, his co-accused, Rex Lupondwana, and my great comrade and friend Mzwandile Mcgloria Mdingi – intellectuals all.

Warders resented it when a black man was more educated than they were and blamed our ability to recruit others to the armed struggle on our intelligence. The prison authorities insisted 'Bantus' had no reason to revolt when the white government was creating bantustans for them. They said Africans were being 'misled by communists and agitators', and that's why they would single out a man like Masondo for harsher treatment.

About a week after our arrival, Masondo explained there was a structure among the ANC political prisoners on the Island to maintain discipline and give directives on various issues. We were warned that some of the PAC prisoners – being the majority in prison – were often hostile to our members, and that we should not respond when they verbally attacked us. We had to hold back from fuelling tension. Our struggle was against the system.

We were soon joined by a group from East London who had been sentenced to long terms of imprisonment. This group was led by Johnson Mgabela, and included many outstanding comrades such as Douglas Zulu Sparks, Lungelo Dwaba and Stephen (Steve) Tshwete. Within a short space of time, our membership on the Island was also boosted by the committed communist comrades Harry Gwala and Steve Dlamini from Natal. Gwala was a Marxist-Leninist theoretician. Henry Makgothi, Peter Magano and Joe Gqabi, who were all senior leaders of the ANC from the Transvaal, arrived not long afterwards.

The PAC prisoners displayed an amazing revolutionary enthusiasm and confidence in their cause. Their battle cry, 'Izwe lethu!' (Our land!), rang throughout the prison and they never missed an opportunity to shout it, loudly. Even when they went in and out of the ablutions, the cry rang out.

Every night, once the doors were closed, someone from the PAC would call the cell to attention. We in the ANC found this uncomfortable. Selby Ngendane was often the speaker in the cell, and he delivered tirade after tirade against us, the Congress Alliance and the communists. His attacks on socialism surpassed even those of the apartheid regime. He would give a distorted history of our struggle to misguide rank-and-file prisoners – most of them peasants who believed deeply in their fight for the land – by projecting the PAC's leaders as being of the calibre of Ghana's first post-independence prime minister and president, Kwame Nkrumah, and other giants who resisted colonialism. But since many PAC prisoners were serving short sentences and were soon released or transferred to the mainland, its numbers shifted continuously.

Nonetheless, Ngendane maintained his stance, accusing the ANC of 'abandoning African nationalism' by allowing whites, Indians and communists to 'dictate' the liberation of the masses. This took place even as the PAC was bitterly divided on the Island, with Ngendane torn between two leaders, Clarence Makwetu and Christopher Mlokoti, who were both sentenced in 1963. It was only when another PAC leader, Zeph Mothopeng, arrived on the Island in 1964 that the rifts began to heal between them. Then the authorities sent Mothopeng into isolation in 1965, followed by Ngendane in 1966. We noted the effects of their absence.

The number of ANC prisoners was to exceed that of PAC members by 1967, and the PAC's power base dwindled considerably. The arrival of John Pokela in 1967 brought some sense of balance to its internal divisions, as Pokela had every intention of trying to unite rival groups and bring them within the 'real' PAC. But the ANC had such significant control by then that the PAC could no longer dominate the cells or the quarry.

Our numbers were bolstered mainly by comrades from the Eastern Cape, who brought other views into our space. Joe Gqabi, for instance, was shocked at the stance of the PAC, and said we should not allow their unjust attacks to carry on. He suggested that whenever we were lambasted, we should demand the right to reply. There was much discussion in our ranks as to whether this was the correct approach. Many of our elders felt we should just continue to ignore the PAC, but it was ultimately decided we should respond. We then tasked certain comrades in the cells to intervene whenever the diatribes began. This surprised the PAC leadership. Finally, they reluctantly agreed to our request for a formal discussion. We chose some of our senior comrades such as Harry Gwala, Stephen Dlamini, Henry Makgothi and Zola Nqini to present our side of the debate. They related our history, the role of the working class and the contribution of the communists and trade unions, as well as the national and class nature of our struggle and our policy of internationalism.

Naturally, the PAC leadership had reason to be concerned about the effect this calibre of speaker would have. They immediately wanted to put an end to this kind of freedom of speech. We responded by saying they should then hold their meetings in their own space, as would we, and after that, whenever they proselytised among us, we would instantly respond. That gave us a sense of power, which we needed. Yet, again, one could not but admire their devotion to pan-Africanism. It was a pity the PAC's internecine conflict was a reflection of their poor methods – an inability to objectively analyse the concrete situation of struggle. Still, we never doubted their commitment.

Once there was an influx of ANC prisoners, many of the younger prisoners demanded political classes from us, and the PAC could no longer hold back the tide. Such classes happened everywhere, sometimes spontaneously, at lunchtime at the quarry, and in Harry Gwala's cell. I too learned from him. As he became a close friend of mine, I also saw his frustration and anger with the leadership of the Communist Party. A member of its Natal district committee, he had never agreed with its decision to dissolve under pressure from the regime in the 1940s. He had felt very bitter, too, that when the party was reconstituted in the 1950s, he was excluded. He thought that many of those closest to him had betrayed him, and at times his entire ideological orientation was clouded by this belief.

Yet we all benefited from Comrade Gwala's deep knowledge of leftist politics, even as some of our own older comrades in the ANC objected to his being our teacher. They wanted to have more control over the political education offered to the young arrivals. Would his words promote working-class struggle above national struggle? That he explained issues such as 'the domination of the bourgeoisie' was a problem for them, and they became irritated with him, accusing him of organising a clique within the organisation in prison. They questioned under what 'structural authority' he was conducting such brazen lectures, often on Marxist labour theory.

Gwala received support from Steve Dlamini. They would explain that their lessons were in fact conducted under the direction of the South African Congress of Trade Unions (SACTU), which was entitled to go about its own activities without getting the permission of the ANC on the Island. We had seen how poorly the PAC had countered its divisions in prison. Now, suddenly, we faced our own. Before we knew it, a period of much confusion was unleashed among us over ideology. Without warning, comrades were presenting arguments about the nature of our somewhat loose structure on the Island, their thinking mirroring the ideological clashes which the ANC was facing outside as well, although we didn't know enough about them at the time.

We had hardly any knowledge of what was really going on

underground or in exile, except here and there from new arrivals. But it felt possible that just as we had overtaken the PAC in terms of numbers and solidarity, our own unity could easily collapse, especially if we were unable to offer enough political security. Inasmuch as that situation had come about so quickly, our consultations with our leadership also had to happen in haste, and often in the isolation cells. It was there that we started to rely on a senior comrade, Milner Ntsangani, who had extensive experience in ANC organisational matters. We weren't holding together; we needed discipline.

And so Comrade Milner and others devised a structure that followed some of the principles of the M-Plan, which had been effectively implemented in the Eastern Cape. First, we had to contend with the legalities of a banned organisation mobilising in prison. We had to protect the membership from further persecution for furthering the aims of a banned organisation because we had seen what happened to members of the PAC when they had done so. The authorities were especially cruel to them.

Secondly, a more tight-knit code had to be shared among us. A disciplinary committee (DC) was established under which comrades were grouped into units of five in each cell, with a group leader for each unit. Four cells made up a section in prison, and thus section leaders were also elected. The DC became the highest leadership organ on the Island. It was responsible for giving guidance on all issues and prison matters. We adhered strictly to democratic centralism and consulted widely with our members. Once we took a decision, it was readily accepted, but we were careful not to expose the existence of an ANC structure in prison and so we put security measures in place to protect it. If there was any infiltration, it would only affect a unit rather than stir up trouble among us all. I was named chair of the DC and worked with Henry Makgothi, James Kati, and comrades Nqini and Magano, who served as the communications person. But the composition of the DC was kept a secret.

We further set up a political education committee chaired by Jacob Zuma, which included comrades Steve Tshwete, Harry Gwala, Stephen Dlamini and Mzwandile Mdingi. This area remained factional for some time, however, with many being strongly opposed to the sectarian approach of our SACTU comrades. Certainly, this didn't help the cohesion of the movement.

For me, factionalism goes against the principle of collective leadership and reliance on the people. Such sectarian tendencies also lead to cults of personality. I felt that since the working class was in the leadership of the struggle, our political education needed to focus on the theory and practice of Marxist-Leninism. But such discussions went on for years: class contradiction versus class struggle. The Freedom Charter could be framed as either a socialist or a bourgeois document. Leaders in the isolation cells who felt the Freedom Charter simply sought to unite progressive forces eventually preferred that there be no political lectures in the cells, at the quarry or during walks to and from those places unless these were authorised by the DC. And, indeed, that helped us become more organised.

We alternated lectures on labour theory with lectures on national struggle. The political committee submitted a programme of study to the DC at the beginning of every year. Lectures on Marxist theory, the Communist International, and the history of the Russian and Chinese revolutions were accompanied by history lessons in colonial and imperialist exploitation, the wars of resistance, the formation of the ANC and its allies, and the birth of MK. Robben Island slowly came to be known as a 'university of revolutionary politics,' although it didn't start off that way. It took long and painful work.

The political committee would prepare for the talks by involving comrades acquainted with a particular topic under discussion. The proposal would then be disseminated to representatives of each cell on a Saturday. On Sunday, we'd have a compulsory lecture in all the cells. Some comrades would later gather in the quarry during the week at lunch hour to revise and expand on the lectures.

We also observed certain anniversaries – 8 January to mark the formation of the ANC in 1912, Africa Day on 25 May, the adoption of the Freedom Charter on 26 June, and Women's Day on 9 August – by having special political discussions. Others, like 7 November, which marked the October Revolution, and 16 December, the day MK launched itself, became important as well.

Literature was hard to come by. As I mentioned earlier, many of our study materials from Unisa were censored. Yet we somehow got hold of three volumes of Maurice Cornforth's *Dialectical Materialism*, and the first volume of Karl Marx's *Das Kapital*. When we were fortunate enough to lay hands on political material of this kind, we would spend days and nights copying pages out by hand to share among us. I have especially strong memories of leading discussions about *Das Kapital* in a cell with a small group of comrades.

If disciplinary action had to be taken, a comrade would be removed from the structures of the organisation for a certain period. This was regarded as an extreme punishment. In one case, we had to withdraw the sanction within days because the prisoner quickly became depressed and suicidal. But that kind of response to our internal solidarity mechanisms led to an outstanding level of discipline. Comrades were not allowed to engage in the smuggling of food, for instance, and there was low tolerance for any anti-social behaviour.

Belonging and togetherness made us all feel as if we were part of a large political family. The underground we set up eventually achieved much-needed unity. Comrades felt a degree of comfort in being part of a tightly knit structure that could attend to their needs in prison and was able to provide effective leadership. We could fully express our opinions on all matters, but once a decision was taken, we were compelled to abide by it, irrespective of our personal views.

Morale was kept very high. The authorities were bent on demoralising and dehumanising us political prisoners. Still, they battled to bring us down. Even during the darkest days when we were breaking stones in the quarry in the cold winter months with little clothing to keep us warm, we never regretted our actions. And to this day, I have no regrets.

Eighteen
The shock of what we did not know

AFTER MANY YEARS, THE authorities allowed sporting activities for prisoners on Saturdays. We formed clubs and held highly competitive games, alternating each week between rugby and soccer. From 1966, Prisoners' Association football games were organised by our own governing body, Makana FA. Although I'm not the sportiest of people, I did belong to one of our clubs, the Rangers. That said, I was not very good, and was put into the C division. It was rare for me to actually play, and my comrades joked that I was useless!

Sometimes, there would be disputes during the football matches, and a committee was established to adjudicate them. That suited me far better, and from the beginning I was made the chair of the committee. Prisoners referred to me as 'the judge'. One day a ruling I made was overturned by an appeals committee headed by Dikgang Moseneke. Considering his later huge achievements as a jurist, I consider that one of my most humbling moments: not so much painful as instructive.

Another comrade who was less of an asset in the actual games than he was behind the scenes was Comrade Shirish. He was a key part of the group who cleared and prepared areas for a football pitch, and was particularly wily in how he tricked the authorities into providing many of the resources needed for that good work. Inmates made creative use of all and any resources they were able to lay their hands on. James Chirwa, a comrade from Malawi, even made soccer nets from discarded nylon found on the seashore.

We had indoor games, too, and bridge became popular, as did chess. About six years into our incarceration, the authorities decided that movies could be screened in a common hall. The fare was tame; we could only watch non-political dramas, mostly about spies and war. But I have good memories of us sitting there on benches in the darkened room covered with our threadbare blankets.

At one stage, a church organisation donated speakers to be installed in the cells so that we could listen to music in the evenings. We were allowed to order songs from home and comrades mainly went for American jazz, rock 'n roll, and country music. I asked my family to send me some Indian classical music. Some of my African comrades found it difficult to enjoy my music selection as the sitar, which is the base instrument, wasn't familiar to their ears. The warders were worse. One of them was so convinced that the loudspeaker was broken because of the strange, high-pitched sounds on my new record by the world-renowned Ravi Shankar that he reported a 'technical challenge'. We Indian prisoners had a good laugh about that.

We were also later allowed our own cultural activities. Jacob Zuma established a choir and introduced traditional dancing. At weekends, especially Sundays, he would entertain us with choral music and we enjoyed the performances of dancers, especially some excellent groups from the Eastern Cape, who received rousing applause. Zuma was someone who remained cheerful, no matter what. He kept our morale up. He could bring prisoners from more traditional backgrounds closer to those of us who had grown up in the cities, and vice versa. I always saw that as a primary skill of his.

As time went on, we were also able to obtain assistance from the International Red Cross, which played a role in improving our conditions. The pity was that their representatives were only able to come once a year – not in the 1960s, but from the 1970s – although they were at least able to meet with us privately. This was a relief. We could talk freely, and then they would make a report and recommendations to the government, which it would either accept or reject. Most times, the government would reject their recommendations. But the Red Cross succeeded in some ways, for instance by getting us better bedding – higher-quality blankets, and even new ones. They also improved our uniforms, and even provided a supply of warmer clothing. We didn't even have socks before their intervention. Our food become more varied after their lobbying, and we were even served boiled eggs. That was a real treat.

But the minister of prisons, Jimmy Kruger, took pleasure in visiting us to remind us that we were enemies; that there was no such category as 'political prisoner' in South Africa. We were all criminals, convicted for 'criminal offences'. I once argued with him that if we were not political prisoners, then we should be granted the same rights and privileges as those given to common law prisoners: remission of sentences, contact visits and newspapers, among other things. He said the things I was referring to formed part of the rehabilitation of prisoners – attempts to change their behaviour. 'With you people, you will never change', was his remark. And that was true.

A news blackout on the Island was intended to depoliticise us. Newspapers and radios were allowed for rehabilitation in regular prisons, but such was the determination to keep us detached from society that we weren't considered capable of being 'restored' to normal life. So we established a 'news committee' headed by Sunny Singh, whom I had known from the time I recruited him into MK in Durban, where he was a key member of my unit. Sunny found a way of smuggling papers into prison. The prisoners held him in high esteem as an intellectual, and he was a great support to us all. He never relented. He wouldn't allow us to become completely isolated from the world.

At times we used the common law prisoners to smuggle in newspapers, as they worked in the main food distribution centre and brought uncooked food to the kitchen. They could conceal newspapers in bags of maize meal and forward these to our news committee. In return, they would send shoes to our section when these needed repairing, as we had shoemakers among us. But such opportunities were few and far between, and we could be without news for months at a time. Even a newspaper which was weeks old was cherished. We would analyse every sentence of every article and examine the adverts. Every caption to every picture, and every headline mattered. That's how deprived we were. Once or twice a small radio was smuggled in. That was breathtaking for us. But the batteries soon ran out or the authorities found our treasure.

Such was our longing for news that when a prisoner went to the mainland for a court appearance or any other reason, he was tasked with memorising all the posters on the lampposts around the city and had to report back. And when a new prisoner arrived, he was bombarded with questions: we demanded to hear anything and everything they knew about the latest news.

In the early years, a group of prisoners worked in the Island harbour area. We would gather with them every evening so they could relate the 'news' they'd picked up. Often, this bore little resemblance to reality, and in some cases it was just wishful thinking. But it was news.

Our preferred paper was the National Party-supporting *Die Burger*, which published propaganda for the apartheid system. It gave us information about the activities of our organisation, which was always a source of inspiration to us.

On one occasion when Jimmy Kruger visited, I asked Ezra Sigwela to keep him occupied in the carpenter's workshop so that I could steal the newspaper from his unlocked car. We often stole newspapers from the authorities and once even from a visiting priest.

But we missed out on so much. In June 1976, we had no idea that the Soweto uprising was taking place until a month later when the leadership in the isolation cells smuggled a note to us saying they heard rumours that this had happened. It was only with the arrival of the first batch of prisoners who had been arrested and sentenced as a result of their involvement that we got to know the details of the uprising. As we spoke to the new batch of prisoners, we gained a vivid picture of the agonies that had taken place after young people confronted the police with stones and burning tyres on 16 June. It was shocking to us in the ANC that we had known nothing while the country burned. It troubled us. It stirred the old fight in us.

Their arrival on the Island also marked our most substantial encounter to date with Black Consciousness (BC). Previously we had known little about the movement. It was only when a senior BC leader and organiser, Mosibudi Mangena, arrived in 1973, along with students belonging to the South African Students Movement, that we first got to understand their ideology and motivation. Among the most prominent BC students were Stone Sizani and Amos Masondo, who later became the first black mayor of Johannesburg. It didn't take long for Amos and Sizani to join the ANC once they were on the Island.

Soon we were interacting not only with a few BC members, but also others in the leadership who had been sentenced after they organised a rally in Durban in solidarity with the free people of a newly independent Mozambique under Frelimo. Having been schooled in the revolutionary theory of national and class struggle for so many years, and having the Freedom Charter form the basis of our non-racial position, we closely interrogated Black Consciousness. Many of our white allies had joined MK, only to be imprisoned; some became important leaders of the liberation movement. It went against our principles to even consider excluding them from our movement. But BC was a complete commitment to black life.

For the most part, our BC compatriots were anti-communist and were inspired rather by the American civil rights movement. Some were also ignorant of our own history, including the Defiance Campaign of 1952, or believed the true struggle began with the formation of the BC movement in 1969, at a time of severe suppression of political activities after the Rivonia Trial.

Yet BC's new militancy in challenging the status quo had an impact on us. Nelson Mandela even proposed that he refuse to obey any instructions from the prison authorities as a means of developing our own militancy, but there was no consensus among the leadership on the matter, and the issue was referred to the disciplinary committee. We called a meeting of senior comrades and, after a lengthy discussion, concluded that such a move by Comrade Mandela would amount to 'adventurism'. In Marxist-Leninist terms, this means 'militancy without the masses'. His proposal was duly rejected and, true to form, he accepted the views of his comrades.

Still, there was no denying the ideals of BC, which stood boldly against the apartheid regime as its organisers went about mobilising young black people to stand on their own and be proud of their blackness. BC remains a feature of youth politics today, although I still believe in the basis on which the ANC was founded. The BC movement was created to fill a vacuum. We didn't necessarily see it as meant to replace the ANC and

PAC. But the problem for us was that there were some who believed BC was a successor to the ANC and PAC.

Nonetheless, as with the PAC and the ANC on the Island, the BC movement underwent its own period of dissent and splits. Among the most prominent of its members to join the ANC on the Island was Mosiuoa 'Terror' Lekota, who ultimately dissociated himself from BC in a painful schism that even led to some physical fights. Comrade Terror spent two periods on the Island, like me. The first was six years; the second was supposed to be twelve, but on appeal he spent only a few months with me in 1989.

Not long after the first BC prisoners arrived, the authorities began separating us from them. The warders called them 'klipgooiers' (an Afrikaans term for 'stone-throwers' or 'troublemakers') and dismissed them as somewhat less dangerous than us. They thought we would have a negative political influence on these militant young minds but soon realised their folly in isolating them from us.

The many years in prison had taught us that it was in everyone's interest that we abide by common regulations. Yes, we were required to wake up when the morning bell rang and wash and make our beds. When the guards opened the cell, we had to stand in twos to be counted and then collect our breakfast in single lines. When addressing officials, we stood up and spoke to them. Yet we would not permit warders to be rude to us, and if they were, we would respond likewise. If a warder swore at us, we would swear back at him. Many of the warders were young, some still teenagers, and we felt it unbecoming for us to be constantly bickering with such uneducated oppressors. In any event, it was better for us to keep them as far as possible away from us so that we could continue with our political education and other activities.

The new BC arrivals were not so co-operative, however. They brought the spirit of the Soweto uprising with them. They carried with them the mood of the masses outside. This perpetual conflict between the BC cohort and the warders meant that the latter needed us ANC members to draw our young comrades into line, simply to keep unity among prisoners. This had an irony to it, but it didn't matter. It gave us great joy when the BC members were again mixed into our sections. We learned so much from them about events outside.

The shock of what we did not know

The newcomers were excited to live among us, and were inspired by being in the same prison as comrades like Mandela, Walter Sisulu and Govan Mbeki. Many new prisoners did not belong to any organisation. Some who had been arrested in the townships were activists without a political home, and once they were convicts on the Island, we saw that they needed political education. We were, after all, entitled to bring into our ranks whoever was willing to join us. This was always going to be tough for the BC and PAC leadership to accept.

The BC movement claimed that the youth coming into prison belonged to their organisation and accused the ANC of poaching their members. They had the support of the PAC, and at one stage they decided to boycott members of the ANC by not playing sports with them or dismantling the joint study classes with members of the ANC. Steve Tshwete and I discussed the matter at length with Mosibudi Mangena and Eric Molobi, and agreed that prisoners were free to join whichever organisation they wished. The vast majority of people coming into prison after the Soweto uprising joined the ranks of the ANC.

As the 1970s drew to a close, there was growing optimism among us and an ever-increasing sense of the mass struggle that lay ahead. We used the time in prison to prepare our cadres and, indeed, many of them would become leaders of the Mass Democratic Movement during the bloodiest decade of apartheid, the 1980s.

Nineteen
Crossing the lines

WHEN POLITICAL PRISONERS HAD done their time, they were usually taken from Robben Island to their home town, where they were immediately banned and confined. A month before my release in 1979, I was moved from Cape Town to Leeuwkop Prison in Johannesburg, en route to Durban. The first part of the journey, which took more than fourteen hours, was in the company of a friendly brigadier. One talks. I can't say if the conversation mattered or went anywhere, but he asked me questions about life inside. We spoke about how the food could be improved, and prisoners allocated work that was more meaningful. It's a long time to spend in a car with your oppressors. You switch on your voice and switch it off.

It was all part of the dislocating and unfamiliar experience of seeing the outside world after fifteen years on the Island. I wasn't physically free yet, but I could witness ordinary people in their colourful clothing, children laughing and playing, women shopping, the buzz of the streets, and nature passing in a blur from the windows. We stopped at a petrol station and the brigadier bought me a can of Coke. It was the first time I had seen such a thing, as I had been in custody since 1963. I didn't know how to open it. I got a fright when I did.

I spent two weeks in Leeuwkop before I was driven to Durban by a prison lieutenant, who was not familiar with my home city. Once there, I had to direct him to Durban Central Prison, where I had to be registered. It was sad that I could not return to Greyville to serve out my banning order. It had been my home for so long, but it had been flattened in the meantime. There was nothing there, except for a few factories. I felt as if my whole history had been uprooted.

A few black warders were immediately sympathetic towards me and interested in my experiences on Robben Island. I was able to get them to courier letters to some of the Black Consciousness Movement prisoners on trial in Durban. Notable among them was a very bright law student, Penuell Maduna, who wanted to understand the conditions on the Island, and what to expect if he and others were sent there. But I felt an anxious confusion during those communications. What was my role? What would happen now? How was I going to continue my activism in the political world outside but underground, which was now new to me just as Robben Island would be to activists like Maduna. None of us had ever been free. None of us were free at that moment. We still had to fight to secure any kind of liberation.

The Security Branch visited me on my last day in Durban Central and served me with the anticipated banning order restricting me to Reservoir Hills. I was told I was only allowed to be in the company of two people at a time, was not to communicate with anyone other than my family, and had to report weekly to the police station. I was prohibited from entering any educational premises, factories or workplaces.

My family was waiting for me at the gates of the prison on the day of my release, but the security police instead took me out through the back and informed them I was already at my uncle's home and that I could be arrested for breaking my banning order. The regime would not tolerate grand welcomes for former prisoners. In the end, though, none of that mattered in the joy of being reunited.

It was revitalising to see members of our family whom I had missed for fifteen years. Some I had last seen as children and they were now grown up. It was dazzling to hold babies in my arms, and to hug and kiss people. It was strange to move around a garden at night and view the stars. I remember that on a few occasions after my release I said to my aunt after dinner that I would be 'going back to my cell', by which of course I meant my room. It certainly took time to adjust to living a normal life.

It was exciting to watch TV for the first time, and to listen to my favourite Indian music from my youth. I felt I would never be able to eat enough curry and rice and sweets. But the damage had been done to one's mind and mental health.

Although I was able to establish contact with comrades in the underground, I was kept under surveillance. The security police often parked their car near my uncle's house. At times I wondered what they were really trying to achieve in this way, as I quickly found out that, far from suppressing the resistance of the people, the regime's chokehold only seemed to propel us into greater activism.

Pravin Gordhan ran the unit with which I had many clandestine night meetings. He had established a network of structures linking 'legal' work with secret work, and the underground at home with the leadership in exile. I was possibly even more fearless under banning orders than I had been before I went to prison. After a while I simply left my uncle's house and stayed in the Asoka Hotel in Reservoir Hills. Initially I had demanded to stay in an apartment in town that belonged to our comrade from our sabotage days, Poomoney Moodley, who had been a constant source of contact between the underground at home and prisoners on Robben Island. But the police refused, so I moved to the Asoka. The hotel, which belonged to a comrade, had a predominantly black clientele and it soon became clear that the security police were not going to be able to keep tabs on me.

Eventually I was allowed to stay in Poomoney's flat as a banned person, and this made it easier for me to go to meetings in the evenings. I would take a brisk walk to a certain area and was there picked up by a member of Comrade Pravin's unit. I was later told by a younger comrade, Mahomed Kamdar, that they would observe me venturing out at night while walking to the prearranged site. Once I got to know him, I would often visit his family home. His younger sister Shaida became one of our operatives.

After getting out of prison I needed to reconnect with the outside world both socially and spiritually. For fifteen years there was no spiritual guidance for Muslim prisoners. When travelling to Westville police station I had to pass the Soofie mosque in Westville. As they were related to me, the Soofies embraced me with warm hearts and open arms. The Soofie family became a second home of mine and reignited my interest in

Islamic prayers and practices. Moulana Roef, his wife Shanaaz and their son became my spiritual mentors; they also protected me while I was underground in Durban in mid-1985. The Soofie family was interrogated by the police in that year in an attempt to establish my whereabouts. They even raided the Soofie mosque in Springfield, looking for arms which they suspected I had stored there.

The Soofies have a long presence in South Africa, dating back to 1895, when Hazrat Soofie Saheb arrived in Durban and established a number of religious sites. He built numerous mosques and orphanages. At the invitation of the Soofie family, Nelson Mandela gave an address at the Springfield Mosque complex in 1993, urging those present to support the new democratic dispensation.

One of the issues confronting the underground in the early 1980s, shortly after my release, was how we should respond to the Tricameral Parliament. This had been set up by the PW Botha government to deal with the question of political representation for Indians and Coloureds, seeing that, according to the National Party policy of 'separate development', African political aspirations had been directed towards the bantustans. The Tricameral Parliament consisted of three separate houses, the 178-member white House of Assembly, the 85-member Coloured House of Representatives, and the 45-member Indian House of Delegates. Each house would look after its own ethnic affairs but on matters of common interest they would all vote together, with the numerical majority of the white house ensuring that whites would continue to hold the upper hand.

Some comrades demanded that we stand for election to the House of Delegates so as to make it ungovernable from within. They insisted that we had to stymie collaborators from the community occupying that space. There were others who felt that a boycott was the only correct tactic. The debate became so intense that Pravin Gordhan went to London to consult the ANC leadership in exile. Among the people he met was Dr Dadoo, whose message was one of boycott. And that proved effective, even though it left room for collaborators.

The consequences of the Tricameral Parliament were radical in our circles. It brought together a whole range of opponents and dissenters, including activists in civil society, workers' organisations and left political formations, who came together in a powerful movement that was launched as the United Democratic Front in 1983.

One of the difficulties my comrades and I faced was the presence of infiltrators, who were everywhere among us. A certain 'Ismail' would visit me while I was banned in Reservoir Hills. He always brought his wife and children, and appeared to be a straightforward family man, sympathetic to the struggle like so many other community members who arrived to express solidarity. 'Ismail' claimed to be a businessman whose work meant he often travelled to Swaziland. He intimated that he was able to establish contact with our ANC comrades there and volunteered to act as a courier for us.

I tested him by using him to bring into the country banned literature like *Sechaba*, the official organ of the ANC, and the SACP magazine, *African Communist*, for distribution in our underground structures. Later, he began passing messages to comrades in Swaziland, and brought replies back to us. It was fortunate that our national intelligence department had recruited a black security policeman as a source through our internal underground work. He told head office in Lusaka that Comrade George Naicker and I were soon to be arrested. 'Ismail', whom we'd code-named 'Librarian', had supplied the security police with information about us.

Someone was immediately dispatched to spirit us out of the country. Our destination was Zambia by way of Swaziland and Mozambique. To me and George, the experience of exile was completely unknown. We'd been activists, then prisoners and then underground operatives. Exile was not something we had considered or expected at that time, even though we knew numbers of our comrades had been given no choice but to leave South Africa.

It was December 1980: I had been out of prison though banned for nearly two years. But my life had barely been my own since I was fourteen anyway, and I didn't have much of a life beyond that contained within the movement. Of course I would go. What else could I do? I would be imprisoned or die if I refused.

I received the news from George, who phoned me with a coded instruction to 'meet for a bite' on a certain day at a specific restaurant at ten in the morning. None of this was within the bounds of our banning orders, but I went all the same. As I was walking to the restaurant, a car pulled up. The driver was a Swazi comrade, Grace Cele, and George was in the car. Comrade Grace told us we should be ready to leave within four hours as we were to be detained at any time. There were no goodbyes to family and friends nor a chance to pack a bag. By two o'clock, we were on our way to the border by car.

The gate was already closed by the time we got there, and so we had to sleep in the vehicle overnight. We were then dropped off at a certain point very early in the morning when it was still dark and had to make our way across the border fence. In retrospect, this was easy: we simply extended the wire to fit ourselves through and then stepped over. We kept walking as we had been instructed until we got to a road, which we crossed. We hid in a secluded spot there to wait for Comrade Grace, who made her own way through the border gate in the conventional manner. Incredibly, or so it seemed, she soon arrived, and we were on our way to Manzini, the central commercial town in Swaziland where the ANC had set up its base.

Our first contacts in Swaziland were comrades Ivan Pillay, who had been part of the BC movement before he joined MK, and his partner Rajaluxmi 'Rajes' Pillay, whose father was the activist TVR Pillay. I stayed with them for a week so they could brief me thoroughly on what was happening in our southern African structures. George and I also met Shadrack Maphumulo, who was responsible for the underground units in Natal, and Leonard Tyron, who was involved in the urban areas of the Transvaal.

There had long been a divide between the political and military structures in Swaziland, with MK units based there falling under a Revolutionary Council (RC) ultimately responsible for operations in South Africa, including the infiltration of guerrillas. At that time, Joe Slovo was chief of staff of MK and served on the RC. MK structures were reorganised after the ANC conference in Maputo in 1983. Political and military machineries were then combined with a Politico-Military Council (PMC), led by OR Tambo, which provided overall leadership. The PMC was the umbrella body for the Regional Political Military Councils (RPMCs) and Area Political Military Councils (APMCs), which included both rural and urban machineries. The Natal Urban Machinery was at that time led by Muziwakhe Ngwenya, better known as 'Thami Zulu', and the Transvaal Urban Machinery by Siphiwe Nyanda, more popularly known by his 'travelling name' or nom de guerre, 'Gebuza', after one of King Shaka's generals.

'Thami Zulu' is, however, a name that has haunted the ANC for decades. He was a commander from 1983–1988 when he and the rest of the Natal Urban Machinery were recalled to Lusaka for investigation by the security department, or Mbokodo, under Comrade Zuma's command. This was after nine ANC guerrillas were murdered by an apartheid hit squad on the Swaziland border. Comrade Zuma was also commander of the Natal rural machinery. 'Gebuza' was to face a completely different challenge in that his brother, Zweli Nyanda, was murdered by the apartheid forces.

Swaziland was an ANC regional command existing in a state of high stress. The South African regime seemed to be playing a game with us by detaining and even assassinating cadres who operated in and out of Manzini while ensuring it did not completely destroy our operations. Its goal was rather to destabilise our machinery but to keep the ANC alive across the border for purposes of leverage. As Swaziland was largely dependent on the South African state for its economic stability, the kingdom would thus remain under pressure in a way that suited the apartheid regime.

King Sobhuza II and his government would not recognise apartheid South Africa officially and accepted the ANC's representation in exile, but it was almost impossible to prevent the South African Defence Force (SADF) or the South African Police (SAP) from entering his country's borders. This was especially true after Sobhuza's death in 1982. He had been supportive of the anti-apartheid struggle, once telling Moses Mabhida that if our cadres crossed through Swaziland on the right, he would ask his police to look to the left. It became more difficult for us during the interregnum, and especially after Mswati III became the youngest absolute monarch in the world in 1986 at the age of eighteen, four years after his father died. Mswati objected even less to incursions by the apartheid regime, and the intervening years – in which Sobhuza's wives, Queen Dzeliwe Shongwe and Queen Ntfombi Tfwala, served successfully as regent while Mswati completed his educated in the UK – created a dangerous situation for us.

Death, or the threat of death, was everywhere around us, all the time. In 1987, for instance, two comrades, Paul Dikeledi and Cassius Make, were assassinated by an apartheid hit squad. They had just arrived in Swaziland on a flight from Mozambique. Their taxi was followed from Manzini Airport and forced off the road near Mswati's palace. A Mozambican woman, Elisa Augusto Tsanine, who had met them at the airport and who was with them in the taxi, was also killed.

In view of the threatening situation, arrangements were quickly made in Swaziland for us to move to Mozambique, which was the next step on our journey into exile. A comrade escorted us across the Namaacha border, taking us through the fence and leaving us there with instructions on how to get to the police station, where we were warmly received as South African freedom fighters. The police on duty immediately phoned the ANC desk in Maputo to inform them that we were safe, and within a few hours we were picked up by another group of comrades and driven south-east to the capital city.

It was a great feeling to cross over into Frelimo territory. Yet it was also a strange and dreamlike trip. It only took about ninety minutes to reach Maputo, though the journey certainly had its dangers too, because anti-government rebels from Renamo were active in the area. In some ways we were all so attuned to the possibility, or probability, of being captured and tortured that we were almost expecting it. It was a surprise somehow when we reached our destination unscathed. Though we didn't discuss it, we probably all had the same thought: we were prepared for whatever might come.

Jacob Zuma, Joe Slovo and John Nkadimeng were there to receive us. Ronnie Kasrils was also in the city. They were the official link between South Africa and the ANC head office in Lusaka. Maputo was a place where activists from all points on the globe gathered. Here we mingled freely with foreign supporters of the Frelimo movement – expats who lived and worked there to assist the young Mozambican government. There were comrades from Latin America, other parts of Africa, Asia and a number of conflict areas around the world. We rubbed shoulders with Cubans, communists from eastern and western Europe, and other South Africans wanted by the apartheid regime, prominent among them Ruth First.

I first stayed with Theresa Cardoso, a Mozambican of Portuguese origin who was highly supportive of us. She could have left for Portugal in 1975 when Mozambique gained independence but she decided to stay.

She lived two houses away from Indres Naidoo, who had been with me on Robben Island. His place was a home away from home for many ANC people.

But there was nothing pleasant or calm about the circumstances under which we stayed in Maputo and tried to live some semblance of a normal life. The civil war and the economic sanctions imposed by Western powers and South Africa also meant that Mozambique had severe food shortages, even if rationing made it bearable for most. Many other basic items were simply not available. The fact that we in the ANC were supplied with food and other necessities by our friends in eastern European countries and supporters from Scandinavia, especially Sweden, was both a relief and posed a moral question. While we never went hungry, our Mozambican hosts were battling to keep their people fed. ANC cadres were supplied with tinned food, oil, flour and maize meal, at the very least, and bundles of excellent 'second-hand' clothing arrived mainly from the Scandinavian countries. We called these supplies 'impando', though I never knew why.

Despite the hardships, the long queues for bread and milk, and the constant threat of military attack, Maputo had a vibrancy beyond compare. I took solace in the company of people like Sunny Singh, Sue Rabkin, Albie Sachs, Mohammed Timol and Rashid Aboobaker. There was a strong bond among ANC comrades. Our experiences were diverse; our pain common. In Mohammed's case, he was marking nearly a decade since he had been told that his beloved brother Ahmed had died, having, according to the inquest, 'jumped to his death' from the tenth floor of John Vorster Square – a place of many atrocities. Mohammed battled terribly with this. As long as I knew him, he vowed his family would ultimately get justice for his brother, whose funeral he couldn't even attend as he himself was in detention. By coincidence, Comrade Rashid was at Ahmed Timol's memorial service at a sports ground in Vrededorp, Johannesburg. Mohammed and Rashid didn't know each other, but Rashid, who was a politically conscious teenager, was writing Matric at the time, and responded to a community call to attend the service. Only after a new inquest was opened into Ahmed Timol's death in 2017, were the findings of the original inquest overturned, and the judge found that Timol had been killed at the hands of the security police, after being gruesomely tortured.

At the time I knew Mohammed Timol in Mozambique, Mohammed worked in ANC intelligence under Jacob Zuma. He married Julie, a Mozambican of Indian origin.

We spent many evenings as a group at Sue's apartment, where she made hearty dinners for us. Joe Slovo was a frequent visitor and I came to appreciate his wry humour. There was so much going on in the background to these sociable encounters that I sometimes wonder how we managed to relax. There were more and more attacks by our soldiers within South Africa, many of them organised by Slovo and Rashid and aimed at strategic economic and military targets. We had political arguments on issues such as armed struggle versus political struggle, and we discussed the role of the Soviet Union and the direction the Mozambican government was taking under Frelimo.

We also spent time at Jacob Zuma's flat in Maputo, where we would often meet Slovo and Ronnie to remain updated on what was happening inside South Africa. Zuma had left the Island five years before I was released, and so the two of us were able to fill in the information gaps each of us had.

Yet possibly my most enjoyable meals were with Sunny Singh, my former cellmate and trusted friend. I would sometimes go to the market near the beach to buy fresh fish, and he would cook spectacular curries for us in his flat. Even now the memory of buying fish is still vivid for me. Fishermen pulled their dhows straight up onto the sand to sell their catches, and traders, mostly women, would lay the fish out on newspapers for their customers. Sometimes there was crayfish, which reminded me so much of Robben Island; at other times, octopus and giant tiger prawns. Once you've tasted them in Maputo, the same dishes never taste as good anywhere else in the world.

* * *

A few words are needed to tell the subsequent history of the police informer 'Ismail'. Apparently unaware that we knew his identity, the security police sent him to make contact again with us, this time in Swaziland. Upon his arrival there, our comrades Ivan and Rajes Pillay told him that they did not know where George and I were and encouraged him to proceed instead to Maputo. Once there, Indres Naidoo told him that we had already passed through – we had by then left for Lusaka – and so he went back to South Africa to inform his handler.

Rajes and Ivan had also proposed to him that he go on a crash course in Maputo, and he was encouraged to do so by his handler. But the 'crash course' was a set-up by our comrades to lure him into a trap. ANC security took him into custody in the Mozambican capital city, and once they found recording devices hidden in his car, he confessed. Subsequently he was sent to Camp Viana in Angola and given a chance to be 'rehabilitated' within the movement as a secretary. But he tried to desert and was then held at Camp 32 (the Morris Seabelo Rehabilitation Centre, or Quatro).

'When he disappeared, it was a big joke to us,' a security policeman told me during my abduction from Swaziland in 1986. 'Only his family was worried.' The regime generally treated its informants with this kind of disdain. This was especially the case with the askaris – those former comrades who agreed to collaborate with the enemy.

Later, I would find out that 'Ismail' or 'Librarian', whose code name as a police agent was Raymond Dlangamandla, had himself approached the police in 1969, 'complaining of the number of thefts in the Indian areas committed by Africans living in Wattville, Benoni', where he lived. He was thereafter paid R30 for any information he supplied to the regime. This is according to the ANC's second submission to the TRC.[5] His real name was Muhamad Mustapha.

Among 'Librarian's' assignments in Durban had been to befriend Comrades Shirish and Kisten, who, in turn, introduced him to Comrade George. That's how I, and many other activists, met him. 'Librarian' would report back to his apartheid handlers on every encounter. In the ANC's submission to the TRC, it said that 'on four occasions, when given material like cassettes, leaflets and literature by Rajes and Ivan Pillay in Swaziland, he took the material to his handler before he took it to George. He was reporting all the content of his meetings with Ivan and Rajes.' This was a good example of how challenging it was for even the best of us to identify infiltrators.

Twenty
Lenin and the blue Black Sea

IN 1980, SHORTLY AFTER George and I had been smuggled out of South Africa to Swaziland and then Maputo, we were flown from Maputo to the ANC headquarters in Lusaka. It was my first time in an aeroplane. ANC secretary general Alfred Nzo gave us a warm welcome. Within a day or two of our arrival, we went to the ANC's head office at 250 Zambezi Road and had a meeting with him, OR Tambo, Chris Hani and other members of the National Executive Committee, which is the highest organ of the organisation. George and I were debriefed about our years on Robben Island. As we spoke about our imprisonment, our leaders' questions about the dynamics between us in the ANC and other political organisations in the cells and the quarry triggered memories and maybe even brought to light issues we hadn't acknowledged before. The fact of being able to talk about our experience behind bars was somehow helpful. It was as if we were putting links together in a chain.

In retrospect, as George and I discussed our experiences with our senior comrades, we could see that it was to the ANC's benefit that 1976 had brought greater support for our organisation. By the time we were released, the PAC was on the downturn, its leadership all but silenced. For its part, Black Consciousness had been systematically crushed by the state after Steve Biko's murder in 1977.

Once we had been debriefed, Nzo suggested that George and I go on a holiday to one of the sanatoriums, the health and recreation spas, in the Soviet Union. Apparently, this wasn't very unusual, as some of our comrades had also travelled there for medical treatment. But it was extraordinary for us: neither George nor I had ever had a holiday. Joe Nhlanhla, the ANC's national administrative secretary in Lusaka, and Sankie Mthembi, who was an important part of the ANC's diplomatic initiatives in the Nordic countries, went with us. The Aeroflot flight made a brief stop-over in Luanda to pick up some Russians who worked in Angola.

Our journey was a revelation. We were with top comrades in the movement whom we hadn't previously known, and among Russians, those eternal enemies of the apartheid state. It felt as if I had left my old life behind for a short while. Our first destination was the 'party hotel' in Moscow, a surprisingly luxurious venue set inside a hangar, which had nothing to do with cocktails and dancing and everything to do with communism, the Russian Revolution and Lenin. There we met a few young ANC recruits, students from South Africa who were studying at Patrice Lumumba University. We were given some rubles to spend in Moscow and we had time to walk around like tourists.

We went to Lenin's mausoleum on Red Square, where his preserved body has been on public display since soon after his death in 1924. A queue of patriots, 'pioneers' (young communists) and the curious stretched for miles, although we were able to reach the front more quickly as guests of the government. This was one of the strangest sights I have seen in my life. Upon a black granite floor and surrounded by black granite walls lay Lenin under a warm light. We were told the room was kept at a constant temperature and humidity, and that his skin was kept clear of bacteria and mould with a regular mild bleach wash. His old silk suit – which had already been changed a few times when we saw his body – was laundered from time to time. I won't ever quite forget that.

A contrast to that sombre space was the colourful changing of the guard by the Separate Red Banner Kremlin Regiment, yet even if the actual ceremony was colourful the history was sorrowful. Until today, many Russians and older former Soviet citizens referred to it as the Great Patriotic War, and events like the Battle of Moscow in 1941 are

ABOVE LEFT *Ebie demonstrates how prisoners in the stone quarry were forced to break stones all day.*

ABOVE RIGHT *Ebie opening his former cell in the isolation section on Robben Island where he was incarcerated between February 1989 and February 1991*

LEFT *Ebrahim at a reunion of political prisoners who were part of the Bamboo span, who had to pull seaweed from the ocean, on Robben Island in September 2005*

Ebie and former political prisoners of the Bamboo span during a reunion on Robben Island, September 2005

LEFT *Ebrahim addressing parliament as the Chair of the Portfolio Committee on Foreign Affairs 2002.*

RIGHT *Ebie and Shannon at Thabo Mbeki's inauguration in 2004*

Former political prisoner Paul Langa hands Ebie the master key to the prison on Robben Island.

Ebie with his brother Essop, sister-in-law Fatima, nephew Saleem and his wife Nadia at Mbeki's inauguration

Ebie and Shannon during their wedding ceremony with Shannon's mother Sue, brother Craig and sister-in-law Jennifer in the background

Ebie with the Ebrahim family

Friends Devon Curtis (bridesmaid) and Aziz Pahad (best man) at the wedding reception

LEFT *Ebie and his older daughter Cassia at his wedding in September 2004*

RIGHT *Ebie and Shannon gorilla trekking in the jungle on the border between the DRC and Uganda for their honeymoon in December 2004*

Ebie and Shannon at their wedding on 25 September 2004 at the Gallagher Estate in Midrand

Ebie with the first indigenous President of Bolivia Evo Morales and Roelf Meyer the year of Morales's election 2005

Ebie in Bolivia on the invitation of President Evo Morales. To the right of Ebie is ANC Secretary General Kgalema Motlanthe, General Secretary of the SACP Blade Nzimande, and General Secretary of COSATU Zwelinzima Vavi.

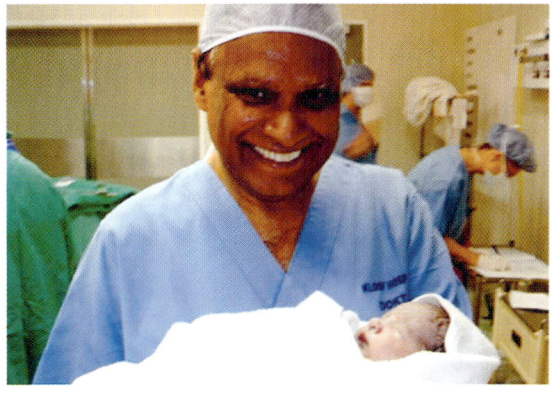

Ebie and Shannon in the delivery room at the birth of their daughter Sarah on 13 November 2006

Ebie and his close friend Henry (Squire) Makgothi at Ebie's 70th birthday celebration in July 2007

Ebie and his daughter Cassia at his 70th birthday celebration

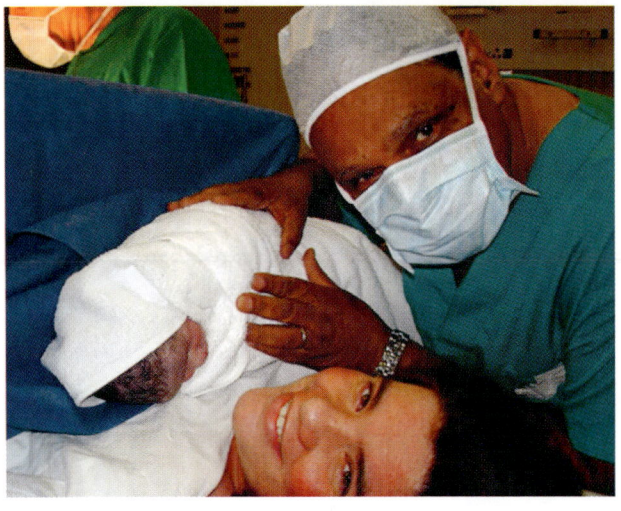

Ebie at the birth of his son Kadin on 13 September 2008

Sarah with her new-born brother Kadin

Ebie at his swearing in as Deputy Minister of International Relations and Cooperation in May 2009 (DIRCO)

Ebie and Sarah

LEFT *Sarah and Kadin*
TOP RIGHT *Ebie and his son Kadin*
BOTTOM RIGHT *Ebie at a BRICS meeting with Russian Foreign Minister Sergey Lavrov in Moscow 2013 (Dirco)*

Ebrahim and Chinese Assistant Foreign Minister Zhai Jun in Beijing September 2011 (Dirco)

commemorated in ways we have never quite matched to memorialise our national tragedies in South Africa. In June 1941, Hitler ordered Operation Barbarossa, the German Invasion Plan, to capture Moscow. Nazi forces invaded the Soviet Union using Blitzkrieg tactics to destroy entire Soviet armies. This was during the coldest European winter of the twentieth century, around minus 45 degrees celsius. Just as we in South Africa were treated as inferior by whites, the Nazis portrayed Russians as *untermenschen* ('inferior humans'). Unbelievably Moscow survived, although the German atrocities were incalculable.

A week later, we were in a plane again on the way to the Crimean city of Yalta, situated on the dark-blue Black Sea, where we stayed at a famous sanatorium. Crimea is full of picturesque old summer houses and grand palaces from the imperial era, and it attracted all kinds of travellers to its charms. It is like a paradise compared to most of the Russian coastline, which faces the Arctic and chilly Northern Pacific. The resort offered me an experience of a lifetime. I attended music concerts and went to movies. I had lunch watching the waves on the beach at Sevastopol, which was full of battleships and monuments. And even though I had been through years of bad food, icy prison cells and shocking labour conditions, the doctors at the sanatorium found me to be generally in good health. I was in my mid-forties. It seemed a lot of time still lay ahead of me.

Twenty-one
Skylark in the bush

ONCE WE WERE BACK in Lusaka, I was posted to the ANC treasury department with Dulcie September, who became a good friend. We shared an ANC house. We would cook for the others on Sundays, but I was only an assistant, as Dulcie was the chef and she brought her childhood to our kitchen with her Cape Malay dishes. Many people remember how her sense of humour could change everything on a difficult day. She was witty; she understood laughter, and I loved that about her. She was also a devoted collector of memorabilia and could bring to life the most vivid stories about places she had visited.

I missed her when she was appointed as the ANC's chief representative in France, Switzerland and Luxembourg. I believe one of my lowest points was when I got the news six years later that she had been assassinated in Paris. That her murder was never properly investigated continues to eat away at me. The unsolved killing of Comrade Dulcie remains one of our deepest injuries as a movement. It left me devastated. I look back on my Lusaka days with her uppermost in my mind, even though there were other great comrades I spent time with there.

In the 1980s, the apartheid regime was committed to destabilising Botswana, Lesotho, Mozambique, Swaziland, Zambia and Zimbabwe through support of rebel groups and the destruction of infrastructure.

Those of us who had newly arrived in exile had an intense time of it trying to make sense of how our leadership intended to take the struggle forward. Our comrades had had experiences that were different from ours, and that affected their outlook, tactics and strategy. Yet we were neither less nor more than each other in what we had gone through. In prison, one was perhaps safer, but not free to come and go in any way. In exile, one was free to come and go in some limited ways, but one was never safe, and many of our comrades in exile lived in as much fear as those of us who had been in detention and prison and tortured.

Our movement operated of course on three fronts: underground in South Africa; behind bars, most famously on Robben Island; and in exile. George and I had had experience of two of those fronts, and now we had little choice but to try to embrace the third. Those who had gone straight into exile were perhaps more emotional about getting home to fight on the streets of South Africa for our freedom. It was an urgent matter for some of them. We, on the other hand, were more resigned to whatever new route faced us.

Comrade OR Tambo was definitely in charge in Lusaka. By the time we arrived there in 1980, the ANC leadership was working according to *The Green Book*, a pivotal politico-military report produced to underpin a new direction for 'people's war'. The document was the result of a trip taken to the newly unified Socialist Republic of Vietnam in October 1978 by comrades OR, Alfred Nzo, Joe Slovo, Chris Hani, Moses Mabhida, Joe Gqabi, Joe Modise, Thabo Mbeki and Mzwai Piliso. There, they met Vietnam's 'Red Napoleon', General Vo Nguyen Giap, in Hanoi and studied how to prioritise propaganda in order to build mass political support on the ground. Mac Maharaj has explained *The Green Book* very well. Armed activity was meant 'to keep the perspective of people's revolutionary violence as the ultimate weapon for the seizure of power', but the time had come 'to concentrate on armed propaganda whose immediate purpose [was] to stimulate political organisation'.[6]

But this was a monumental challenge for us, some seventeen years after MK had been launched, almost independently of the ANC itself, to drive the armed struggle. When I was jailed in 1964, MK was in the ascendant, propelled by the Communist Party. The ANC under Chief Luthuli was at odds with itself over the strategy it should pursue although

Mandela and others kept our spirits alive. Then in 1969 the ANC's Morogoro conference brought MK under its full control for the first time. The conference also resulted at last in membership of the ANC being opened to all races, as membership of MK had always been, though only Africans could be members of the ANC's National Executive Committee. Thus, by the time I was released, the ANC and MK were inextricably linked. The problem now was that the armed struggle could not succeed without mass mobilisation, and the only way our people could get behind MK and the ANC was if they were made aware of our activities. At the time, the PAC was still trying to undermine us at every turn.

Consequently, no matter the precipice on which we stood, Lusaka offered me a revolutionary reunion. I was especially happy to see Kay Moonsamy and Dr Randeree, two comrades I had worked with in the Natal Indian Congress until my detention and conviction in 1963. Both were members of the Communist Party. Both were arrested and charged in 1964 but were fortunately granted bail, giving them a chance to escape into exile before they could be jailed. Dr Randeree was editor of *Sechaba* for some time in Lusaka, but he was also a general practitioner. His home on a plot a few kilometres outside the city became a safe, supportive gathering place. His work in our movement eventually took him to Canada where he subsequently passed away. Comrade Kay was also deployed to the ANC treasury department under Thomas Nkobi, 'Comrade TG'.

It was my privilege for the time I stayed in Lusaka to work with Jack Simons and his wife Ray Alexander, 'Ma Ray'. They were an inspiration to many of us. Jack and Ray were unusual. They pursued their service to political life with fearless energy. I enjoyed going for walks with them because they would impart such wisdom that one would be electrified by their thinking.

I also met Dr Yusuf Dadoo in Lusaka while he was visiting there from London. As chairperson of the Communist Party, he was apologetic about the fact that the underground structures of the SACP hadn't contacted me on my release from Robben Island. It was true that when I was back in Durban, banned, I had expected that contact would be made with me, and I was frustrated that nobody reached out to George or me, even though we had both been loyal members of the party before our imprisonment. One learns to live with these disappointments.

It was inevitable that I would go for military training so that I could be deployed in the frontline areas, if necessary. We all had to know what it was to be a soldier. The ANC had been building a military infrastructure in Angola as its main rear base since 1976, and there were many transit and training camps there. But Angola was only just beginning its catastrophic civil war, to which some of our recruits would be deployed as combatants.

No one told me exactly how long I would be there, so I took only light baggage and left the rest of my belongings with Dr Randeree. Three of us were booked on a commercial flight, and I travelled without a passport, although the ANC had supplied an official letter. Our destination was the transit camp, Viana, or Camp 001, where we were vetted. All cadres entering Angola for military training were scrutinised there, and there were about four hundred people in the camp at any one time until it closed in 1989.

This was undoubtedly a fraught time for the movement. Our leadership tended to react harshly to anyone who was suspected of working for the enemy, and we were only too aware of the consequences of such suspicion. To some extent, that response was the result of the destruction of Novo Catengue training camp in 1979 when a number of cadres were killed there after the SADF staged an aerial bombardment based upon the intelligence of agents planted within MK. The fear of betrayal had also come with the sudden and overwhelming influx of recruits who went into exile after the Soweto 1976 uprisings. It was difficult at times to identify agents posing as young revolutionaries, but they brought death to us, or the potential of death. This explanation by Vladimir Shubin, who acted as a key liaison between the Soviet Union and MK, may give you more background:

> During the first two years of [Novo Catengue's] existence, 932 new recruits were interviewed, 26 confessed to being enemy agents, and a further 35 were still under interrogation. The spies were ordered to find out the location of ANC houses and camps, their daily routine, the identity of the people who lived there, and the system of protection and defence.
>
> Special attention was given to finding out the names and location of the leadership. However, a number of [the] regime's agents continued operating within the ranks of the ANC, and a network of

infiltrators was uprooted in 1981. They carried out various subversive and dangerous acts, such as the attempted mass poisoning of cadres, supplying intelligence which led to the bombardment of one of the MK camps in Angola, sabotage of equipment [and] attempts to encourage indiscipline.

Moreover, some agents supplied Pretoria's security services with information which led directly to the assassinations of leaders and the arrest, torture, and imprisonment of ANC cadres.[7]

The apartheid regime's cross-border attacks accelerated change in the way our movement operated. Although the regime had always been a violent instrument, it was now organising forays by its army to take revenge on us outside South Africa. It was waging a conventional war in Angola, and, some believe, at the same time helping the Americans in their proxy war against the Soviet Union. Those were still the days of the Cold War. When Angola gained independence from Portugal in 1974, the People's Movement for the Liberation of Angola (MPLA) won the right to form the new government of Angola. This led to a break with the National Union for the Total Independence of Angola (UNITA), which had previously been united with the MPLA in the fight against colonialism. The apartheid regime and the United States assisted and funded UNITA in their battle with the MPLA, which was in turn supported by the Soviets and the Cubans. Cuban soldiers were also sent to Angola to train guerrillas and operate in the bush. We didn't know it at the time, but that horrific civil war would go on for thirteen years, until 1988. Throughout that time, the MPLA, the Soviet troops and the Cuban soldiers were our brothers and sisters. We operated side by side.

We MK operatives might have been soldiers, but we didn't have an army. We might have aspired to become guerrillas, but we didn't even have the opportunity to train in the appropriate terrain. MK consequently took strain from within and without.

Our department of national security and intelligence was having to play a greater role, and that meant our comrades had to become specialists in a whole range of areas of warfare if we were to stand a chance against an apartheid force that was growing in military strength. The East Germans and the Soviet Union were especially supportive in terms of training. This is another reason why screening procedures were so important.

Not long after I was sent for military training, dozens of our comrades at Viana camp, where we had been vetted, demanded to have complaints about conditions addressed. But once Comrade OR had examined their issues, there was a delay in taking action, and so there was a mutiny in 1984.

Life in the camps was very tough.

I was sent to a camp called Funda, set deep in the jungle. We travelled for about half a day in a truck to get there and found it wasn't much more than a clearing where mostly tents were set up, with three men sharing one apiece. It was a spartan existence. There were only a few wooden structures. A bell woke us up before sunrise for breakfast, which was always porridge, and we would then assemble for military exercises. Thereafter, we would walk with our towels and soap to a stream to wash and collect drinking water to take back to the camp. We used purifying tablets to make it palatable – but only slightly. The water always had a disconcerting taste.

Next came instruction in firearms, explosives and military tactics. Some of our trainers were Soviets, who gave us disciplined political education. I wouldn't hesitate to name the trainer I thought was the best of them all: Comrade 'T-Man', a South African whose real name was Ernest Pule. He knew the history of the ANC and the struggle inside and out. It was no surprise that after liberation he became a general in the South African National Defence Force.

We left Funda rather more quickly than intended as the site was infested with mosquitoes, and we were thoroughly bitten, night in and night out. I contracted malaria, although we were regularly given quinine tablets as prevention, and I had to be treated by a medical officer. We were then transferred to Caxito, a much larger camp. There we were taught to handle different types of weapons, from AK-47s to bazookas. This was a far cry from my early days as a saboteur in Durban when we improvised. I occasionally shared stories of those early days of MK with other comrades in the camp, and there was much raucous laughter. Those of us who had survived that haphazard and dangerous bomb-making period considered ourselves the lucky ones. Yet telling stories like that was rare. We tended not to disclose details of our past activities for security reasons.

I performed night duties a few times a week at Caxito, where our training included long hikes through near-impenetrable bush. But after a few months, the commander tasked me to listen to the SABC, BBC, Radio Moscow, Voice of America and other radio stations, and compile news bulletins for the assembly every morning. I remember the first-ever item I read to the camp was about the death of reggae superstar Bob Marley. That upset the comrades. Marley had a large following; he was an activist, like us.

For me, though, collecting bulletins and presenting them to my fellow soldiers was a source of mighty comfort. I enjoyed it. News aside, I also got to hear All India Radio or Akashvani, the national public radio broadcaster of India, and listened to the music, which reminded me of Ma and carried so many vibrant memories. I especially loved the Bollywood playback singers – Mohammed Rafi, Lata Mangeshkar, Kishore Kumar, and the 'skylark', Geeta Dutt. It seems incongruous now that I once listened to those immortal and enchanting Indian cinema songs in the Angolan bush – I might even have lip-synched.

Despite it being hot and humid inside our training areas and notwithstanding the complete absence of even the most basic of comforts, our morale was high. There was a constant sound of the singing of freedom songs, and the thumping of dancing feet in boots. I never again experienced that level of fervour. It was also a time of fear. UNITA was brutal, and many MK soldiers were killed by UNITA rebels. Burials of the dead took place at camp. It was hard on the mind.

But our underground structures within South Africa were simply not ready to receive trained MK soldiers. Our chances of returning to South Africa thus became less and less real, resulting in more dissatisfaction for some and sorrow for others.

After six months of being in the camp, I was sent back to Lusaka, where I was to stay with Joe Nhlanhla. But not long after I arrived, there was an alert that there might be an attack by South African forces, and many of us had to leave for Tanzania. Security alerts were common in Lusaka. Usually we would be instructed to move out of our houses overnight. But an imminent military strike was another thing altogether.

I wasn't opposed to going to Dar es Salaam, though, because I could meet my brother Gora there. We had last seen each other in 1962 when he was living in Johannesburg as a student at Wits. I was on trial when he escaped the security police dragnet in 1963. I accepted his decision to join the PAC because I knew we belonged to different political camps. When we saw each other again in Dar es Salaam, he had two children, Yasir (named after Yasser Arafat, the chairman of the Palestine Liberation Organisation, the PLO) and Zareena, who were living in Tanzania with their mother, Xaviere, a French translator from Paris. Gora had also reached the heights of becoming the PAC's foreign secretary.

I cherished our reunion. We discussed the fact of our father having passed away while I was in prison, and Gora was grateful to get news about our mother, our younger brother Essop and our sisters. He missed the family very much, and it seemed life in exile had brought him some regret. But that was true for both of us. Essop had certainly taken on our role in caring for our parents. How does one properly express that kind of gratitude to your brother? We felt it deeply.

Gora was bright, and I could easily see why the PAC needed him. He could argue its case in the most challenging environments, and although I never had political discussions with him, I understood that he played a very significant role in keeping the PAC alive internationally. He introduced me to his wide circle of friends and comrades in Dar es Salaam, which was full of revolutionary figures in the 1980s. Gora was a prominent revolutionary himself, representing the PAC at the Organisation of African Unity and the United Nations. He'd also had the experience of living in Beijing when he worked for the Afro-Asian Journalists Association in the 1960s. It is said that without Gora the Chinese communist government wouldn't have paid any attention to the PAC at all, but I think the far more important aspect of his time in Beijing was his meeting Xaviere there.

One of his friends who won my admiration in Dar was Karrim Essack, a South African Marxist, lawyer, journalist and lifelong activist, who drove a VW Beetle, which he also used as an office. His modus operandi was to stop along the road and interview his clients in his car. Karrim was a frequent visitor to North Korea, and he would always argue with me that North Korea was the only true socialist country in the world.

I also met the representative of the PLO, Ali Halimeh. Gora vacated his apartment in Dar for the PLO to use as an office. Ali was later the Palestinian ambassador to South Africa some years after our liberation, having been a key contact between the ANC and the PLO during apartheid.

Tanzania holds a special place in ANC memory, and its Solomon Mahlangu Freedom College (SOMAFCO)[8] in Morogoro was an important part of that. Established in 1977 on a sisal farm donated by the Tanzanian government under President Julius Nyerere for the ANC's Mazimbu Liberation Camp, SOMAFCO was funded by foreign donors, and incorporated a pre-primary and primary school. I was overjoyed to be reunited with Henry 'Squire' Makgothi on my trip there. He was in charge of SOMAFCO, which was named in honour of our MK comrade Solomon Mahlangu, who was hanged by the apartheid government in 1979 after re-entering South Africa in 1977 and clashing with police in Johannesburg. I listened to my comrade's many stories about how, when he first arrived at Mazimbu, he found open bush, with a few mealies growing here and there. Initially there were only tents, and the 'kitchens' were open fires. Our comrades had to build an educational institution and then an entire community from scratch, which they succeeded in doing. It wasn't surprising that Squire later became the deputy secretary-general of the ANC in exile. Squire and I were lifelong friends until his untimely demise.

But Tanzania wasn't good for my health, as I rather suddenly became ill with another bout of malaria which was more severe than what I had experienced in Angola. Dr Manto Tshabalala, one of the ANC's foreign-trained medical doctors who was based in Tanzania at the time, quickly put me on a drip and I gradually recovered under her treatment.

Twenty-two
Life underground in Swaziland

I WANTED TO BE DEPLOYED in the frontline areas so that I could be nearer the people at home. Once I was back in Lusaka, the leadership decided I should go to Swaziland as the head of the Political Military Committee there. Mac Maharaj wanted me to go to Botswana, but Moses Mabhida insisted on Swaziland, which was my preference too. And so another chapter began.

Before I settled in Swaziland, I travelled back to Maputo. Under President Samora Machel's government, Maputo was as vociferous a socialist city as when I had left it a year or two before. But it was also breaking under the bloody civil war between the ruling Frelimo and the rebel Renamo group.

In Maputo I was made familiar with the workings of the 'senior organ', chaired by Jacob Zuma. This section dealt with the political underground in South Africa by means of a political committee based in Swaziland. It played a critical role in the implementation of the plan contained in *The Green Book*. For us in the ANC, the corridors between Mozambique, Swaziland and South Africa were crucial for the infiltration into South Africa of cadres and arms. This meant that Swaziland, code-named 'the Bay', became increasingly unsafe as the apartheid regime used the vulnerability of that country to try to crack down on us.

Our cadres were being murdered and kidnapped with seeming ease in 'the Bay', Maputo and Lesotho. A parcel bomb had killed Comrade Ruth First, and Comrade Albie Sachs lost his arm in a car bomb in Maputo. I was greatly affected by the death of Zola Nqini, when the regime attacked the house where he and others were staying in Lesotho, murdering many innocent people. Comrade Zola was an outstanding cadre, who displayed great potential for lifelong leadership. Here is what Comrade Phyllis Naidoo wrote about him and the terrible day of his death in her book:

> Homes were few in the ANC community. Zola's home was one of the few. Zola was employed at CARE (a US aid organisation) until a week before the raid when his appointment as chief representative in Lesotho was confirmed. The media description of Zola Nqini was that his alias was Bra Z. Any black journalist or worker on any of the papers would have told the writer that 'Bra Z' is slang for brother. He was brother to all. It was a term of endearment. He was very dear to us all… For Bra Z, how quickly and anonymously death came. His shirt and pants were placed over a chair, and he slept in his underpants. The bed and the floor were covered in blood.

I think I still miss him, I wonder what he could have become.

My time in Swaziland coincided with the most intense period during which the Swazi police and South African security forces worked together. They devised a strategy whereby the Swazi police would arrest a cadre and lock him up in a remote police station. They would then inform their South African collaborators, and that same night the South Africans would raid the police station and kidnap the comrade. Many fell victim to this tactic, chief among them Glory Sedibe, whom we knew as September. He was badly beaten after his capture, and ultimately decided to become an askari.

Or so we initially heard. But the story wasn't quite as simple as that. The historian Jacob Dlamini has explored Sedibe's character in the book *Askari: A Story of Collaboration and Betrayal in the Anti-Apartheid Struggle*. Dlamini writes that Sedibe's 'actions form but one layer in a sedimentation of betrayals in which he himself was betrayed by the Royal Swazi Police, and may have been sold out to the Swazis and the Security Branch of the SAP for "sordid monetary gain" by some of his own comrades in the ANC'.

September went on to betray me as well as comrades Simon Dladla and Mandla Maseko.

Once I arrived in Swaziland, I had to find safe and secure accommodation. Since I had crossed into the country illegally over the Mozambique border fence at night, over the Easter weekend, I had to be inconspicuous or else I was doomed. Our modus operandi was to meet cadres from home in charge of operational units inside the country. Pravin Gordhan was key here. He had a wide network both in the underground and in the mass democratic movement, and was successful in linking the two, especially at the time of the formation of the United Democratic Front.

Pravin and his unit played an important role in giving strategic direction to comrades on the ground. So did Moe Shaik, a student at the University of Durban-Westville, who was by nature a militant. Moe expressed his militancy quite openly, causing some consternation among a few comrades. We had to call Moe to Swaziland to speak to him and ask him to be less outspoken, as his conduct risked exposing him to the security police. We wanted him to assume a lower profile so that he could be a more effective underground operative – which is what he became. This was important for us in exile. Moe's unit was named after a great comrade, Mandla Judson Kuzwayo (MJK), and became a valuable resource in intelligence gathering and a superb communication channel. The MJK unit and those of Pravin, Shadrack Maphumulo and Archie Abrahams (Billy Whitehead) played a crucial role in the political development of South Africa.

We needed the brightest minds to advise us. One who stands out is Professor Ismail Mohamed, a brilliant mathematician, who had worked at the University of London, the University of Zambia, the University of the Western Cape, the University of Lesotho and the University of the Witwatersrand. His relentless activism had also seen him being fired from his job, detained and persecuted. He would visit me in Swaziland with his daughters Elaine and Jennifer who were active in our underground movement. His son Andrew had joined MK and gone into exile. Professor Mohamed would brief us on the political situation in the country, enabling us to make the correct strategic decisions.

We were under strict instructions in MK to avoid civilian targets.

Comrade OR Tambo would be very upset when innocent people were killed. The trouble was that when the South African security forces attacked and killed our cadres – and innocent people – in the frontline states, cadres operating inside South Africa would want to take revenge. Some would say, 'If we bury our people, they must bury theirs as well.' I argued that this was not the policy of the ANC, and that as a liberation movement we needed to assume the moral high ground. At the same time, one could understand the feelings on the ground when the regime conducted its deadly raids.

The murder of Comrade Gebuza's brother Zweli Nyanda, also known as 'Douglas', still raises deep feelings. Zweli had a recruit in his unit named 'Fear', who was part of the military machinery. 'Fear' had come from ANC headquarters in Lusaka and was present with Zweli in a house in Manzini on the night of an attack by apartheid troops. Zweli was the direct target of the apartheid murderer Eugene de Kock, who was commander of the notorious Vlakplaas hit squad farm. When the unit to which De Kock was attached attacked the house in Manzini, Zweli tried to make a run for it. De Kock shot him from behind nine times while a colleague of De Kock's shot him a further two times once he was already dead. De Kock earned a medal for that murder.

'Fear' later claimed he had climbed out of a window to escape the attack, but we would find out that he was a security police plant, and it was he who gave the agents of death the location of the house and the identities of the people who would be there that night. 'Fear' had been part of our military machinery based in Swaziland. It turned out that he had sent many of our people to their deaths. His real name was Edward Lawrence, and his other aliases were Ralph Mgcina and Cyril Raymonds. When he was finally arrested by ANC security, I was told that he confessed, and claimed his family had worked for the South African police force for many years.

'Fear' himself had been working for the Special Branch since the 1970s, when he was instructed to join young Black Consciousness and ANC supporters who were leaving the country to become part of MK. He was to 'study [our] internal situation, gain experience and remain dormant', according to the ANC's submission to the Truth and Reconciliation Commission in 1997. 'In 1983, whilst deployed as a leading cadre in the Natal military machinery in Swaziland, he was arrested by the Swazi police. He knew that one of these policemen was working for the [South Africans]. During questioning, he revealed information about his unit in Swaziland.' 'Fear' collaborated in the attack on the house in Manzini where he lived with Zweli and others. He alerted the security forces when the comrades were asleep, unlocked the back door, switched off the outside light, and broke his bedroom window to 'escape'.

Another comrade killed in the raid was Keith McFadden. According to the People's United Democratic Movement (PUDEMO) of Swaziland, Keith and his brother Gavin were 'instrumental in the logistics of MK when the ANC needed to smuggle weaponry into South Africa'. PUDEMO later paid tribute to their father, Percival McFadden, upon his death in 2016 'for the contributions he made to the Swazi and South African struggle as he gave himself up to it so much that he risked his family by opening his home to host revolutionaries'. The McFaddens were people who mattered to us.

'Fear' also exposed a farm at Malkerns in Swaziland and another house in the suburb of Fairview, where the ANC kept materiel. Those were subsequently raided, and the weapons captured. Weeks later, having been identified as a spy, 'Fear' was being interrogated by our operatives when he complained of agonising stomach pains. It was decided to consult a doctor, but by the time the doctor arrived, 'Fear' was already dead. The doctor suspected he might have ingested poison. To this day, 'Fear' occupies one of the darkest places in my mind.

Twent-three
Hélène Passtoors

INTERNATIONALISM WAS VITAL to keeping the ANC going, financially as much as politically. It had a strong psychological component to it, too. If we, as cadres, were embraced by a solidarity network, we felt we were not alone. Among the foreigners who supported our struggle were Hélène Passtoors and her husband, Klaas de Jonge. Hélène was a Belgian activist whose work as a linguist led her to live in Africa for some years in the Congo from 1967. She moved to Maputo with Klaas, a Dutch anthropologist, and they became close to Joe Slovo and his wife Ruth First. It was after Ruth was tragically killed in Mozambique in 1982 by a letter bomb sent by the apartheid regime that Klaas got involved in our armed struggle.

It didn't take long for Slovo to recruit Hélène into the MK in 1981 and put her talents and skills to good use. I met Hélène on a trip I made to Maputo to confer with our leadership. Hélène was working underground with Rashid Aboobaker, who was MK's Special Operations commander in Mozambique at the time. She was then separated from Klaas. Hélène worked in Maputo as a lecturer at Eduardo Mondlane University where Ruth had been research director of the Centre for African Studies.

Joe had groomed Hélène to become a pivotal member of the ANC's Special Operations team under his and OR Tambo's leadership. As a white woman and a foreigner, Hélène was able to carry out extensive reconnaissance missions without being easily detected. She looked for potential targets, such as strategic coal export and oil import lines, as well as identifying South African Defence Force and police vulnerabilities and possibilities for attacks. One target was a training base for the rebel Renamo movement in what is now Limpopo province. Hélène also transported weapons and established arms caches, setting up 'dead letter boxes'. This involved burying equipment in remote areas. A map with a sign indicating the location of the cache would then be passed on from the frontline areas to operatives inside the country.

I was taken with this Belgian woman, who daily put her life on the line for the cause of South Africa's liberation. It did not take long before Hélène and I began to have a relationship. Hélène then decided to move to Swaziland, where I was living under a passport given to me by the Indian government in the name of 'Ahmed Zaheer'. A South African Indian family by the name of Badat ran a business in Swaziland and, like many such families, they were supportive of the struggle. There was a two-bedroom house behind the clothing shop they owned in Manzini, and when I was first in the country, I rented it. I would meet with our political machinery there clandestinely at night, although it was important that I kept my accommodation a secret even from most of our comrades, especially those in the military units, as many were being infiltrated into South Africa. It was preferable that if they were arrested and tortured, they would genuinely not be able to reveal our whereabouts.

By the time I met Hélène, I was no longer living in the house at the back of the Badats' shop as we had to change our accommodation underground at least every six months. I moved to a house with a garden in Mbabane, but I was robbed of most of my possessions there, so I had to move again, this time to a house on top of a hill. This is where Hélène, her daughter Brigitte and three sons, Yves, Philippe and Fabrice, came to live with me. The boys didn't stay with us for extended periods as two were at school in Maputo and the other at the private Waterford Kamhlaba United World College in Mbabane, where many ANC leaders sent their children to be educated. It was a pity we had a burglary there, too – Hélène's radio was stolen – and we were compelled to find another home. I then rented a house at the end of a road in a secluded area. But this was not paradise either. There were MK operatives in hiding on the same street a short distance away, and one day there was a police raid on their house and a shootout ensued. Those kinds of incidents kept us on edge.

Ronnie Kasrils asked Hélène to reconnoitre for me, which meant she would check roads that I intended to take and followed me to my meetings. I often touched base with contacts from South Africa in hotels, although these were especially precarious spots as many agents lurked there. Hélène also dropped Ronnie off at places where he had to be present, and picked him up again, or met him to courier information or materials between us. She did the same for Comrade Nkosazana Dlamini-Zuma and me, acting as a go-between. Nkosazana, a good friend of mine, was a doctor based at a hospital in Mbabane, and I would often visit her at her home for dinner. Yet Hélène and I were disciplined about keeping our work and our private lives separate, as I was in the political machinery and she in the military. We made a point of not discussing what we did. We even had workspaces that were out of bounds to each other.

This was the first time in my life that I had been a family man. I would take young Brigitte to school until she turned sixteen, when Hélène gave her a light motorcycle for her birthday; this meant Brigitte could become a day scholar at Waterford. Fortunately, we could still have dinner together in the evenings. Hélène was impressed with my ability to cook a delicious mince curry, and we savoured the Indian treats my family would bring from Johannesburg on occasional weekends.

Hélène, the children and I would go on day trips to explore the countryside. It was comforting to have the company of an instant family. She was particularly fond of my own extended family and always delighted at the news that Essop and my sister-in-law Fatima were coming to visit with their sons. She developed a strong bond with my sister Ayesha, who brought us sumptuous food when she came to see us. Those were wonderful times for me to reconnect with my siblings and nieces and nephews, and I looked forward to their visits. On one memorable trip my brother Gora's children, Yasir and Zareena, who were otherwise living in Paris, joined us. I remember how all the cousins spent the day swimming together. It seems so simple. It meant so much.

Behind the scenes, Hélène's and my life in the movement went on. Throughout the period when Hélène was with me, she liaised between Special Operations cadres in Swaziland and commanders in Maputo. But it was inevitable that our time as a family would end. Both of us ended up returning to South Africa on secret missions. But Hélène went through absolute hell. That she is still as positive and as bright as ever remains an inspiration to all of us.

A decision was made by the ANC to transfer Hélène into South Africa in 1984, so she could carry on her work for us there. Although I was clear on the need-to-know principle under which we all operated, I was thrown by her departure. I was worried, too.

She moved into an apartment in Yeoville, which was still designated 'whites only' in terms of the Group Areas Act, though it had a famously multiracial, bohemian character. Next to Hillbrow and Soweto, it was Johannesburg's most well-known place. It was later revealed that the security police not only knew Hélène was there but had rented an apartment directly opposite hers so they had a view of her flat.

A short while after she left Swaziland, I too was instructed by our leadership to go home – covertly, of course. I was to set up new communication channels and draft detailed reports on the scale and tempo of resistance to apartheid. The aim was to provide a clear picture of events on the ground. It had always been the intention that we cadres should return and begin to operate from within South Africa. I had to operate under a suitable structure, and the leadership in Maputo instructed Yunis Shaik, who led the MJK unit, that his unit should take care of all my logistics and security.

On 23 January 1985, I was taken to an area near the border fence where a peasant farmer, an ANC supporter, met me. We set off together to walk through the bush to get onto a road on the other side of the border. Our trek included traversing a few minor rivers. That was how porous the border was with South Africa, though this too would change within a few months as the regime cracked down even more harshly.

Unfortunately, once we were on the South African side, we noticed some unusual activity and my companion felt it wasn't advisable to complete the crossing. He took me to his small house near the fence, and I spent the night and the following day there. I had to stay inside a room so as not to be noticed by the neighbours. It was a relief when we got news from comrades that my pick-up had been aborted but would take place the next night. That's when I successfully entered South Africa.

Yunis and Shirish Soni, who was also part of the MJK unit, were there to fetch me. Shirish was a businessman who owned a clothing factory in Durban, but he was also a committed MK operative. Although that was the first time we had met, we would go on to have a long association. Shirish drove us to Durban, where we arrived in the early hours of the morning. I stayed with Yunis's father, Lambie Rasool, for the rest of the night. The Shaik family had a long history of involvement in the liberation struggle, so this wasn't a strange arrangement. Lambie had earned his activist stripes as a trade unionist. Their sons – Yunis, Moe and Shamim (Chippy) – became activists, and Moe and Yunis were first detained in 1980. I had frequently met Yunis on his trips to Swaziland, and I received a warm welcome from the family, and a tasty dinner had been prepared for our arrival, which I really appreciated.

Moe had found me a flat in the Overport area opposite his own, so that we would be able to signal to each other by flicking lights in our apartments in a particular way if there was a security danger. I did have to use a disguise, though, and grew a bushy beard, wore longer hair and was never without a pair of glasses. Comrade Nkosazana Dlamini-Zuma had helped me in creating my disguise, and it was she who suggested I dye my hair grey. We had a good chuckle about that. The disguise proved so effective that one day when I had to go and see a dentist and spotted one of my close relatives in the waiting room, she looked straight at me and showed no sign of recognition. It hurt that I couldn't greet her with a hug after not having seen her for so many years, but I had no choice.

Phumla Williams, my comrade in Swaziland, was to be my contact person while I was in Durban. She had stayed at my house in Mbabane for a while. But the contact ended when she was herself infiltrated into South Africa. In 1988 Phumla was to experience the most terrible torture after she was arrested in Soweto. Her capture and interrogation left me shocked and greatly pained as I had some idea of what she went through.

When our contact ended on my return to Durban, I had to turn to Hélène to communicate with Maputo. I couldn't risk calling her on her home phone, which was believed to be bugged by Military Intelligence (MI), so I rang the Linguistics Department at Wits where she was a doctoral student and was lucky to reach her. We agreed to meet in Johannesburg. In retrospect, that was a bad idea.

I flew to Johannesburg from Durban. Hélène picked me up at the airport, but Military Intelligence (MI) was monitoring her movements and photographed us together. When I was detained in 1987, the security police told me it took them a while to identify who I was because of my disguise. They thought I was an operative named 'Ahmed' and, of course, my passport from the Indian government identified me as 'Ahmed Zaheer'. The photographs MI took were sent to an agent in Swaziland – a highly placed cadre, and askari, in our movement – who confirmed that I was the man in the photo. The security police were furious, as they had been looking high and low for me, and there I was, right under their noses.

I gave Hélène a report to send to Lusaka via Maputo, with some verbal instructions. She also undertook to arrange money for me from headquarters to cover the work I had to do in Durban. We then parted, but Hélène popped in to see me on her way to Swaziland about a month later, as I had to pass another secret document to her. We did that in the parking lot at the Snake Park on the Durban beachfront, and she then carried on with her journey to Swaziland by car. But we were again being watched by MI. Their decision, MI agents told me later, was not to arrest me on the spot, but to keep on monitoring me in the hope I would lead them to others in the underground.

I picked Hélène up at the airport in Durban when she flew back from Swaziland. She had booked in at the Blue Waters on the beachfront, the hotel having 'international status' at the time. This meant that race was not a barrier to entry, and we could go to her room together. Of course, it had been bugged by the Security Branch. So we turned up the volume on the TV and sat on the balcony, which was too far for the bugging device to pick up clear sounds. Hélène gave me a sealed envelope containing cash for my mission and documents about the important conference the ANC was about to hold in Kabwe, Zambia. Our view from the balcony was over an army camp situated next to the Blue Waters, and she wondered out loud whether it could be a military target for MK. After all, the hotel room offered a perfect view of it in its entirety. We laughed about that.

But we also had an important issue to discuss: the plan of how I was to be smuggled back into Swaziland. Hélène even had maps to indicate where I should cross. Once we were back inside the hotel room, where we could be recorded, we stopped talking about my plan and tried our best to hold each other tightly and remember how it felt to have human contact. The state made a big deal of that hug during Hélène's trial in 1987. Not only did it try to stir some kind of disgust for us as a 'mixed-race' couple, but it tried to make a case that our encounter was engineered for me to give her military instructions from MK. That was not the case. I will, however, admit that we shared a kiss, and when the state raised this in the courtroom, even the judge in Hélène's case started laughing. He asked the witness, a security policeman, whether this wasn't normal, since Hélène and I had been romantic partners for some time.

It's memorable that *The Star* newspaper in Johannesburg ran a story on its front page about us in reference to the security police recording, under the headline 'The Kiss', detailing the events described in court. That was all the information the state had on us, however, as the batteries on their equipment ran out the next day and nothing more could be recorded. Meanwhile, Hélène and I were able to be reacquainted, catch up and even enjoy a meal at an Indian restaurant before we parted.

I drove her to the airport for her flight to Johannesburg, but we didn't know that this would be the last time we would see each other until after we had both undergone torturous detentions. We were allowed but one exceptional visit in Pretoria Central Prison after my trial ended in 1989, before I was transferred to Robben Island again. I had the awful experience of seeing her through a glass partition. That is an event which left me empty and hopeless.

After six months of being inside the country, I needed to present my findings in person in Swaziland. It would have been best to do this at the ANC conference in Kabwe, in June 1985. As this took place in Zambia, the Zambian army had to protect our delegates as there was a serious concern that the South African regime would bomb or attack the venue. It did not, but the decisions taken at the meeting would be used by the regime as reasons for its increasing cross-border violence.

I wanted to be among those supporting the intensification, not deceleration, of the struggle. I believed this would capture the growing revolutionary mood that I had reported as part of my work back at home. I was frustrated that I wasn't able to get to Kabwe in time. Some have described Kabwe as a 'council of war'. Yet, if its tone was militant, it was also conciliatory. Even though we intended to seize power at last, our leaders weren't talking war. They were essentially talking peace, which was breathtaking considering that the SADF had recently killed fifteen of our people and a number of Botswana citizens, including women and a child, in a raid on a building in Gaborone.

A new National Executive Committee was elected at Kabwe, which drew support from many organisations in the world, including the OAU Secretariat, the Swedish Social Democratic Party, the British Labour Party, the British Council of Churches, the French, Dutch and West German Anti-Apartheid Movements, the American Committee on Africa, the All-India Peace and Solidarity Organisation and the Socialist Unity Party of New Zealand. A rally in support of the conference was held in London, attracting around twenty-five thousand people.

Kabwe was a symbolic moment too. The delegates agreed ANC membership should be open to all, irrespective of race – not only among the rank and file, but also on the NEC, as 'comrades from other racial groups have laid down their lives for the cause of freedom'. The committee was thereafter made up of twenty-five Africans, two Coloureds, two Indians and one white. Non-racialism was formally adopted as a principle. Kabwe would also cement the relationship between the ANC and the SACP – a central issue for those who had left the ANC to form the PAC in 1959.

Then came August 1985. We were all waiting for a promised speech by President PW Botha. Although we in the movement didn't believe for a moment that he would announce 'reforms' that would match our demands for liberation, some people in the world thought he would. But he did not. *The Guardian* reported it this way:

> The president's speech was a defiant restatement of existing neo-apartheid policy, a castigation of critics at home and abroad, and a questioning of the role of the media in the reporting of violence in the townships.
>
> As if to underline the president's tough stance, the government put a curfew on the township of Soweto. Restrictions have already been imposed on Eastern Cape townships under its emergency powers. Stricter control measures relating to school boycotts and the transport of petrol in Soweto and Alexandra were also ordered.
>
> Botha adopted a defiant stance, as when he called the leaders of the

rebellion in the black townships 'communist agitators on the payroll of their masters far away'.

Our situation in the frontline states worsened after that, and some of the most appalling violence against our people inside the country took place following Botha's 'crossing of the Rubicon' speech.

I listened to the speech with some of my comrades underground and we concluded there was an even greater need to fight back against the regime while it was at its weakest point. Why do I say 'weakest point'? This is because the world was then turning its back on the South African government, with even the United States and Britain angered by Botha's refusal to make good on his promise to reform apartheid. The nature of resistance had also changed. To me, it recalled the resistance of the late 1950s and early 1960s when the apartheid government's ability to suppress the mass movement had been constrained. Meanwhile, the Anti-Apartheid Movement was gaining ground internationally, as were sanctions and boycotts of South Africa. The problem was that being at its 'weakest point' in a global context did not diminish the regime's military capacity. And Botha loved the military.

My exfiltration was arranged by Hélène and comrades in Swaziland. I asked Hélène to provide security on the South African side and trusted her implicitly. The plan was that comrades Moe and Shirish would drive me to a spot near the border with Swaziland, close to the town of Ermelo. Hélène would wait for me at the Ermelo Inn to give me further instructions. Another comrade was assigned to pick me up at a T-junction close to the border post. He was to leave a can of Coca-Cola under the road sign to indicate he was in the vicinity.

Hélène had carried out reconnaissance of the area in the afternoon, and then again an hour before we arrived from Durban. This was to ensure there were no roadblocks or any other suspicious presences. She was concerned that there was a man making a fire at the T-junction where I was to be picked up. She hovered around in the area and noticed a white man sitting in a car parked on the roadside. He didn't seem to have a particular purpose. He then got out and walked around for a bit, seemingly waiting. He finally drove off.

Hélène was anxious enough to recommend we abort the exfiltration, but I was feeling under pressure and insisted we proceed. It was the middle of winter, a freezing evening in June, when we set off. Moe and Shirish, who were ordinarily good-humoured and talkative, seemed subdued. One could feel the tension. I was usually the quiet one, but the heavy atmosphere in the car was even too much for me, and I desperately wished someone would say something. Moe was driving. We all knew the consequences if we were to be stopped. We were praying. My stomach was contracting in knots. So many people's lives depended on my safe and successful exit.

The first sign of trouble was our seeing lights in the distance at the top of an incline not far from the border post. Unfortunately, this was serious. It was indeed a military roadblock. The arrangement with Hélène was that she would drive ahead of us, and if she saw anything suspicious, she would blink her brake lights so as not to alert any cars in front of her. The problem was that the results of all reconnaissance done within the hours before had come back negative: no roadblocks. This one had taken Hélène by surprise. She blinked her brakes as she went over the hill and saw the soldiers in front of her. But we weren't over the hill ourselves yet, so we missed her signal.

Furthermore, the military wouldn't have been expecting traffic, as it was evening and the border post was already closed. It was not a residential area. So why were they there? Naturally, it would have been a huge mistake to do a U-turn, so we had no choice but to proceed straight into what could very well have been an ambush. There is nothing like driving into your enemy's arms when your impulse is to speed off in the opposite direction. But Moe was as cool as could be. He told the soldier who came to his window that we were lost and trying to find the Ermelo Inn. Just as calmly, the soldier pointed us in the right direction after taking our names and car registration. I gave a fictitious name, but Shirish had to tell the truth as he had hired the car using his real name.

Just as we drove off, breathing a collective sigh of relief, Moe spotted two cars in the rear-view mirror which had stopped at the roadblock seconds after us. My heart was palpitating, especially when the cars turned left, following the same route as ours. One's sixth sense is invaluable, and it was beginning to feel as if our luck might have run out. We were voicing all kinds of scenarios, but what convinced me that things had gone awry was that when we passed the T-junction where I was supposed to have seen the can of Coca-Cola, there was nothing there. This was a bad sign.

My instinct was for us to outmanoeuvre the Security Branch and make it to Hélène at the Ermelo Inn first. We drove at top speed. Moe and Shirish waited in the car while I ran into the hotel to find her. She and Brigitte were near the casino, and after a quick briefing, we agreed we were all in real danger, and they needed to grab their things and leave. I then ran to the car and threw myself into the back seat, shouting, 'Go, go, go!' Moe put his foot on the accelerator and we heard the wheels screeching as we took off.

The rest of the night was something of a blur. My mind was racing. What should we do now? There was no choice, really. We had to go back to Durban. I always knew my mission into South Africa carried serious risk, but it is only at moments like these that one realises just how nightmarish one's situation really is. By this time, the security police had traced my place of residence in Overport. The MJK unit picked up an increase in surveillance of the area and believed I would be arrested. So Yunis contacted Pravin, who agreed that I should be transferred to his unit as it could take better care of my security. Yunis gave his word to Pravin that he would never reveal my transfer, no matter what happened. I owe a debt of gratitude to Pravin for sheltering me and later making sure I could leave the country safely.

The ANC leadership in Maputo was adamant that I could not be captured. I was one of the only leaders of the political underground who had full knowledge of all the units in the Durban area, their members and operations. I hurriedly packed my things in Overport and went to the Roadside Hotel near the Umgeni River, where Yunis had booked a room for me. He said someone would contact me, and I should stay put until they had done so.

It was an intense moment. Yunis fetched me at the flat. Before we parted, we hugged each other. There were tears in his eyes. The dragnet of the security police was closing in, and we all knew it. I had no idea if I would see Yunis again.

It took only an hour before Thiruth Maistry, a member of Pravin's unit, arrived to fetch me at the Roadside Hotel. He drove me to a house in Reservoir Hills which had a room in the basement. I was to stay there until we could try again to get me over the border. I thought this would be just a few days, but the days turned into weeks and the weeks into months. My life seemed to be in a perpetual state of limbo, but there was nothing I could do about it except practise patience. Given the ferocity of the manhunt under way, I was unable to leave my hideout even to get some air or go for a walk. I would spend my days in a locked room. The TV and daily newspapers, which Thiruth brought me, were my only solace. Thiruth was in fact the only person who saw me during that time. He delivered meals to me from the outside, and I think I had more curry takeaways than I ever thought possible. There was no phone to call anyone, nor did I hear any visitors in the home above. It was like a peculiar form of house arrest. The story of Anne Frank, and how she hid in an attic to avoid capture by the Nazis during World War II, played in my mind.

I knew this would be very tough on my family as they would no doubt be going through their own traumatic ordeal in view of the Security Branch's desperate search for me. One weekend, Essop, Fatima and their young sons, Saleem, Enver and Nazeem, took a road trip from Johannesburg to visit Fatima's mother, who happened to live in Reservoir Hills. They had no idea that I was in hiding nearby. Essop decided to use his company van, which was quite spacious and suited to a weekend drive away. But they were followed by the security police on their way back to Johannesburg. As the family reached Pietermaritzburg, they were pulled over, much to Essop's horror, as he didn't even know I was in the country.

He was detained and taken to CR Swart, the Security Branch headquarters in Durban, and given a rough interrogation. He was grilled about when he had last seen me and the nature of his trips to visit me in Swaziland. It was agonising to hear years later of how they had beaten my brother, and repeatedly pushed his head into a bucket of water, demanding answers to their questions, answers he couldn't and wouldn't have given.

The police kept Essop's van and dusted it from top to bottom for fingerprints, as they were sure he had been hiding me inside at some point. Meanwhile, Fatima and the children were taken back to Fatima's mother's house. Shortly afterwards, the police took Saleem, who was only sixteen, to CR Swart, and showed him a number of photos so that he could point me out if I was in any of them. They specifically showed him a photo of me in disguise with a long beard and glasses, but he was emphatic: there was no way that could be me. The askari in our ranks in Swaziland had already identified me, although that didn't help the agents locate me in the basement.

After a few weeks, Thiruth told me that comrades Moe, Yunis, Chippy, their father Lambie and Shirish had all been detained, also at CR Swart. This was under section 29 of the Internal Security Act of 1982.[9] We were well aware of how many people were being killed in detention, and history shows us that by 1982 at least fifty-six people had been murdered under section 6 of the Terrorism Act. When Thiruth gave me that terrible news, I felt as if someone had stabbed me in the gut. It was obvious they would be going through hell. The Security Branch would not let up until they had me in their clutches. Until then, they would brutalise everyone attached to me, non-stop.

Moe, Yunis and Shirish were indeed severely tortured. Yunis's torture could only be described as the most sadistic, and to this day I wonder how he ever managed to recover from the extreme brutality exacted on him by the security police. When he recounted his torture at a re-opened inquest in 2021, it left me completely broken and in tears.

Shirish was badly affected, and his mental condition deteriorated to the extent that he spent time in a psychiatric hospital. An application was brought for his release, leading to a Natal Supreme Court judge saying that if a person held under section 29 'was incapable of being interrogated, the detention of that person was unlawful'. The *Weekly Mail* reported in June 1987[10] that 'a number of experts [gave] evidence [with] the state psychiatrist and senior lecturer in Psychiatry at Natal University's medical school, Dr Angelo Lasich, [saying] Shirish was unlikely to recover from his mental disorders unless he was released'. Lasich noted that 'further interrogation would serve no purpose as his mental health prevents him from giving any answer which can be regarded as reliably satisfactory in any respect'. Shirish was then released in February 1986.

But he was detained again in June 1987, and went through the same life-threatening mental agonies, with the result that his lawyers went back to court arguing that he was 'suffering from severe anxiety, bordering on psychosis'. A doctor described him as 'gravely ill' in papers. Yet police arrived at St Aidan's Hospital, to which he had been admitted, and told him that since the court action, he was being detained under a different law – section 31, which related to the holding of potential state witnesses. The intention was for him to give evidence in my case, as I was on trial at the time, with police claiming he had 'made a statement during his previous detention which could be related'. They insisted even though Shirish's psychiatrist, Dr Ashwin Valjee, feared he was 'a candidate for a mental breakdown which could result in brain damage'.

Moe suffered greatly in endless interrogation sessions and prolonged solitary confinement over many months, but he never gave the security police anything they demanded of him. He and his brothers had showed exceptional courage. It is difficult to put into words the deep sorrow and regret that I felt, knowing my comrades were enduring such mental and physical suffering. It was one of the worst things a human being can experience. I was the most wanted person in South Africa at that time. The police were raging with anger. But my courageous comrades never gave me up; not one.

Comrade Lambie was released from detention after a month, along with Yunis and Chippy and a cousin of theirs. Chippy was not even part of the unit, and thus detaining him was a purely vindictive act. He came out of detention well and strong. Yunis was later rearrested and detained.

There was an even more shattering outcome to this. The stress of their ordeal resulted in their mother, Kaye, having a heart attack. She died while Moe and Yunis were behind bars, and they were taken to her funeral in shackles. Moe spent nine months in detention, and both he and Yunis were released without ever being charged. Chippy was detained again when I was in detention and was kept in solitary confinement for a year. These are destructive events that have weighed heavily on my conscience ever since, but sadly these are also burdens one carries; they are scars from our struggle. My comrades underwent despicable torment so that I could escape. It is difficult to live comfortably with that thought. I simply can't.

At the time I was in the basement, I was also aware that Hélène was in danger. I didn't know if the Security Branch had arrested her, and Thiruth Maistry was not privy to everything that was happening. I wondered whether she had found out that the Shaik brothers had been detained. The chances were that she had been captured before that information reached her. One day while I was sitting solemnly in that quiet room,

I found out that Hélène had been arrested. So had Klaas. That was a blow that left me reeling. At the time, I was far more concerned about Hélène – how she would cope with isolation and detention, and what would happen to her children.

When Pravin was at last able to make contact with ANC headquarters in Lusaka to draw up a new plan for my exit, my sense of foreboding was overwhelming. But so was the adrenalin. It had to be done. On the morning of my escape, I left the isolation of the basement like a creature emerging from hibernation. It was as if I was feeling the warmth of the sun for the first time, and I found that sensation, and even the feeling of fresh air, exhilarating. I prayed I would never have to go into the darkness like that again. Sadly, that was not to be.

That morning, I was picked up by a comrade and his wife. They were in the front of the car and I sat in the back trying to conceal myself as much as I could. They had devised a system of communication whereby we would drive to town 'A' and wait at a telephone booth for a call from an advance group in town 'B', which was further along the route. The caller in town 'B' would then get in his car and check whether there were any police roadblocks between towns 'A' and 'B'. Once the road was clear, we would proceed from town 'A'. This went on until we reached the Swazi border, at a point where one could more freely cross over. There I met Totsie Memela who, according to prearranged plans, was awaiting my arrival. She then drove me to Manzini.

Comrade Totsie was an exceptionally dedicated young comrade from Soweto, who was responsible for the infiltration and exfiltration of many of us in the underground, including Gebuza, Ivan Pillay and Mac Maharaj. She worked in this way in Swaziland and later in Zimbabwe, and spent time in Angola too. Totsie was also an expert at managing dead letter boxes located on white-owned farms near the borders.

I had been out of Swaziland since January 1985, and in that time many ANC comrades had had to leave Mozambique because of the signing of the Nkomati Accord between PW Botha and Samora Machel in March 1984. According to this agreement, Mozambique undertook not to allow its territory to be used as a launch pad for attacks on South Africa. South Africa agreed to cease its support for Renamo while Mozambique undertook to expel the ANC. Naturally the Accord failed – especially from Mozambique's perspective. South Africa got what it wanted, or to the greatest extent possible, as it continued to support Renamo, and Mozambique's economic dependence on South Africa made it nearly impossible for it to fight back.

Among those ANC members who were expelled from Mozambique was Joe Slovo. He had specifically been asked by the Mozambican government to leave as he was such a high-profile, senior member of the movement. He went to Lusaka. When I returned to Swaziland, he had already been elected the first white member of the ANC's National Executive Committee at the Kabwe conference. The expulsion of the ANC from Mozambique also affected the way the ANC operated out of Swaziland.

I had hardly arrived in Manzini before I was asked to travel urgently to Lusaka via Maputo. In Zambia, I met OR Tambo and Slovo, who separately informed me that the leadership had taken a decision to send more senior comrades back into the country. This eventually led to Operation Vula in the late 1980s. Chris Hani briefed me on the decision taken at Kabwe to create regional political-military committees (RPMCs). I was instructed to report directly to Lusaka as chairperson of the Swaziland RPMC.

At that time, a people's insurrectionary war was under way in South Africa. I saw my role as central to that. I could fully understand Joe Slovo's argument that three vital historical stages had been reached by 1985: the apartheid regime was going through a major crisis; our people had had enough and were ready to make the final sacrifice to achieve freedom; and there was an acceptance that the ANC might govern the country. This was no longer an illusion created by revolutionary imaginations. But the final hurdles still lay ahead of us.

Twenty-four
Dutch support

I STAYED WITH COMRADE Reggie September, an outstanding leader of the utmost integrity, and his English wife Dora when I was in Lusaka. It was at their apartment that I first met the Dutch anti-apartheid activist Conny Braam. At that time she had already been part of the anti-apartheid movement for about fifteen years. She seemed to be pleased to meet me. She especially wanted information on Hélène Passtoors as they came from the same part of the world; Conny was also close to the ANC, like Hélène. We talked at length about the arrest of Klaas and Hélène.

Conny and I had a close relationship while I was in Lusaka. She even took to calling me by my family name, 'Chota', which I liked. Hélène had done the same. Later, it was the critical role she played in Operation Vula which gripped us activists. It was under her guidance that many comrades were trained in communication and disguises. She set up safe houses inside South Africa – although she visited our country for the first time only in 1990 – and arranged for documents to be smuggled into South Africa on a regular basis.

Our friendship was intense but also delightfully 'ordinary', if I can call it that. Conny and I roamed the streets of Lusaka and indulged in the luxury of ice cream – a real treat for people like us in those days. We would take walks after nightfall. Even when I returned to Swaziland to set up the RPMC, I sometimes had to return to Lusaka to liaise with Ronnie Kasrils, and I was glad I could see Conny then. She was also a great letter-writer. Her handwritten accounts of life would arrive from Lusaka and later from Amsterdam.

At times, we met up in Maputo, where we stayed at Helena Dolny's house. Helena was an Englishwoman, the daughter of a Polish father and Czechoslovakian mother, who had taken a gap year to teach at a mission station in Zambia when she was eighteen. That was in the early 1970s. Helena's love for southern Africa grew alongside her support for the liberation struggle. She became part of the anti-apartheid movement and the Committee for Freedom in Mozambique, Angola and Guinea-Bissau in the 1970s and 1980s, as well as a researcher. She also worked for the department of agriculture in Maputo, and as a lecturer at the Eduardo Mondlane University under Ruth First. Joe Slovo first recruited Helena, who was by then an agricultural economist, and her then husband, Ed Wethli, who was also a South African, to engage in reconnaissance. After Ruth was assassinated, Helena and Slovo fell in love and later married.

Helena understood the strangeness of the bonds between people that went beyond politics in the situation we lived. She would lend us her car so that Conny and I could have some free time together in Maputo. Conny and I then made plans to meet in London, but that was never to be. I was abducted by the apartheid forces in Swaziland before we saw each other again. Conny wrote about her response to this news in her book *Operation Vula*, which was published in 2004.

From 1987, roughly 70 Dutch citizens were involved in the dramatic transformation of South African resistance fighters. Using makeup, false teeth, wigs and new outfits, the fighters assumed a different identity and found their way back into South Africa.

The smart phone *avant la lettre* was developed with help from Philips employees to establish communication between Mandela in prison and the ANC leadership in Lusaka. Mandela could now inform comrades of the preliminary conversations he had with representatives of the regime. Our comrades used a method of communication which came before that of social media or emails, to share digitised information between Mandela and the leadership in Lusaka.

The information was sent via London to Amsterdam, where Conny

Dutch support

decoded the first messages and then sent these to Lusaka. There was also information transmitted via floppy discs that were smuggled by a KLM stewardess.

Operation Vula was so successful because it took place in secret. For four years, the people involved in this operation managed to evade the sight of the regime's security forces. Only a handful of top leaders of the ANC, including Tambo, were informed. It represented a unique collaboration between South Africans, Dutch and other internationalists.

Conny did everything she could to mobilise international opinion in support of my release.

Twenty-five
Abduction by intelligence agents

IT WAS A HOT SUMMER morning with bright sunshine pouring in through the window. From there, I could see the hills of Pine Valley, the surrounding mountains and green pastures, as well as the river flowing through. This was Umgugu Reserve near Mbabane, in Swaziland, where many of our ANC cadres sought refuge. This was where I had stayed in hiding for nearly two years. The tranquillity of the valley shielded many of our armed combatants, and its beauty was the backdrop for clandestine meetings with cadres from home.

I was exhausted after a night of meetings that had started at about nine and ended at four the next morning. As the chairperson of the RPMC, I had called together the commanders of various units to get their end-of-year reports. I also wanted insight into their plans of action for 1987. Among those present were Gebuza, Paul Dikeledi and Thami Zulu. We discussed the main points that would constitute OR Tambo's January 8th message, when our president would issue a statement reviewing the activities of the previous year and point to the course of action for the coming year. Those of us involved in internal work were expected to inform head office of the state of organisation in the country, recent political developments and the balance of forces.

Our meeting the previous night had covered the activities of our comrades in the underground in South Africa and the possibilities of armed activities. I had received a substantial amount of money from head office which I had to distribute to the various machineries according to their programme of work, so this kind of gathering was vital for me to find out who needed resources.

When the meeting ended, we all dispersed. I left for home at the crack of dawn, and then tried to get a little sleep. Not long after I put my head down, I heard the phone ring. Very few people knew my number, and when the phone rang it was usually a case of dire emergency. I was taken aback by the sound of the phone so early in the day. I immediately recognised the voice of Lindiwe Sisulu, a very special comrade, the daughter of our leaders Walter and Albertina Sisulu. Although she was part of MK, Lindiwe was lecturing at the Manzini Teacher Training College at the time. She was so bright. We shared a love of history, which was the subject in which she had earned her honours and master's degrees.

'Are you OK?' she asked.

'Yes,' I replied. 'What's wrong?'

The concern in her voice had my heart beating faster.

'Haven't you heard?' she asked, and then she told me the SADF's Special Forces had raided some of our comrades' homes during the night. They had entered Swaziland seemingly with impunity and, we suspected, with the assistance of some hostile elements in Swaziland itself. Among those abducted were Swiss nationals Corinne Bischoff and Daniel Schneider, who were working in Swaziland. The soldiers blew their front door open with explosives, forced them out of their house, and threw them into a police van with a few other people. That weekend, Pik Botha, the South African minister of foreign affairs, defended the kidnapping of what he called 'terrorists'. He maintained South Africa had the right to defend itself. The Swazi government remained silent, but the Swiss government strongly protested against the kidnapping of its citizens. Thanks to the pressure the Swiss exerted, Corinne and Daniel were released within two days and transported back to Swaziland by helicopter.

The soldiers had also kidnapped our good comrade Grace Cele, who had assisted George and me to escape from South Africa in 1980. In another attack, they killed a thirteen-year-old boy who ran out of his home in panic when they bombed it. In that assault they kidnapped a

Swazi national in what they later acknowledged was a case of 'mistaken identity'. A family and a community had lost a beloved child. We grieved for their loss.

As for my comrade Shadrack Maphumulo, I still don't have the words to express my outrage. He was a registered refugee in Swaziland and lived with his family in a block of flats in Matsapha, a working-class area near the town of Manzini. A disciplined, dedicated cadre with a sound theoretical mind, who argued for the emancipation of the poor and the working class, he was among the co-accused in my 1963 trial. Comrade Shadrack served ten years with me on Robben Island. Close to Jacob Zuma, he was very taken with the lessons in revolutionary Marxism which that great communist Harry Gwala gave us in prison.

I feel uncomfortable giving such a graphic description of his fate, but I cannot otherwise express the horror of that night. The South African soldiers raided his flat by blowing open the door. They then shot him in the stomach in front of his children, and dragged his bleeding body down a flight of stairs and threw him into the boot of their vehicle. By the time they crossed into South Africa, Shadrack had already died from blood loss. The rest of the victims were blindfolded and their hands tied behind their backs. Corinne told us later that she could feel a dead body 'knocking against her' as the soldiers drove away at high speed. I suppose we can't imagine the precise sensation, but we can understand the terror that everyone in that army vehicle must have experienced at that moment.

I tried to gather as much information as I could, first establishing that the commanders who had been with me the previous night were safe. I rang Jacob Zuma in Maputo to tell him about the raid and especially about Shadrack – a very close friend of us both – but I battled to have a conversation. I broke down and wept.

On Monday, 15 December, I was in my house, which I regarded as 'safe', as very few people knew about it. At about nine thirty, while I was watching TV, there was a knock at the door. Dumisane Zwane, a seventeen-year-old Swazi teenager who had been living with me and doing work in the garden, went to answer, thinking it must be the neighbours. There were two black men on the doorstep, who claimed they needed a wheel spanner as their car had broken down. I fetched my keys and went to my car outside. When I was about to open the boot to assist them, one of them drew a gun. They threatened to shoot me if I moved or made a sound. I knew there was no escape. They ushered me back into the house. One held a gun to my forehead while the other tied my hands behind my back and blindfolded and gagged me. They also tied Dumisane's hands and feet and put him on the floor. In the freedom struggle, you were prepared for all sorts of danger, which perhaps explains my calmness as this ordeal was taking place.

They searched the house, collecting as many documents as they could, and put them in a steel case. They seized all the money I had, which may have amounted to about R4,500, as well as a combination radio and cassette player and all my cassettes, a Walkman, and a suitcase with clothing, and then steered me into the back seat of my own green Mazda 232. I was made to lie down. I could hear my captors conversing with people with Afrikaans accents. It seemed a group of men had surrounded the house, probably to kill me if I tried to escape.

I was driven to a house in Mbabane, removed from the car and made to sit in what seemed to be a garage. My captors went inside to make some phone calls. I was then put into the boot of the car, and we drove towards what I would later discover was the border fence. Once we stopped, I could hear more conversation. I was then taken from the car and made to walk down an incline before my blindfold was removed. We were right at the fence. They made me go through the barbed wire of about three or four fences. I could see the bright lights of the Oshoek border post, in what is now Mpumalanga, as it was the dead of night. I found myself on the South African side of the border, against my will.

One of my abductors, who said he lived in Soweto, told me I would have 'nothing to fear' if I cooperated with the police. They would even furnish me with a passport to go to Zambia as an agent of theirs. They informed me they had picked up my trail on the Friday during the raids into Swaziland when they were at the flat of a South African refugee by the name of 'Maphumulo', who was staying a little distance from Manzini. It could only have been Shadrack's home. They saw me in that area early in the morning, which would have been around the time I was leaving the meeting with the MK commanders.

My captors steered me up an incline onto a tarred road. As we waited for others to arrive, one of them told me about a detainee by the name of 'Wally' who had tried to flee from a police vehicle at Uncle Charlie's Junction in Johannesburg. He said the escape was planned because the police had tried to turn 'Wally' into an askari, but he'd betrayed them. His escape gave them a chance to kill him. This was as straightforward a warning as I could have got.

Later, two cars arrived and parked a short distance apart. As we approached the cars, white men armed with rifles closed in on me. One put leg irons on me, my hands were untied and I was handcuffed. The metal container with the items removed from my house was put in the boot of one of the cars. I was forced into the back seat and we drove off. There was a South African intelligence agent in the front next to the driver and one in the back. The car had a radio to enable the agents in the vehicles to remain in constant contact.

After a long while, dawn broke on 16 December – the day of the launch of MK and our armed struggle in 1961. They in fact asked me, 'How do feel to be arrested on your freedom day?' The men attempted to interrogate me in the car as we were driving, but I refused to speak at that point, and certainly would never have answered any questions. 'Tell us where you planted bombs today. If you don't tell us, you will die tonight.' I looked at them in disgust. They continually said they would torture me, and that by evening I would be standing on hot bricks and 'would talk'. They vowed they would otherwise deny me food and water. 'What terrorist acts have you planned for this freedom day?' they wanted to know. 'We are going to kidnap and kill you bastards one by one,' they boasted. They also played my cassettes while we were driving. Most were recordings of my favourite Indian music, which wasn't what they had hoped to hear. As the sun rose and I looked at the hills and valleys of the Eastern Transvaal with cows grazing in the fields and people waking up to enjoy a public holiday, I wondered where I would be when the sun set.

The men in the car seemed confused as to where to take me. They kept stopping and making phone calls from telephone booths. I later found out one option had been to deliver me to Vlakplaas, the torture farm operated by Eugene de Kock. Fortunately, the head of intelligence, Niël Barnard, who was on his way back from Natal, instructed that I be taken to the Security Branch head office in Pretoria. Had I been sent to Vlakplaas, it would have been like disappearing into a deep, dark hole of continuous torture and probably death.

We had to pass through an army roadblock, but a policeman in the 'escort car' in front of ours made sure that nobody asked us any questions. The only times we stopped were for the men to have coffee. We finally reached Pretoria in the late afternoon and parked alongside a building. The agents radioed someone. We waited for about fifteen minutes before the men became impatient and drove off. After more radio communication, we stopped again, and after a short while another car pulled up behind us and I was transferred into it. We drove a few more blocks until we reached the Compol building, where police intelligence was located.

I saw the words 'Police Museum' on a lintel. Indeed, that is where the police museum and its grisly collection of crime evidence had been situated since 1968. The building has retained a kind of terror for me. It looks as if it belongs in 1800s Paris, which is not surprising as it was built in the late nineteenth century in the Beaux-Arts style popular in Europe at the time. There are lots of sculptural decorations of fruit and flowers. This was the epitome of 'civilisation', yet what was happening inside the building during the 1980s, a century later, was quite the opposite.

I was pushed inside by two intelligence agents, who passed through strict security checks, and I was then made to sit in an office, still in leg irons and handcuffed. A tall man walked in and introduced himself as Brigadier Schoon. This was the heinous Willem Schoon, although I did not know it then. He was the head of the deadly C-section – the 'anti-terrorism' unit of the Security Branch, which was closely linked with Vlakplaas. It was Schoon who gave the orders for the murders of Griffiths Mxenge in 1981 and of Jeanette Schoon (Curtis) and her young daughter Katryn, in 1984 – and he could have had me killed at any time. I knew my life was hanging by a thread.

Schoon asked me whether I had been assaulted. I said no. He asked me why my eyes were red. I told him it was probably lack of sleep. He said he would arrange for me to see a doctor. Another brigadier, introduced as 'JH' Cronje, was also present. He told me I was to be detained. Cronje was in fact the infamous Jack Cronje, a former commander at Vlakplaas, the sort of person who, like Schoon, could have overseen my death. Cronje was later charged with four violent and deadly incidents of murder committed around the time I was in leg irons and handcuffs in front of him. Furthermore, Cronje, like Schoon, was instrumental in the murder of Griffiths Mxenge. Cronje would end up receiving a huge pension, and Schoon later retired at the age of 55 in 1989 as the secret hit squads were being exposed.

A Captain Naude then read from a typed piece of paper to inform me about the terms of section 29 of the Act under which I was being detained. It meant I would be kept incommunicado: no lawyers, no family and no visitors of any description for periods of six months at a time. He asked me to sign the paper. I refused. I insisted that the paper did not state that I had been abducted from Swaziland. He said I should sign it and write about my abduction in my own words under my signature. They removed the handcuffs, and I added my testimony to their paper. At no point did any of these security policemen deny that I had been abducted. They simply replied that I was 'now with them'.

I was handed over to Naude and a Warrant Officer Savage, who were told by Schoon that if I 'played ball', they should also treat me 'in a nice way'. They were to be my interrogators. They went through the papers from my house in Swaziland which they had packed into the steel case, including the passport given to me by the Indian government under the pseudonym 'Ahmed Zaheer'. I was also known as 'Roy' and 'Roy Zaheer' in Swaziland. I acknowledged that the contents of the case were mine, so that I could prove I had been kidnapped from Swaziland. They also went through all the goods they had packed from my house. That night I was held in an isolation cell with a small single bed at a nearby police station. I fell into a deep sleep.

A telex was sent about my detention to attorneys Yunus Mahomed and Associates – who were known as the 'struggle' lawyers – only on 29 December 1986. But on 16 December, I was somehow relieved that I was being detained under section 29, for the simple reason that my detention would be recorded and it would not be easy for the apartheid police to kill me and deny any knowledge of my existence. But I remained determined not to cooperate.

Twenty-six
Surviving torture in John Vorster Square

THE NEXT DAY, I WAS examined by a doctor, as Schoon had promised. I complained to him about my abduction. He didn't respond to that specifically, as he said it was his job to examine my physical state; nothing more.

Two days before Christmas, there was a first attempt to interrogate me. I was taken to a room in the Compol building where there were two white men and a black man. They wore badges saying 'Besoekers/Visitors'. I don't recall the names of the white men, but the black man was September, the askari, who I was told was now working for the security police. The interrogation didn't succeed as I still refused to answer questions. Instead, I kept complaining that I had been kidnapped and demanded that I be allowed to see lawyers and returned to Swaziland. I maintained that my abduction was illegal. They used all manner of threats but failed.

After a week, two other security policemen from Johannesburg visited me in my cell. One was Nicolas Deetlefs, the other Warrant Officer JC Farquhar. They said they 'just wanted to greet me'. Deetlefs mentioned that he had interrogated Hélène Passtoors and therefore 'knew a great deal' about me.

The next day they took me to John Vorster Square, where Ahmed

Timol[11] and many other political detainees had been tortured. Ahmed Timol's body was so sadistically tortured in 1971 that it is believed that he had significant brain injuries before his body was disposed of from the 10th floor. During the re-opened inquest in 2017 into Timol's death, his comrade Salim Essop testified about his own torture at the time in John Vorster Square. Salim had testified that there were teams of torturers who were working on shifts, who brutally assaulted him for days on end in a vault. Essop was so severely tortured that he ended up in hospital unable to walk.

Torture in security police headquarters had become the norm. Security policemen like Lieutenant Theunis 'Rooi Rus' Swanepoel had gone abroad for specialised training from the French in torture tactics. Swanepoel was infamous for carrying out electric shock torture, burning people, breaking their bones, hanging people upside down from open windows in high rise buildings, and depriving detainees of food and water for up to three days at a time.

By the time the ANC was unbanned in 1990, over 70 detainees had been brutally killed in detention. We mourn the loss of these brave cadres and wait for the circumstances surrounding their deaths to be exposed.

John Vorster Square had an unassuming grey and blue exterior, as if intended to dull the truth behind its walls. My mind was racing as we approached it. There were a lot of people in there who were suffering. Of that I was certain. I knew I had to do my utmost not to break down once I was inside.

I demanded to write a letter to the minister of law and order. Deetlefs was ordered to give me a piece of paper and a pen. I wrote a letter complaining about my abduction and my missing property, and handed it back to Deetlefs. I was then put into a cell where the windows were welded with iron bars. I could see the street below where there were people shouting up at prisoners, most of whom were criminals. They were discussing their cases – what to admit and what not to admit in court. Someone opened the grille of my cell to ask whether I was 'OK upstairs' – he pointed to his head. I said yes, and he responded: 'Well, we'll see about that.'

I knew what was happening once they moved me to cell 221 where I was bombarded with terrible sounds. I knew those horrific noises were being deliberately filtered into my cell to destabilise me, and I used all my resources to fight back. But soon it became too much for me. I became uneasy and anxious and couldn't sleep. I tried to put wax paper into my ears, but it didn't help. As the noises grew louder and more insistent, I began to become a bit disorientated. I complained to the station commander who came in the mornings to open the door, look through the grille and close it again. He peered at me, laughed and slammed the grille shut. I recalled the words of Deetlefs: that if I survived, I would not be human.

I knew that the political underground and many lives depended on me to survive this torture, but the confusion that results when you're going through it requires unimaginable strength, moment for moment. I pray my children will never have to experience even one second of torture in their lives.

The doctor usually visited detainees every second Thursday. On my first visit to him, I complained about the chaotic sounds. He maintained it was other prisoners who 'always make a lot of noise'. But he nonetheless gave me sleeping tablets to use every second night. He found my blood pressure very high and said the medication would also help that. As the banging and clattering continued, I felt my mind was being held together by a very thin, tight thread which could snap at any moment.

One morning I was taken out of my cell to meet the inspector, a retired magistrate named Strydom. In view of allegations of torture and deaths in detention, and as result of the public outcry both within the country and internationally, the regime was compelled to appoint such a person to periodically visit detainees. I complained to him about the noise, too, and he accompanied me to my cell for an inspection. He agreed the cell was constructed in a peculiar manner and asked the policeman escorting him why this was so. There was no explanation. Naturally, the cell – which was on the second floor – was completely quiet when he inspected it. But he told my captors that I should be moved immediately and put in a 'normal' cell, number 217.

I was interviewed there by a Colonel Grobler, who was tasked to look into my allegations of abduction. After taking a lengthy statement from me, he promised to investigate what he called 'man stealing'. According to the police, the word 'abduction' was usually applied to the kidnapping of girls by men. They said they were unfamiliar with its use in the context to which I was applying it. I never heard from Grobler again.

I stayed in this cell for a few days, grateful that it had windows so I could at least see the sky. I even spotted Comrade Raymond Suttner in the prison yard, with a canary on his shoulder. Initially, I experienced the relatively normal background sounds of life going on. But then the noises started again. This time, the noise was like dripping, as if from a shower, but coming from outside the window. Soon I could also hear a grille being loudly opened and shut. This would go on for ninety minutes or so and then stop, and then start again in the early hours of the morning.

My nerves now seemed to crack. My hands were trembling. I felt as if I had pins and needles all over me. I couldn't lie or sit still. I had to walk around the cell for hours, even when I was drinking tea. I once again became utterly destabilised. I couldn't concentrate on anything. I couldn't eat because as I picked up my plate, my hands would shake. I told all of this to the doctor when he saw me the following Thursday. I was in a state of nervousness and panic. He decided to send me to the Johannesburg General Hospital for psychiatric observation. I was pleased about that as it would enable me to get out of my situation and seek help. But this didn't happen.

Instead I remained in the cell on the Friday, Saturday and Sunday, and every night the dripping and banging became more intense. I was now frantic about getting to hospital, even though I still had medication. A constable would come in the morning to give me three pills as prescribed, and in the evening another one would come and give me another three. I knew I was only entitled to one pill in the morning and two or three pills in the evening, but I had the feeling that the low-level policemen bringing me the tablets were not intentionally giving me more than I was supposed to have, though I didn't tell them.

On the Monday morning, Deetlefs and Farquhar came to fetch me. I immediately thought I would be going to hospital at last. When we were leaving, I made a mental note that cells 221 and 217 were the first and last in the passage, and that each had some pipes going into the floor above, while the cells in-between had none. Deetlefs and Farquhar taunted me from the moment we got into the car but I did not respond. I soon realised I wasn't going to the hospital after all. We were in fact on our way to Pretoria, back to the prison there. I'm convinced Deetlefs wanted to avoid having me medically assessed in a clinical environment. He said he bet he would break me down and that in the end I would talk.

On our arrival, I was seen by a state psychiatrist, Professor JA Plomp, who said he had been told I was suffering from 'withdrawal symptoms' as I had been 'deprived of alcohol'. I told him I did not drink at all, and that I had been kidnapped from Swaziland. I described the torture I underwent at John Vorster. This was what I vowed to myself to repeat again and again. He was very impatient and didn't want to hear about my abduction. He said I was 'taking up his time.' Yet he prescribed more anti-anxiety medication – Ativan and Lexotan – and told me I would be 'fine'. Many years later, I read Plomp's two reports on me. He spoke as if I was doing well and showing no signs of depression or ill effects from the detention. Plomp didn't regard me as a suicide risk – and I would never have considered myself to be one either.

I was then put into a small cell where there was music playing. Plomp had advised that I needed 'enough light', fresh air, the ability to move around, contact with warders and reading materials. I was thankful that the grille was indeed left open, leading into a passage where I could walk. I was given a tablet in the morning and another at night and gradually began to stabilise. But as soon as the pills stopped, I would experience the same symptoms as at John Vorster. This was of concern to me. I would have preferred not to take medication. The truth was that I had no choice.

One evening, I heard prisoners being brought in on the floor below me. I found out they were members of the PAC who were on trial, so, at night, I communicated with them by shouting through my window. One was Ahmed Cassim, who had spent five years on Robben Island and who joined the PAC while in prison. These men had access to lawyers; their instructing attorney was Priscilla Jana. Little did I then know that this great woman and committed activist, who had been banned herself, would come to play a significant role in the rest of my life.

I had some plastic bags in my cell in which I carried my toiletries and clothes, so I tore up the bags and tied them together to make a long string, which I threw out to the cell below. The prisoners there sent back a pen and paper on which I detailed, in tiny letters, the events of my kidnapping and the torture I had undergone. I also wrote that I would rather die than reveal any information to the state. I attached the paper to the end of the string and dropped it down again from out of my window. The PAC prisoners were able pass the letter on to Priscilla Jana.

On or around 27 February 1987, an envelope containing my note was delivered to her offices in Abbey House, Commissioner Street, in Johannesburg. My brother Essop would detail this in an affidavit he filed before the Supreme Court in March 1987. 'A black person, who was not known to the receptionist, Mrs Mogotsi, requested her to hand the envelope over to Mrs Jana. He did not give his name to the receptionist.' Essop was determined to establish it was indeed I who had written the note, and was able to confirm my handwriting, which he knew very well.

A week or so later, I was seen by the psychiatrist again. He told me a legal application had been made on my behalf, resulting in a ruling that I should not be interrogated by the security police, and that the inspector of detainees should take a statement from me to be presented to court. This was thanks to Essop. He had taken the matter of the validity of my arrest and the lawfulness of my continued detention to the Supreme Court, his affidavit noting that I was not in a position to bring the application myself, and that he, Essop, had 'a duty' to 'protect' my welfare as he was one of my closest relatives. He wrote: '[My brother's] continued detention causes me emotional agony and anxiety and affects my own wellbeing and sense of security.' The minister of law and order and the commissioner of the South African Police were the first and second respondents.

In his affidavit Essop explained that the last time he saw me, in Swaziland in 1984, was at a family gathering, and I was 'fit, strong and mentally quite normal'. He told the court I had 'always been an energetic, vigorous and lively person', but I had now 'become a nervous wreck' and 'felt I was going off my head'. This was no understatement. I feared I would not survive what was to come, and my brother intuitively knew I had reached that state of mental agony and exhaustion. Some weeks later, the inspector duly came to see me and took a lengthy statement in which I recounted my abduction from Swaziland and my torture.

Meanwhile, I spent each day in a state of monotony. I could walk up and down the passage for exercise, but there was always a warder watching me. I would sometimes ask where he was from and if he played rugby. He wouldn't communicate. I asked for, and was thankfully given, a copy of the

Holy Quran, which I read meticulously, and from which I drew strength. I memorised passages to keep my mind active.

Eventually I was removed to a section where only white prisoners were kept. The intention was to separate me from the PAC prisoners once the warders discovered it was they who had smuggled out my letter to Priscilla. My new cell was small with only a washbasin, a bed and toilet and no space for anything else. The grille was kept locked, and I was only allowed half an hour of exercise. I had nothing else to do during the day. That experience was to last two to three months. I was able to sleep at night, though, which was a relief, and it was fortunate that I could see the sky.

But it was increasingly disturbing to be so cut off from the world outside. Even on Robben Island, we got information from the outside from time to time. And of course, Thiruth had brought me papers when I was hiding in Reservoir Hills. When I had the PAC prisoners below me in Pretoria, I at least got some updates from them, as they had access to newspapers through the privilege of awaiting trial. One day they sent me a cutting which showed that PW Botha had made a statement to Parliament referring to my kidnapping, saying that 'a terrorist and very senior member of the SACP' had been arrested. Both those descriptions were a lie.

After about five months, I was called into an office and informed that I was being released. But this was not a moment of joy. Immediately, another police officer in the same room put his hand on my shoulder and said he was arresting me on a charge of high treason, and that I would be appearing in court that day. The only good thing about all of this was that I was out of detention and would thus have access to lawyers. Indeed, I appeared before a magistrate that day, with the esteemed Advocate Ismail Mahomed representing me, and was refused bail. The magistrate ruled that I was to appear in the Supreme Court with two other prisoners. What had happened was that the court which decided that my detention be investigated after the original application ordered that a report be submitted so it could hear my case. An optimistic view might have been that the court would demand my release and order that I be sent back to Swaziland, but optimists didn't belong in apartheid-era courtrooms.

It seemed surprising that I was suddenly being linked with two other prisoners, since I had been abducted alone – unlike the others who were abducted from Swaziland on the Friday night before me. There also hadn't been any mention throughout my detention of other comrades directly linked to me. As it turned out, the police found it convenient to attach me to the trial of two other men who were already charged with high treason. I was simply added as an accused, even though I had never previously set eyes on ANC comrades Mandla Maseko and Simon Dladla.

I was then put into the awaiting trial section. Again, there were slight advantages, including being entitled to receive newspapers and visitors. This meant I could see members of my family, many of them for the first time since I went into exile in 1980. I found the experience overwhelming at first, as I had no idea who exactly would come or when. All I knew was that I had half an hour for two visitors at a time.

My first family visit was from Essop. I entered the visiting cubicle on edge and in anticipation. It seemed no matter how many times one was imprisoned, and in how many settings, one could never quite be oneself. That person one truly is, is not there behind bars because one's conversations are limited and also monitored. The visit seemed to be over before it began, and I realised I hadn't asked any of the questions I had wanted to. Fortunately, I saw Essop again, as well as my sister-in-law Fatima who I was very close to and had grown up with in Durban. At least during this period, I could be reunited with my sister, brother, nieces, nephews, cousins and even friends.

I also remember getting a visit from Mohammed Bhabha, a comrade and lawyer who was closely following my case. He has often recounted that he asked me if I was concerned about the fact that I could receive the death penalty, but I told him that I did not fear that outcome, and that I would do what I'd done all over again. My reply is something that has stayed with him ever since. We became close friends in the decades that followed.

Years later, Lindiwe Sisulu enjoyed relating the story that during this time there were a number of female admirers who would send me chocolates through my lawyer Priscilla Jana. According to Lindiwe, Priscilla said she couldn't possibly give me all those boxes of chocolates, so she had eaten many of them herself!

The most important visit I received was from my daughter Cassia.

We had never met before. Priscilla told me that Cassia and her mother were coming from Washington DC, where they were living, and that I should expect a visit at any time. Although I had seen photos of Cassia, I was looking so forward to seeing her. My emotions were running very high. I was anxious. I didn't know how she would respond to me, a virtual stranger. I wasn't sure what her mother had told her about me.

We first set eyes on each other through the glass partition. I remember she was shy and hugged her mum throughout. I wondered how being introduced to me as her dad in such a way might affect her later in life. The next time I saw Cassia was when my trial started. She still looked at me tentatively, which was completely understandable. I was overcome by how beautiful she was.

Twenty-seven
Trauma

AS FAR AS FRIENDS WENT, there was one person I urgently wanted to see. Hélène had already been sentenced to ten years in prison and was in the women's section in the same jail as I was. She made a request to visit me, and the authorities asked whether I would like to see her. I was very keen, but it was painful and unfulfilling for us both, I think.

We had only half an hour with the glass partition between us, and she was accompanied by a white wardress and I by a white warder. The best we could do was to enquire about each other's health and ask about our respective families. I had been warned not to discuss my trial with her.

I was glad to see that Hélène looked well, albeit in prison uniform, and she seemed to be in good spirits. The circumstances were, however, unbearable. I wonder if you can imagine it? All too soon we were taken back to our cells and, unbelievably, it would be nearly fifteen years before I saw Hélène again.

It was heart-breaking to later find out the details of what Hélène had experienced during detention. Every word sent shivers through my body. Her ex-husband Klaas had contacted Hélène, as he was smuggling an arms cache into South Africa from Zimbabwe, where he was living at the time, and needed her assistance in hiding it in a dead letter box in Midrand between Johannesburg and Pretoria. Hélène, who was living in

Yeoville in Johannesburg, was concerned that he had called her, which was against security protocols. Nonetheless, she and Klaas met up to bury the weapons. Unfortunately, an off-duty policeman saw them engaged in 'suspicious activity' in a field at night and followed them. This soon led to the involvement of the security police.

Although they were hoping to catch a whole underground network through Hélène, they decided instead to arrest her in the Johannesburg CBD when she was on her way to inform her lawyer, Kathy Satchwell, about Klaas's disappearance. Klaas had been arrested as he was leaving South Africa to make his way back to Zimbabwe. Under interrogation, he agreed to point out where he had deposited some arms. He took the security police to a building in downtown Johannesburg, but the police were unaware that the building housed the consulate of the Netherlands. He tricked them by dashing into the consulate and asking for asylum. The security police stormed into the offices and pulled Klaas out, but the Dutch government vehemently protested to the South African government to this a violation of their consulate. Ultimately, Klaas had to be taken back there by virtue of international law, and that is where he remained from July 1985 to September 1987. Hélène, however, was taken to the notorious security police headquarters at John Vorster Square.

I knew Hélène's daughter Brigitte was six months pregnant at the time; that was one of the reasons why she had been staying with Hélène. They knew something had happened to Klaas because Brigitte had flown to Harare to spend a short holiday with her father, but he did not arrive to fetch her at the airport. Brigitte called Hélène to tell her, using careful language, as she knew her mother's phone was bugged. Hélène's work for MK and her detention and imprisonment took a huge toll on her children.

We all knew her interrogators would not treat her gently. She held the keys to a trove of information, and they didn't care how they extracted it – out of a woman, out of a foreigner. But what they did not know was that Hélène was as solid as they come. Deetlefs, the same sadist who tormented me, was her chief interrogator, and he used every form of mental torture on her, to no avail. They put Hélène in a 'special cell' with no windows, daylight or ventilation. It was sound-proofed with perspex plates, and there was a video camera running 24/7. A dim light burned day and night. It causes the most severe headaches as the light is not strong enough for reading but is too bright for sleeping. Her cell had double doors fixed with a heavy chain and padlock.

We found out later that the security police had tested a novel form of surveillance on Hélène. She had seen strange activity in her cell when electric wiring that led outside to a lift shaft was installed. She believed that the wires trailed into a room packed with electronic equipment. When a man identifying himself as a technician came to see her in her cell and made idle conversation, she guessed he was trying out a hidden microphone. Something had been placed in a pillbox-shaped hole in her cell wall which had been pasted over. At times, weird noises came out of the hole. It made no sense at first, but as time went on, bizarre, disorientating events took place: for instance, her cell was sprayed with the insect repellent Doom. Without any ventilation, Hélène virtually passed out.

To Deetlefs, Hélène was nothing more than a terrorist. This gave him the right, in his understanding, to attack her mind in any way he liked. The result of that kind of treatment is that the prisoner engages in a deadly struggle just to stay sane. Other cadres tortured by Deetlefs insisted he was a quintessential psychopath. I would agree. In Hélène's case, he preyed especially on her emotions and her love for me. At one stage after I had been abducted and was also in detention, he offered to let her write me a few letters in the hope that one of us might incriminate ourselves or expose information that could link me to MK's military machinery. If they could prove I had given Hélène instructions, it would add to their case. But nothing worked. Deetlefs couldn't break Hélène.

So he got worse. One day, Hélène was surprised when she was served what looked like homemade spaghetti for lunch instead of the usual pap. The food arrived in a large plastic container, and she was told it was from 'someone who cared that she had lost too much weight'. Receiving food from outside was unheard of, so she thought it could only have come from Deetlefs. She had very little appetite and was able to eat only a small portion that night and a small portion the next morning. Soon, she felt extremely ill. She lay down with a sense that she might be losing consciousness. Most terrifying was that within a short while she became completely incapacitated – unable to walk or move. She was in effect becoming frozen on the mat on the floor of her cell.

When Hélène realised that something dreadful was happening to her, she quickly wrote a letter to her children as she thought she was going to die. She remembers Deetlefs hovering over her, taunting her. He prodded her. She started having alarming hallucinations that her father's head was on Deetlefs's body. Hélène was only taken to the district surgeon two weeks later. He ordered that she be hospitalised. State psychiatrists then prohibited Deetlefs from seeing her after they noticed he was manipulating her in his daily visits.

We now believe that her spaghetti was laced with Scopolomine – a drug used by some sinister government agencies when interrogating prisoners. It's dubbed a 'truth serum', and it exploits the nether regions of human consciousness, putting the individual in a state of semi-consciousness. The idea is that the person being interrogated will, as a result, not have the mental focus to lie and evade the truth.

About two years later, when I was on trial, Hélène was again subjected to manipulation by Deetlefs. He organised for her to be transferred from Pretoria Central Prison, where she was being held with other white female political prisoners, to Kroonstad Prison, where she would be alone again. Kroonstad was a remote institution where he likely felt he would have more of a free hand to do with her as he wanted. He orchestrated Hélène's transfer in the middle of winter in the Free State, where it gets so cold that it snows. She froze in her cell with inadequate clothing to wear, and developed frostbite on her hands and feet.

Deetlefs made sure that Hélène was badly treated in other ways, too – all against prison rules. She twice received an official-looking 'Supreme Court order' to appear for the state in my trial, but on the appointed day nothing would happen. These were obviously further attempts to break her. She would never have considered giving evidence against me, but even her lawyers were prevented from seeing her, as the state pretended she was their witness.

She eventually went on hunger strike to have some of her prison 'privileges' restored, but when she received food, she had another collapse, similar to what had happened at John Vorster Square. Again, she was sent for medical care only after two weeks, as she ended up having an epileptic fit. It seemed clear that she had been poisoned again. After her eventual release, Hélène's friend, the former political prisoner Thandi Modise, told her that she too was poisoned in Kroonstad Prison and almost died.

Hélène's psychiatrist, a Chilean exile from the dictatorship of Augusto Pinochet and a specialist in understanding all forms of torture, examined Hélène's and Thandi's symptoms. He concluded that they were poisoned with a neurology drug used in pharmacological torture, which is the unethical, illegal or abusive use of a chemical substance that changes cognition, perception, behaviour, mood and consciousness, usually for purposes of torture. Apparently, such drugs remain visible in the blood for ten days, which could explain why Hélène wasn't taken to a doctor or a hospital for at least that length of time.

Once Hélène had been back in Europe for a while, she took up journalism and then accepted an opportunity to be transferred to Chile. Here she was finally able to be treated by experienced psychiatrists who had dealt with many cases of detainees psychologically tortured by the Pinochet regime. That was the kind of care she needed at the time. We can only be thankful that she and Thandi, two stalwarts of our struggle, survived the hell to which they were subjected.

More than thirty years after Hélène's nightmare, the former security policeman Paul Erasmus privately said that his colleagues in the Special Branch kept Scopolamine and other chemical drugs in a cupboard in an office at John Vorster Square. These were for use on selected detainees.

Few South Africans can imagine the trauma that freedom fighters like Hélène went through out of their commitment to the liberation struggle. In Hélène's case, she was tried and convicted for treason in 1986 in a much-publicised trial. She got ten years in prison. In mitigation of sentence she stated that she had 'acted out of a general human duty against racism and fascism'. Her four children and her mother travelled to South Africa for the trial and sentencing. It was devastating for them. Imagine knowing you would effectively lose your mother for a decade. That knowledge alone causes damage.

Hélène spent three years behind bars in Pretoria Prison alongside comrades like Barbara Hogan, Marion Sparg, Jansie Lourens and Trish Hanekom. There was a massive campaign by the anti-apartheid movement in Belgium and the Netherlands to put pressure on the PW Botha regime to free Hélène. She was released early as a result, but even that event was shrouded in secrecy. Apartheid foreign minister

Pik Botha later admitted that the regime had done a 'deal' with the Belgian government in exchange for Hélène's freedom in 1989. While the archives for this period are still closed, it is suspected that Belgium may have agreed to continue importing cheap coal from South Africa in violation of UN sanctions imposed on it.

Hélène returned to her home country, where she was constantly harassed by right-wing elements who targeted her as an 'evil communist and terrorist'. Being Hélène, she put up with that dreadful stress. She worked at the ANC office in Brussels and focused on international solidarity. She and other comrades were under constant threat – so much so that they had to receive protection from the Belgian security services. This was around the same time that Godfrey Motsepe, the ANC's chief representative in Brussels, narrowly escaped two assassination attempts and our beloved comrade Dulcie September was killed in Paris.

Hélène didn't receive an MK pension as she was not a South African citizen, and it was argued that she 'lived abroad'. Yet she lived a humble existence. She richly deserved the Companion of OR Tambo Award given to her in 2011 in recognition of her dedication to our struggle. We organised a dinner in her honour afterwards, an event that marked an extraordinary reunion of comrades who had worked with her out of Swaziland and Mozambique. These included the Shaik brothers, who had a major impact on my life, and Ivan Pillay and Shirish Soni. Six years later, the SACP also honoured Hélène for her bravery and commitment.

Around the time Hélène came to South Africa to receive her national order, my wife Shannon, who was doing research for this book, found a phone number for Deetlefs. There were two numbers in the telephone directory of that time, and when Shannon called the first one, she reached Deetlefs's son, who confirmed the other number was his father's. It was amazing to us that he was not even trying to hide. He felt completely safe and vindicated in post-apartheid South Africa.

Shannon got through to him, and asked him questions about Hélène. He didn't know Shannon was my wife, or that Shannon knew Hélène. Deetlefs was unmoved by the process South Africa had been through during the Truth and Reconciliation Commission. He was still full of hate and venom towards the ANC, and ranted about Hélène, offering to shed more light on her 'evil ways' in person to Shannon. His total lack of remorse or change of heart makes one question the compromise at the heart of the TRC process, 'truth for amnesty'. Deetlefs never even applied for amnesty, while Hélène did.

Ebrahim with Iranian Deputy Foreign Minister Hossein Amir-Abdollahian in Tehran in May 2012 (DIRCO)

Ebrahim with Pakistani Foreign Minister Hina Rabbani Khar in Islamabad in January 2013 (DIRCO)

Ebrahim in Palestine, May 2010 (Dirco)

Ebrahim is welcomed by officials in his ancestral village in Chasa, India in 2008.

Ebrahim presides over a meeting of the United Nations Security Council during South Africa's Presidency of the Council in 2012. (DIRCO)

LEFT *Ebie and Kadin on an elephant ride in Chiang Mai, Northern Thailand in December 2012*

RIGHT *Shannon, Ebie, Sarah and Kadin in the garden in Bryntirion estate, Pretoria*

Ebie, Shannon, Sarah and Kadin in a shoot for Sutra magazine

Ebie and Shannon

Ebie

Ebie and Sarah going to the father-daughter barn dance

Ebie at Boulder's beach in Cape Town

Ebie giving a speech on Mandela Day

Ebie and Shannon with Arjum Wajid at Nelson Mandela's memorial service in Soweto

LEFT *Ebie and Albie Sachs*

RIGHT *Ebie, Sarah and Kadin in Zermatt, Switzerland with the Matterahorn in the background in December 2017*

BOTTOM RIGHT *Ebie with his comrades from the MJK unit: from left Yunis Shaik and his wife Devina, Moe Shaik, Ruweida and Shirish Soni*

Sarah and Kadin performing a rap about Ebie's life at his 80th birthday, July 2017

Ebie and his great niece Nasneen who baked his 80th birthday cake

Ebie and his brother Essop

Ebie, Ronnie Kasrils and Hillary Hamburger at Ebie's 80th birthday party

TOP *Julie Mohamed, Angela Sibanda with the family at Ebie's 80th birthday party*

LEFT *Ebie and Kadin at a diplomatic function*

RIGHT *Ebie in the Kruger National Park*

Ebie at the opening of parliament in February 2019

Ebie and Shannon at his last opening of parliament in February 2019

Ebrahim is bestowed the Pravasi Bharatiya Samman Award by Indian President Pranab Mukherjee in Kochi, India on 9 January 2013.

Ebrahim is bestowed one of Spain's highest honours – the Order of Civil Merit – a knighthood at the rank of Knight Commander, from the King of Spain Felipe VI at the residence of the Spanish Ambassador Juan Sell in July 2015.

At Ebie's Knighthood, from left is Zaida Enver, Fatima Ebrahim, Shannon, Sarah, Kadin, Ebie, Ambassador Juan Sell, Saleem and Nadia Ebrahim.

Ebie and the Directors of In-Transformation Initiative: from left is Ivor Jenkins, Ebie, Mohammed Bhabha, Roelf Meyer and Patience Zonge-Hwenha

Twenty-eight
On trial for treason

THE *WEEKLY MAIL* WROTE that I was 'the most senior ANC official to stand trial since Nelson Mandela and the Rivonia trialists in the early 1960s'. But I was not at my strongest when our trial began in Piet Retief, a small town on the border of Swaziland, far removed from our family and lawyers. It was four and a half hours' drive from Pretoria and communication was very difficult. This was going to be an ordeal, but I was comforted by the sight of the court benches packed with members of our families, ANC supporters and well-wishers.

The indictment said I had given instructions to cadres Mandla Maseko and Simon Dladla to plant landmines on farms in the Eastern Transvaal. Among the alternative charges were several counts of attempted murder arising from four landmine explosions in that area. No one had been killed, but the state described the explosions as 'cold-blooded' and 'barbaric' acts. The claim was that I had been part of the Elias Motsoaledi 'command', or the Transvaal 'command', which directed 'landmine warfare'.

Yet rather than having given them instructions, I met my co-accused, Mandla and Simon, for the first time when we went on trial. They had been arrested inside South Africa at a roadblock in 1986. Simon – who held a Swazi passport – was the driver of the car that transported Mandla, a trained MK cadre who was being infiltrated into the country to carry out military actions. Both were young men in their thirties. The court showed they had travelled together in this way on four occasions, and that Simon had transported other operatives in this manner, too. I had personally never been involved in military activities, and had certainly never planted landmines.

When the trial began, Advocate Ismail Mahomed argued that before the court could even examine the indictment, it had to consider my abduction, as it was an illegal act, and the court therefore had no jurisdiction to try me. My application contended that South African agents were responsible, 'acting within the scope of their duties but not necessarily on express authority'. My advocate pointed to evidence that included the use of rifles, handcuffs, leg irons and car radio communication devices, the attempts to interrogate me in the vehicle on the way to Pretoria, and the ability of my captors to pass unhindered through an SADF roadblock. I had also been given a receipt for the goods which the men had taken from my house in Swaziland, which would indicate they were au fait with what had happened that night. Advocate Mahomed said: 'Each of these pieces of evidence might of themselves have the weight of feathers. Taken collectively, they are like a ton of bricks.' His argument was that the law required 'a balance of public interests': 'To break the bonds of international peace and good neighbourliness is far greater than the harm and prejudice to the community of a particular offender.'

The state prosecutor, Harry Prinsloo, tried to dismiss his argument as inferior to the charge against me, which he said was 'the most serious crime a person can be charged with – high treason'. I was at that time still carrying an Indian passport issued by the Republic of India in Lusaka in June 1981. I had also been given permission to enter and remain in the kingdom of Swaziland by the Swazi government in July 1985. It was noted that Swaziland had not even protested against South Africans entering its sovereign territory to remove a foreigner and thus it was unlikely it would insist on my being able to return. Had Swaziland complained, the matter would probably have been heard before an international tribunal. The state prosecutor maintained that the police knew nothing of my abduction, and that I was 'handed' to them in Pretoria by 'unknown persons'. The argument between Mahomed and

Prinsloo took the whole day.

I could see that the use of a variety of agents and security policemen throughout my abduction, our arrival at the Compol building, and my being informed that I was being detained under section 29 was purposeful. The men who held a gun to my head in Pine Valley were not the same ones who were waiting at the cars alongside the border, and those in turn were also not the same as the men in the car to which I was transferred in the streets of Pretoria the same evening. There were also different policemen who made themselves known to me before I was told I was being detained. So, legally, it was a challenge to prove that an abduction by the Security Branch or the South African regime had taken place.

Still, some of my evidence seemed irrefutable. For example, how were the security policemen in Pretoria able to unlock my handcuffs and leg irons if they were not in cahoots with the men who had placed these on me in Swaziland? The way the Security Branch responded to that was to say that I wasn't in handcuffs and leg irons when they saw me in Pretoria. This was a total lie, but it would be difficult for me, alone, to disprove it.

Justice Hekkie Daniels adjourned the court to consider the arguments. After a few days, he ruled that it was not of concern to the court how I got there, although if an illegal act had been committed, I should have other remedies. However, as long as I was in court on charges, he had the right to try me and sentence me if I was found guilty.

After numerous adjournments, the trial continued in Piet Retief, and was then transferred to Delmas, another small town in the Transvaal. It finally ended up in Pretoria and went on for months.

My co-accused, Simon and Mandla, also had a powerful case. The judge heard that Mandla had been armed with a Makarov pistol and a grenade when they were arrested in June 1986. He was shown to have had military training and political education in the USSR, Angola and Mozambique. His indictment claimed he had 'without duress, drawn a detailed map for the police showing the positioning of four landmines in the Breyten and Volksrust areas.' Indeed, MK had switched its focus more to the rural areas at that time, after the proliferation of attacks in the urban areas seemed to have isolated the countryside. Without attacks there, we couldn't expect the people in the rural areas to see what we were doing as their military wing. Without that understanding, we couldn't expect a political reaction on the ground, like the mass protests which were happening in the urban areas.

After November 1985, there was increasing landmine warfare in the border areas of northern Natal and the northern and western Transvaal, from where our cadres could also more easily escape into the frontline states of Mozambique and Swaziland. MK had had deep discussions about whether white farmers, who would most likely be affected by landmines in those areas, could be regarded as 'legitimate targets', since OR Tambo demanded that there be no loss of innocent lives. It was decided that since most of the farmers not only supported apartheid but were also part of the SADF's rural commandos, they were reasonable targets. We were insurrectionists whose aim was to mobilise our people to become our political army, while we were their revolutionary army. This was essential to our strategy and tactics at the time.

But my comrades Simon's and Mandla's 'confessions' to planting landmines along those border areas, allegedly targeting white farmers, had been extracted through torture. Bags had been placed over their heads as a form of suffocation, and they were blindfolded and taken to a room used for torture. There, they were stripped naked and tied to a chair, and wires were placed on their genitals to administer electric shocks. Predictably, the judge rejected their harrowing accounts in the same way as he had my abduction.

I want to emphasise that this trial was not a straightforward matter. It could have resulted in our receiving the death sentence. We could have been hanged. The regime had already executed many of our cadres at the gallows.[12]

This is where 'September' enters the picture. Glory Lefoshie Sedibe – his real name – has never left many of us, in our memories. I'm sure he even appears in our nightmares. September went into exile in 1976 to join the ANC and was sent to East Germany and the USSR for intelligence and security training. In 1984, he was appointed head of our military intelligence for the Transvaal, based in Swaziland. He wasn't a member of the military rank and file.

September, or, as he was called at the trial, Mr X1, was the 'secret' chief witness against me. He had in fact been kidnapped from Swaziland, six months before my own abduction, by South African security police in cahoots with Swazi policemen who collaborated against ANC cadres. After he was captured, he was held prisoner and tortured for about three months before he became a paid employee of the regime, a Vlakplaas operative. After that, people claimed to have seen him in cars with security police when there was a raid on MK houses. We believed he was an askari.

'Mr X1' was brought to court to say I had instructed him to plant landmines in farming areas to kill farmers. Under cross-examination, he denied he had been abducted by South African agents and maintained he had voluntarily handed himself to the police, as he was 'tired of struggling'. Although I knew who September was, and had met him on many occasions in Maputo, I had had no operational dealings with him, nor was I involved in instructing anyone to plant landmines. It was the practice of the security police to fabricate evidence against the accused in political trials, especially when they had no concrete evidence.

But there was something more about September. It is notable that when the ANC was unbanned, he contacted Jacob Zuma and said he would supply us with information of atrocities committed by the Security Branch. But before he could do that, he died, allegedly as a result of poisoning. In a later interview that the Vlakplaas commander Eugene de Kock gave, he confessed that the security police had poisoned September because they were afraid he would reveal their apartheid agents who had been infiltrated into the liberation movement. This was a pattern in many parts of the country whenever the security police 'disposed of' black people who had collaborated with them or informed on the liberation movement, for fear they knew too much.

So we knew that he was an askari and expected what he would say in court. All the same, September affected me deeply. He was arrogant when he took the witness stand. He was confident about his position. I didn't quite know how to get my head around that. He was somehow different from Bruno Mtolo, who had turned and testified against us in 1963, or Adrian Leftwich, who betrayed other white students sympathetic to the struggle. It was as if September had bought into the regime. This was actual betrayal, on a profound and destructive level.

I couldn't understand why so much false evidence was brought against me, because I never denied membership of the ANC or that I was actively involved in the overthrow of the apartheid regime. I suspect the security police were bitter against me for refusing to cooperate with their interrogation. They had failed in the most basic way and were determined to see that I was sentenced to death.

The state called three other witnesses – X2, X3 and X4. I had never seen those people before. I described them in court as being of 'despicable character', people who would 'sell their own souls for a sixpence'.

Evidence in my case was even led in the UK, to show that I would not have given orders to September, as I didn't have military tasks within the ANC. My lawyers applied to examine the policies and structures of the ANC in hearings with the organisation's leadership, and so the trial was briefly moved to a secret location in London, where senior members of the ANC in exile disputed claims made by September. This was unprecedented in South African jurisprudence. Priscilla Jana had a passport valid for only two weeks in which to conduct the hearings, as her travel documents been taken away from her in 1979 because of her political activities and banning orders against her. Among those who gave evidence for my defence in London were Jacob Zuma, Ronnie Kasrils, John Nkadimeng, Totsie Memela, Johannes 'Joe' Mkhwanazi (of the South African Council of Trade Unions) and Vusi Khumalo (an artist comrade based at Dakawa, the ANC's camp in Tanzania).

The judge would later say that 'although [Ebrahim's] exact position in the ANC was unclear, defence evidence taken from ANC members on commission in London showed that he was so valued that he was not to be exposed to people who might get arrested and disclose information'. He said: 'ANC colleagues spoke of [Ebrahim] almost reverently.' When proceedings were reported by the media, it marked the first time that members of the ANC's National Executive Committee had been heard and quoted in South Africa since the movement was banned in 1960. They testified that I was not involved in military work in Swaziland and it was 'unthinkable that I could have given a military command'.

Ronnie even produced his passport to prove that he had been in London at the time September claimed that he, Ronnie and I had met in Swaziland where I was supposedly given military orders. I'll never forget Ronnie's words: 'It was well known to us that Ebrahim was kidnapped by the South African police, clearly tortured by people who are well known to us and will pay for their crimes when South Africa is free. That is as sure as the sun comes up in the east and sets in the west.' As we know, this did not happen. Our torturers got away with their crimes. Ronnie later told me that when he said that during the hearings, he had specifically looked at Deetlefs, who had travelled to attend the proceedings and advise the prosecutor, who was also a member of the right wing Afrikaner Weerstandsbeweging (AWB).

In August 1987 I wrote to Phyllis Naidoo while I was on trial, saying: 'Well, your son is back to square one.' That is how I felt. I knew I would be returning to the Island, at the very least. I would miss Phyllis's letters and the contact I had had with her.

I was feeling down at the time as the ANC head office in Lusaka had promised to send evidence of support for us from international governments or organisations to present in court, but nothing had arrived. It would take a little while before the movement rallied support and solidarity, appealing to the global anti-apartheid community to call for my unconditional release. When it did, it labelled the apartheid government's violation of international law 'acts of banditry'. Just as the closing arguments were being given in our trial, the US under its new President George Bush Senior included the ANC on its list of terrorist organisations. The UK under Prime Minister Margaret Thatcher took the same position.

Later, too, in December 1988, the Dutch Anti-Apartheid Movement convened a 'Hearing on Abductions by South Africa in the Frontline States' in the Amsterdam city hall. The witnesses included Shadrack Maphumulo's wife Khumbuzile and Corinne Bischoff and Daniel Schneider, the two young people from Switzerland who had been abducted. The prosecutors were Dutch judge Boris Dittrich and American jurist Gay McDougall, and expert witnesses included ZN Jobodwana of the ANC legal department in Lusaka.

Around the same time the Dutch author Rudi Boon produced a publication entitled *Beyond Fear: Ebrahim Ismael Ebrahim versus the Apartheid State*, a copy of which was presented to the ANC representative to the Netherlands, Bobby Sanjee, better known to me as my beloved friend Sunny Singh. Sunny had left Maputo as a result of the Nkomati Accord of 1984. His first *nom de guerre* was Bobby Pillay and he travelled on a Tanzanian passport. He then used the name Kumar Sanjay and travelled on an Indian passport, like I had done. Sunny was deployed to the Netherlands in 1988 and represented the ANC there for about four years. Just as he had been on Robben Island, he was mad about news and media, and excelled in using those to our advantage in the Netherlands.

Rudi Boon's work and the hearing on abductions in Amsterdam were exceptional interventions, and they buoyed me. But back in August 1987, when I wrote to Phyllis, I was feeling pretty much alone. I was also intensely bitter and sad over the murders of Shadrack and comrades Paul Dikeledi and Cassius Make. Paul was murdered in July. He would undoubtedly have been a powerful witness for my defence, but what upset me was the loss of the man himself – to his family, to the movement.

I was also battling with guilt about the Shaik family and others who had suffered as a result of protecting me. 'I have spent many hours in meditation and prayer,' I told Phyllis, 'at times in tears, thinking about the sorrow I have caused so many people and their families. When they put the leg irons on you, you realise the entire nation is in chains.' The militancy of other prisoners helped a lot. There was a will to fight until victory. We were not afraid of the oppressor. 'It is in the face of the jailers that you see their fear of the masses,' I wrote. 'They even fear you when you are in chains.' We all supported each other wholeheartedly.

I was especially moved when my Robben Island comrade Terror Lekota and other UDF comrades Popo Molefe and Moses 'Moss' Chikane gave me a birthday party. They were joined in that celebration by the seven PAC comrades who were also on trial. That mattered to me. Terror, Popo and Moss had been arrested and charged with treason in the Delmas Treason Trial just as I was coming to the end of my own trial. Terror was the UDF's publicity secretary, Popo was the UDF national secretary-general, and Moss was the UDF Transvaal provincial secretary. We were all held at Pretoria Central Prison. They were found guilty in November 1988 and were sentenced to between ten and twelve years in jail. In a joint statement released before they went to prison, they and their fellow trialists said: 'Somewhere in the future lies a date when South Africans will take a second look at these moments of our history. They will evaluate afresh the events now in contention and our role in them. And since the privilege will belong to them, they will pass final judgment. We are convinced that theirs will be contrary to the present one.'

At the time we were variously in the dock, there were sixty-nine other comrades facing treason charges in six other cases. It gave us strength that the world's media were watching, even if the leaders of two of the world's most powerful nations – the US and the UK – were against us.

The *Los Angeles Times* reported in September 1987 that 'civil rights groups see these cases as "show trials" intended to cripple the UDF and other anti-apartheid organisations by removing key leaders, making members hesitant to take their places and discouraging community support'.

That was precisely how it was. By that stage the UDF was a 'broad coalition of 700 anti-apartheid groups with more than three million members'. The newspaper noted that 'other trials are expected following the defection of a senior ANC underground cadre'. It was referring to September.

'Charges ranging from murder, assault and arson to sabotage, subversion and terrorism were pending against 130 other people, most of them local community and youth leaders, in 25 other major cases. Prosecutors said that special courts would be set up to speed up the hearings.'

My Swaziland comrade Lindiwe Sisulu's mother, Albertina Sisulu, was UDF co-president at the time and was facing two years in prison for furthering the aims of the ANC after years of detention, harassment and torture. She told the *Los Angeles Times*: 'Even when we win, and that's not easy under their laws, these political trials do tremendous damage. They take our leaders away from their real work and put our organisations on the defensive. They cost a terrible amount of money, which could be much better spent. They divert our energies and often prevent us from moving forward.' The four thousand people detained at the time would testify to that. Meanwhile, there were thirty-two people on death row, and five were hanged for 'politically motivated crimes' in the year before I went on trial.

While the Delmas treason trialists were being sentenced, a white supremacist named Barend Strydom walked past the Supreme Court in Pretoria to make his way to Strijdom Square, a few minutes away. Once he got there, he set about the cold-blooded massacre of seven black people, who were deliberately killed for the colour of their skin. It is said Strydom intended to commit his murders on Church Square, which is in front of the Palace of Justice, but because of the Delmas treason trial taking place there, too many policemen were in the vicinity that day and he changed his plans. He was himself a former policeman. His terrorism took about fifteen minutes, but its impact continues until today.

Twenty-nine
Statement from the dock

My mother, Hafiza Bibi Khan, was left heartbroken by my imprisonment and trial. She had already been through so much in her life. She had seen my father in chains in prison for travelling to Natal from the Transvaal without a permit. She went to visit him with my brother Gora, and that left them both with lifelong scars. Gora maintained that sight was what propelled him into fighting apartheid to the very end. Then my mother was evicted from her home in Candella Road, Mayville, in Durban under the Group Areas Act. The regime offered her R2,000 for her house, which was everything she had. It demanded she pay R17,000 for another one in Chatsworth, the area to which she was being removed, twenty-five kilometres away. The insult and pain never left us.

My mother was seventy-eight when I was on trial for the second time. She told *The Leader*, a progressive newspaper in Johannesburg: 'The only thing I can do now is pray for my beloved son daily. I ask you to pray for him too.' I could see she was distressed when we were in court. It was important for me to remain calm. 'He told me he is alright. He is the same Ebrahim I knew when he was still in South Africa. Although he told me not to worry, how can I not do so when he is my son? Any mother will be worried.' My mother stayed in Johannesburg to attend the trial until the end. She also wanted to take any opportunity she could to see me, as we had had no contact since 1980.

Everyone's day of sentencing is uniquely intense. In our case, we didn't know if the judge would send us to the gallows or a long prison term. But I wasn't afraid of his verdict: I was a freedom fighter, and I was ready to pay a price. We anyway didn't expect any leniency from a judge who had been installed by the apartheid regime. His duty was to punish severely anyone who threatened the system. My anxiety was more for the people who loved me. How would my mother react? Her health was failing, but she would insist on coming to court. All the family would be affected.

When I entered the courtroom, I was encouraged to see not only members of my family but many supporters. Our defence team were standing strong. Our advocate, Kessie Naidu, argued that any sentence passed should reflect an understanding of the 'tragedy that is South Africa'. He said the crime of treason should be viewed against the background that we, the accused, 'had no say about their own future in the country to which they owed allegiance'.

The Johannesburg sociologist Mark Orkin of the Community Agency for Social Enquiry had conducted an analysis, which we submitted to the court record, that showed 'a steady growth in black support for the ANC during recent years, to the point where it now dwarfs that enjoyed by any other political organisation in the country'.[13] I remembered something my interrogator Deetlefs had said to me in John Vorster Square when he bragged that the ANC and MK were being destroyed. 'We will get you one by one,' he hissed. 'We will rule this country for another two hundred years.' Yet on the day of our sentencing, our people were openly showing the victory salute and singing in defiance of the apartheid state in court. Deetlefs wasn't blind: he could see the end. He wasn't deaf: he could hear the triumph in their voices.

I wrote a seventeen-page statement which I used to address the court from the dock. As I started speaking, I realised I couldn't have cared less about Deetlefs.

> We are certain that this court will decide to impose on us various sentences. Though we shall condemn it as a perpetuation of the system of injustice to which millions of our people are subject, we do not fear such an outcome.
>
> To fear it would mean that, when we joined the struggle for the emancipation of our people, we did not understand the nature of the

enemy we had to confront. But we know who it is that we and the rest of the freedom-loving people of our country have to fight to turn into reality the dream of a South Africa that shall belong to all the people, both black and white.

We have brushed shoulders with the angels of death who guard the king and princes that occupy the apartheid throne. In their hands they carry the gun, the hangman's noose and vile instruments of torture. We know that the throne they defend can only stand if it is surrounded by a moat of human suffering.

As we leave this building to go wherever the court decides, we wish to say to our people, we tried to carry out your behests.

We did our best to live up to what you expected of us as members of the African National Congress.

There are countless others like us who are prepared to sacrifice their very lives to achieve the noble goal of the emancipation of our country. We shall achieve victory soon!

When I was detained both in 1963 and 1986, I refused to answer questions during interrogation. To me this was a matter of deeply held principles.

During this detention, I told the police that I would rather die in detention than betray the trust of a single person or organisation.

When I acknowledged that certain items were removed from my house, it was to establish the fact that I was indeed abducted by the South African security forces.

The factor that led me not to testify in this trial is that I would refuse to answer questions which would give information to the state security police. This in turn would prejudice my evidence before the court.

The judge found me guilty and sentenced me to twenty years, saying he wanted to give me a lengthy jail term so that when I left prison again, I would be an old man, because my previous fifteen years inside had clearly not done me any good. After all, on my release, I had 'gone straight back to the ANC'. Mandla was sentenced to an even longer term, of twenty-three years; while Simon got twelve.

The judge's words had barely left his mouth when the people in court spontaneously stood up and shouted, 'Viva, ANC! Viva!' and 'Amandla!' and began to sing the national anthem, 'Nkosi Sikelel' iAfrika'. Court officials tried to stop them, but they carried on – louder and louder – drowning out the protests. When the singing eventually subsided, a state prosecutor, Louise van der Walt, did something unexpected. She burst out with the words 'Long live the AWB!' The AWB was a white-supremacist, neo-Nazi paramilitary group which was dedicated to creating an independent Boer republic since its founding in 1973. Her colleagues had to quieten her down, but she was heard shouting back at them, 'Why do you have to shut me up when others are allowed to sing?'[14] Van der Walt was one of the regime's prosecutors who had questioned my comrades in London. She attended those hearing with Deetlefs.

We went back to the Pretoria Prison as convicts. We were put in prison garb and given prison food. This was entirely different from when we were on trial. In my isolation cell that night, I thought about the journey I would now have to make back to Robben Island and wondered what the place would be like. It was so familiar to me, so clear in my mind, and yet so far away and distant. I thought about my family and their reaction to my imprisonment. My mother broke down and cried. She was losing me, her son, for the second time.

Yes, twenty years was a long term. With the fifteen I had already served, my time in jail would practically take up a large part of my life. But I thought of how foolish the judge was to even imagine that prison walls would deter people from struggling for freedom and fighting against oppression. We were incapable of being stopped.

A week or two after the sentencing, the three of us were placed in leg irons and handcuffed, put on a military plane, and flown to the Cape Town military airbase. Among the warders there to take us in was Christo Brand, who told me that he guarded Ahmed Kathrada at Pollsmoor Prison, where some of our veterans had been moved from the Island. I asked him to tell Kathy I was going back to our old stamping ground. I didn't think I would ever see any of them again.

We were taken in a van to the Robben Island Maximum Prison embarkation point at Jetty Five at the Cape Town harbour. I once again looked at Table Mountain and Lion's Head, standing in the same place where I had stood more than twenty-five years earlier. The mountains were the same – stoic, forbidding – but I wondered what had changed in the heart of the city over the decade since I had left it. It was, after all, the place where the UDF was launched in 1983, and its people had since been engaged in some of the fiercest street battles with the apartheid police. In the past ten years, an open political culture had grown there. Consciousness was high, and so was militancy.

It was exactly ten years to the month that I had been released from the Island. Then I was so determined I would never go back, but now, once again, I found myself its prisoner. Just as before, we struggled with our leg irons to get onto the boat and then down inside where the prisoners had to sit – only this time, I wasn't wondering what life would be like on the Island but I was telling my co-accused what lay ahead of us. Certainly, I recalled my fifteen years of hard labour, but I also recounted how comradeship and political discussions had helped me, and all of us, overcome the torture and the struggles. As we approached the Island, the familiar melancholy cry of the seagulls sent shivers through me.

Thirty
Second imprisonment on Robben Island

ROBBEN ISLAND WAS A changed place when I returned in 1989. I felt it the moment we docked. I had heard that comrades Walter Sisulu, Govan Mbeki, Ahmed Kathrada and most of our other senior leaders were already in mainland prisons awaiting release, and I had a sense that while their spirits would still have a powerful presence on the Island, it would be all the lonelier there. It was also known that Nelson Mandela had been transferred, first to Pollsmoor Prison in Tokai in the city and then to the Victor Verster facility near Paarl, just under an hour away from Cape Town. I could imagine that he was deeply missed on the Island. Although we had never mingled with our leaders, as they were in the single cells throughout the previous time I had been on the Island, I knew there would be a void without them. We had relied on them for political guidance when there were disputes among us; and just knowing they were there gave us courage on our worst days.

Comrades Simon, Mandla and I were joined on the Island a month or two later by Ashley Forbes and other young revolutionaries, whose presence on the Island showed how much the mass struggle had intensified over the ten years since I had been away. Ashley had been the Cape commander of MK, and I immediately felt an affinity with him as he had been arrested, tried and sentenced to fifteen years' imprisonment (with another nineteen suspended for five years) at the tender age of twenty-four. It's not easy to be incarcerated at that age. I returned to the Island at the age of fifty-one, having started my first sentence at twenty-six. The only difference between Ashley and me, perhaps, was that in 1963 we all accepted we were there for the duration of our sentences, whereas in 1989 there was a sense that the young prisoners would never complete their full term. Victory seemed certain.

Among our most courageous comrades on the Island in 1989 were the medical doctors Vejay Ramlakan and Sibongiseni Dhlomo, who were among the Durban treason trialists sentenced in 1987. Comrade Vejay, who had worked at the King Edward VIII Hospital in Durban and was a lecturer in anatomy, stated in court that 'every doctor had a duty to become involved in the struggle against apartheid because no health worker could ignore that apartheid caused disease'. Vejay and Sibongiseni as well as other comrades (including Bafo Nguqu, Sibusiso Ndlanzi, Vusumuzi Mahlobe, Ordway Msomi, Mapiki Dhlomo, Malusi Majola and Jude Franas) were sent to the Island for carrying out bombings in and around Durban in the name of the ANC. Vejay was sentenced to twelve years in jail for, among other things, ordering the bombing of the home of the House of Delegates leader in the Tricameral Parliament, Amichand Rajbansi. Vejay told the court that Rajbansi 'represented no one but himself, and the oppressed people [would] not forgive him'.

Other brave comrades on the Island in 1989 included, of course, the Delmas treason trialists –Terror Lekota, Tom Manthata, Popo Molefe and Moss Chikane. Terror and I were serving our second term each on the Island.

As soon as we arrived, we were interviewed by the prison authorities in the observational area of A Section to determine the nature of our 'crime'. This was to allow them to allocate us to particular sections of the prison. I was sent to B Section. I'm sure those of us who were placed in B Section, where Mandela and other leaders had been imprisoned for so long, were all affected by that link with them. This section comprised the isolation cells, and they were indeed very small. There was no washbasin or toilet, only a single iron bed and a little table. We were separated from the General Section, where groups of prisoners lived together in larger cells, and where I had been incarcerated previously. Just as before, we were able to make contact with the political prisoners housed there.

The only senior leader from the Rivonia trial whom we found in B Section was Elias Motsoaledi, who had arrived on Robben Island in 1964 with Mandela. There were many things I loved about Elias. He was a keen gardener, for instance, but he only planted flowers. He was so proud of them, and indeed they cheered us up. Elias was a wonderful comrade, a true veteran of the movement, whose political involvement in the struggle went as far back as the 1940s. He was not one of the educated intellectuals but came from a working-class background, which brought its own wealth of knowledge.

Elias had a lot of stories to tell about the movement in its early days and he kept many of us occupied for hours in that way. He was a deeply kind-hearted person. It was distressing, though, to see how his health was failing; he was on constant medication. He was finally freed in 1990 together with the other Rivonia accused, apart from Mandela, who would be released separately not long afterwards. It was sad for all of us when Elias passed away in May 1994 at the age of sixty-nine. He still had so much to contribute.

I also met Tokyo Sexwale again, whom I had left behind when I was released in 1979. He had been trained in the Soviet Union and reinfiltrated into South Africa in the mid-1970s but was arrested and sentenced to eighteen years in jail.

A major change in prison life was that we no longer went to the quarry or the shore to work but mainly did cleaning work inside the jail itself. This gave us more opportunities for political discussions, which we also had when we were exercising in the yard. That too was new. Terror compelled me to run with him and kept count until I did twenty rounds. Then he would carry on alone. In the late afternoon, we would watch birds through our little windows. By the time I returned, the authorities had relented and given permission for a TV set to be placed in the dining room, and then one in each general cell. We all tended to watch the news, but beyond that the prisoners were mostly hooked on the soapies.

There was still an underground structure that gave leadership to the ANC prisoners. I was asked to join. Our task was the same as before: to deal with problems on the Island and organise comrades' discussions through the Central Political Education Committee. I was gratified that our system of the 1960s and 1970s had held up, but increasing access to news, newspapers and magazines for the prisoners meant that the role of political education was somehow less pronounced.

There was great frustration among prisoners at still being held by that time: our members were itching to get out and become involved in what was happening outside. The world was changing. There was increasing mobilisation of people in the country. Even a few apartheid laws were being repealed. Some of our comrades were seeing their appeals in the courts succeed. It was a challenge on every level not to become rebellious inside the cells.

One morning in 1990, the warders instructed Alfred Phala, Matthews Meyiwa and me to get ready for a 'visit' to the mainland. We were taken by boat to the city, and from there in a minibus along the N1 highway to Victor Verster Prison under heavy escort. We were elated to find out that we were going to see Comrade Mandela. Our vehicle entered the iron gates of the prison, but instead of going to the jail itself, we were dropped off outside a house with a charming garden and pool, where we found our comrade. He was just the same as ever, although he was now out of the olive-green prison garb and back in a suit and tie, as I remembered him from the 1950s and 1960s. He greeted us with sincere warmth, asked after our health, and enquired about conditions on the Island. He was very interested in what had happened with us since we last were in jail together in 1979 and asked for details about my abduction and trial.

Mandela then took us into his confidence about communications he had had with members of the government. He was very clear that this was in keeping with an ANC National Executive Committee statement of 1987 that laid out the conditions under which we would be prepared to enter into negotiations with the regime. He carefully explained the way in which the ANC in Lusaka had gone about discussions with various stakeholders, and how he himself had been in contact with our senior comrades under OR Tambo. The details were stunning.

We knew that a number of meetings had taken place from the mid-1980s between the ANC and some South Africans – businessmen, religious and church leaders, newspaper editors, liberal politicians and activists, students and so on. These encounters were widely reported in the South African media at the time. What was generally unknown was that secret meetings had also taken place between Mandela and PW Botha's minister of justice, Kobie Coetsee, and later the head of the regime's National Intelligence Service, Niël Barnard. It was Barnard who had been consulted by my captors in December 1986, after my abduction from Swaziland. He came to be a key figure in my appeal against my conviction in 1991.

Thus, by the time I met Mandela at Victor Verster in 1990, the ANC was on the verge of a complete breakthrough. The news was breath-taking. The point of our visit was in keeping with the ANC's strong tradition of consultation. As I had been out of political circulation since 1986, I was swept up in what Mandela told us and became aware of the intricacies of events which I knew about only in broad terms. It was a privilege to be in that room that day.

We were under no illusions as to why the National Party government was making these moves. The liberation movement had won. Our campaigns over forty years had succeeded. Through our efforts, the regime had been isolated and made bankrupt, and the political initiative was now in the hands of the people. It was a momentous juncture.

Lunch was prepared for us by a prison warder, and Mandela served us himself. He then asked us to acquaint him with details of the new political prisoners whose cases had received prominent coverage in the papers. This was for him to better understand our increased capacity. Our task after that was to convey all aspects of our discussion with him to our comrades on the Island. Other key cadres in prison –Tokyo, Terror and Ashley among them – made the same incredible journey to see Mandela.

Some political prisoners doubted the commitment of the government to negotiating in good faith with the ANC. Many feared 'dialogue' would compromise our aims and objectives, but there was a stronger belief in the leadership of the ANC at that time. Though the movement had been divided into the three zones of exile, prison and the underground since it was banned in 1960, there was unity of purpose. Once our fellow prisoners gave the negotiations their blessing, we conveyed this to Mandela.

The quantum leap was announced to the world in February 1990, when De Klerk opened Parliament with the announcement that he was unbanning the ANC, SACP, PAC and other organisations. This was what

Botha should have done when he made his Rubicon speech in 1985, but he had betrayed everybody. We watched live coverage of De Klerk's address on TV and cheered with excitement. We congratulated each other. We were beginning to reap the fruits of our struggle and believed our prison terms would soon be coming to an end.

Shortly afterwards, De Klerk announced Mandela's release, and we also watched that on TV the whole day with the prison warders. Most ordinary prisoners had never seen Mandela and became emotional when they watched him leaving Victor Verster, accompanied by his wife Winnie and prominent leaders of the UDF. The crowds waiting for them in Cape Town were as overwhelmed as we were. I won't forget the first electrifying sentences uttered by Mandela when he addressed the people gathered on the Grand Parade.

> I stand here before you not as a prophet, but as a humble servant of you, the people. Your tireless and heroic sacrifices have made it possible for me to be here today. I therefore place the remaining years of my life in your hands.
>
> I salute the African National Congress. It has fulfilled our every expectation in its role as leader of the great march to freedom.
>
> I salute our president, Comrade Oliver Tambo, for leading the ANC even under the most difficult circumstances.
>
> I salute the rank-and-file members of the ANC. You have sacrificed life and limb in the pursuit of the noble cause of our struggle.
>
> I salute combatants of Umkhonto we Sizwe, like Solomon Mahlangu and Ashley Kriel, who have paid the ultimate price for the freedom of all South Africans.

We were so proud to be members of the ANC at that moment. We thought we had the experience and capacity to unite the masses against whatever agenda the regime had in mind. We immediately demanded our release from prison, thinking it wouldn't be long in any event. But that was not to be. As the days and then weeks went by without any sign of forward movement, we became angry. There was even a placard demonstration by prisoners on the field next to the General Section.

Our lawyers, including Arthur Chaskalson, who would be the first president of the Constitutional Court, came to see us. They urged us to be patient for a while longer while the ANC leadership was in talks with the government about the release of political prisoners. We were then given forms by the prison authorities to fill out and indicate what activities we were involved in and what organisation we belonged to. We refused. We deemed them irrelevant. Our lawyers visited another time, spending many hours convincing us that they needed a record of all political prisoners in the country, and that we should at least give our names and affiliation.

Mandela then came to see us, accompanied by Jacob Zuma. They briefed us about what was being done to secure our release. That was all good and well, but we decided we had the right to exercise our agency and reverted to that powerful weapon, the hunger strike. We had to protest against our continued detention. The strike lasted an agonising eleven days. This time, all political prisoners, irrespective of allegiances, refused food. We were again seen by our lawyers, who informed us that we needed to call off the strike. But many activists believed those of us who were still there in 1991, a year after De Klerk's speech in Parliament, were somehow being held hostage while 'talks about talks' were taking place behind the scenes. It was a fight to the last for us.

Already we were being treated differently on the Island. As soon as De Klerk had unbanned the liberation movements, the prison authorities relaxed the rules on visits. The restriction on the number of letters was also lifted. Muslim prisoners began to receive halaal food daily from the mainland during the fasting month of Ramadan, and we were allowed to celebrate our festivals. This was a far cry from the early days when I wasn't even allowed a copy of the Holy Quran.

The extension of visiting hours meant I could see our supporters who came from Cape Town, especially from the suburb of Wynberg where Ashley Forbes was from. Wynberg was full of families of activists including the Pandys, the Breys and the Jaffers. Ashley was in love with Yasmina Pandy, who had also been detained for a period, and they decided to marry while Ashley was in prison. We had to dress him in a borrowed suit and tie and send him off to Pollsmoor, where his bride was waiting. They had a Muslim wedding and Ashley returned that evening in a jovial mood. We celebrated with him.

One of my most memorable visitors was Zubeida Brey who was wearing a blue dress, as was her tradition. She arrived with Ashley's wife Yasmina, a talkative and jolly person who lifted one's spirits. Full of jokes, she liked to make us laugh, and she always brought the most delicious cheese bread. Zubeida was part of a group of women who regularly prepared food to be brought to us on the Island. Zubeida and I remained close friends after my release from prison.

Mothers were prominent among our supporters. Aunty Begum, the mum of the Pandy household, was a frequent visitor. She was very active in the UDF along with her three other daughters – Fatima and Rabia, who during the 1980s had long been sought by the police, and Thoraya, who was in the ANC underground and the student movement. Another notable mother, Mrs Jaffer, was active in organising the women of the Cape, but it had been tough for her. Her daughter Zubeida, who was an activist and journalist, was detained when she was pregnant, and yet she was still subjected to severe torture by the security police. Her brother Mansoor and his wife Kay were prominent activists in the UDF. Other friends during that waiting period included Omar and Naseema Badsha, whom I knew from Durban when I was a banned person in 1980. They were calm and encouraging. The blazing support of all these people gave us prisoners hope in the final months. They made us feel we had an extended family in Cape Town, even when we were alone and unsure.

I was grateful to see anyone whom I knew from the early years of the struggle. It brought the past and the present closer, tying the threads of the different phases of our struggle. I was pleased to get a visit from Phyllis Naidoo's sister Cynthia Davids, an activist I hadn't seen since 1963. I was also visited by Jack and Ray Simons, both members of the SACP. I was also happy to see Kader and Louise Asmal after their return from years in exile, which they spent as key activists in the Irish Anti-Apartheid Movement. But my most special visitor was Conny Braam, whom I didn't expect to be in South Africa. When she entered the waiting room, I was overjoyed to see her. We hugged endlessly. First, she updated me on Hélène and her family. It was important to understand what Hélène had been through since her release because she was a golden thread in our final years of struggle. Her own shine and strength had been tested beyond the limit, and we were forever linked to each other.

As for Conny, she had been tireless in her efforts to have me freed after I was abducted. She had also assisted our comrades involved in Operation

Vula to infiltrate the leadership of the ANC into the country in late 1989, putting her own life and safety at high risk. I only grasped what a difficult journey it was for her to come to the Island and see me there when I read her book *Operation Vula*. Those who loved us were in pain, just as we were.

Although we were drawing nearer to the end of our time on the Island, the days dragged by. We seemed to be watching momentous events take place from afar. Many of our ideas were being challenged by what was happening globally. We watched on TV the collapse of communism in the Soviet Union and the destruction of the Berlin Wall. That propelled us into debates about our own ideologies. But we also knew the collapse of Communism would deprive the apartheid regime of another reason for its war against our people. Its obsession with communism was no longer rational.

One day Elias Motsoaledi was called by the authorities and told to pack his belongings as he was leaving the Island. This wasn't a transfer. He was to be released from prison altogether and was going home at last. Elias had been in constant arguments with prisoners about his flower garden, as they wanted to use some of his space against a wall to grow vegetables instead. Sometimes when a prisoner had a visitor coming, they would pick carnations from Elias's garden for their visitors, and he would get very angry. We were joyful for him at his release and said a heartfelt goodbye as he got into the car with the warders. But as he drove away into the distance, he surely knew we would be plotting our next move: to pull up his beloved flower garden and prepare the soil for the planting of vegetables! We agreed among ourselves to share the ground. In our own small plot Ashley and I decided to plant spinach and tomatoes. We took turns to water our garden and very soon Elias's rich soil delivered beautiful produce. We had to watch out for birds coming there to indulge, and that brought its own pleasure. We fed them from time to time as a respite from the harshness of our conditions, and we thought of it as a triumph when young birds attempted their first flight. How dear was freedom.

When we left B Section to join the prisoners in the General Section on sports days, we noticed that the ducks which laid their eggs on the field were disturbed by our activities and abandoned their nests. Prisoners would then collect the eggs and mix them with the hens in the fowl run that was kept in the yard. When the eggs hatched, the ducklings mixed with the chicks and followed the hen wherever she went. Ashley and I noticed that when the ducklings got into a tiny pond to swim, the chicks followed. Some were rescued and others drowned. It was a complicated solidarity.

Sunday was always a special day. An imam, Sheikh Basheer, would visit the Muslim prisoners to give us spiritual guidance. That too comforted us – that people were praying for our release and well-being. A Christian priest ministered to the Christian prisoners in the same way.

There were other means of coping with one's impatience at being released. I registered again with Unisa in 1990, this time to do an LLB. Most of us were then studying. Yet nothing could compare with the work being done outside to see my conviction overturned.

Thirty-one
A landmark legal judgment

My lawyers were determined to contest the high court's jurisdiction to try me despite my abduction from a foreign country. Eventually, in early 1991, Advocate Mohamed was able to argue my case before five judges of the Appellate Division of the Supreme Court.

At the time, there was a clear distinction between 'state-authorised' and 'unauthorised' acts committed on foreign soil. This distinction came about because the apartheid government had been challenged in the 1970s on a matter very similar to mine: the abduction of guerrillas from Swaziland so they could face punishment in South Africa. It was realised that apartheid courts would struggle with the issue of jurisdiction if the person had been abducted by officials. But if the person was handled by 'unknown people', even if they were secret agents, jurisdiction would be less of a problem. That was why the warders, the security policemen and even the doctors had shown no interest in how I was captured, because if any of them had agreed that the state had kidnapped me in a foreign country, it would have been difficult to put me on trial.

Prosecutors presented it in court as if I had popped out of nowhere one day at the police headquarters in Pretoria, and that, since I was there, the police could take me into lawful custody under suspicion of being a terrorist. The circumstances of my original capture were deemed 'irrelevant.'

The appeal proved nail-biting, as there were a few technicalities that could have derailed our case. The apartheid government had an extradition treaty with Swaziland, meaning that under 'conventional international law', it could have applied to have me legally taken into custody in Mbabane. But there was a caveat. Swaziland did not allow extradition for 'offences of a political character', including offences under the Terrorism Act or the Suppression of Communism Act. That was indeed how I had been charged.

But our argument wasn't about any of that. It was that proceedings should be set aside on the basis of an abuse of process resulting in an infringement of my rights. There was a similar case of 'disguised extradition' heard by the New Zealand Court of Appeal in 1978, which is often cited in law journals. The difference there was that the accused was arrested in Melbourne and returned to New Zealand by Australian police officers in the absence of an extradition process. But even though it was policemen who had carried out the arrest, while my capture was by 'unknown persons', the New Zealand appeal court found that a judge was entitled to enquire into the methods used to secure the presence of an accused to determine if there had been a misuse of powers. It said a judge possessed an inherent jurisdiction 'to prevent anything which smacks of abuse of process'.

The Supreme Court in my matter had affirmed its jurisdiction notwithstanding my forcible abduction from a foreign country by two individuals, because they were 'unknown persons'. It claimed that the first time the state became involved was when I was in Pretoria, having been 'delivered' there by people it did not know. But the appeals court in Bloemfontein found that wasn't true, because my abductors had in fact contacted Niël Barnard, the high-ranking intelligence official, while we were on our way to Pretoria, and it was Barnard who had arranged for me to appear at police headquarters, where I was officially arrested on charges of treason.

Justice Jan Steyn held that the 'manner in which the appellant was abducted provides a clear indication of the involvement of ... [a state] agency'. It was important, he said, that

> The individual must be protected against illegal detention and abduction, the bounds of jurisdiction must not be exceeded,

sovereignty must be respected, the legal process must be fair to those affected, and abuse of law must be avoided in order to protect and promote the integrity of the administration of justice.

This applies equally to the state. When the state is a party to a dispute, as for example in criminal cases, it must come to court with 'clean hands'. When the state itself is involved in an abduction across international borders, as in the present case, its hands are not clean.

The case shows that the repression of crime does not grant unlimited powers to government agencies in bringing to justice alleged criminals, even in the absence of a protest by the authorities of the state of refuge.

My legal team took a deep breath. This was a definitive and groundbreaking judgment. I could hardly believe it. In early February 1991, the appeals court unanimously ruled in my favour, that Justice Daniels had in law had no jurisdiction to try me.

The court described how I had been abducted from Swaziland, and that I was shackled and blindfolded, and taken to a building in Pretoria where I was arrested by Brigadier Schoon who was head of C section of the security police. C1 was a subsection of C section, and was the askari unit. One of the men who worked for C1, Almond Nofomela, was recorded as saying he had been involved in two abductions in Swaziland in 1986. The one was a PAC member, and the other was of September. September was now noted to be an askari who had given evidence in a number of treason trials. The finding, in light of Nofomela's evidence on similar abductions, indicated the level to which the police had taken the fight for apartheid in the name of the regime.

On 26 February 1991, a warder summoned me to the reception office where one of the officials told me my conviction for treason had been set aside. I had to be released immediately. I had been expecting this, but when it happens, you're almost taken by surprise. As it was late in the afternoon, I wondered where I would go when I got to Cape Town. I laugh when I think about it now. I can't quite understand why I thought I might be dropped off by the boat and simply left on the quay. I was also concerned that I would not have enough time to say goodbye to my fellow prisoners. What if there were comrades I would never see again?

The boat was leaving in an hour. I was told to get all my belongings.

As I walked back to my section, I was aware of a sudden weight on me, which is why I turned around and pleaded to be allowed one extra night in prison. Once I arrived at Jetty One, the old prison block at Cape Town harbour, I didn't know what would happen after that. All I knew was that I'd be rejoining my comrades outside to face the transition period, which was a very new and challenging space.

Thirty-two
Forging the road to democracy

I STAYED WITH MY BROTHER Essop and his family in Lenasia, south of Johannesburg, for a few months, and was inundated with visits from family and friends. My mother was overjoyed, as the last time we had been able to spend any significant amount of time together was in 1979 and 1980, between Robben Island and my disappearance into exile. She had made a few visits to see me in exile in Swaziland, but we had not managed to have quality time together, just the two of us.

A few days after I arrived in Johannesburg, my old friend Kathy Kathrada hosted a lunch for me, which Mandela attended. Mandela made a speech in celebration of my release. A recording of a portion of that address was played years later at my eightieth birthday party. Mandela said: '[Ebie] emerged as one of the most outstanding pillars of the movement who was not only committed and loyal, but who had the ability to explain the policy of the organisation.' I remember how Mandela used to tell me that Steve Tshwete, Ezra Sigwela and I were 'best able' to explain the policies of the ANC while we were on Robben Island during my first term.

At the time, a young South African filmmaker, Liz Fish, who also attended the lunch, was making a documentary called *The Long Journey of Clement Zulu*, which was about the challenges of reintegrating into society after Robben Island. It focused on my comrades James Mange, Clement

Zulu and me. The film is set in April 1991 in the mists and clouds of Breakwater Pier at the Cape Town harbour, where people were waiting for the Blouberg to bring the last remaining prisoners home at last. The emotions of the released prisoners and those waiting for them are relayed. Her film has stayed with me because there can be no undoing of the past, and yet we feel a deep sense of loss around comrades whose lives were cut short after their release. This was often the case with comrades whose mental and physical health was compromised. Although James and I made it into a new kind of life after prison, Clement battled, and he died horribly only three years after his release. I know many of us wonder if we could have done more for our comrades like Clement.

I myself saw how the mental health struggles of many of my comrades affected their ability to create a life for themselves after prison. It hurts. Many people are still going through hell and have spent decades feeling forgotten. They didn't get the care or recognition they needed and deserved. I'm so grateful that I did.

Five months after my release, the ANC held its elective conference in Durban in July. This was the first of its kind held inside South Africa for more than thirty years and it brought together leading activists against apartheid from our branches throughout the country. We gathered from the underground structures of the ANC, the camps of MK, the Women's League, the Youth League and the ANC's missions abroad. There were foreign diplomats as well as politicians from other parties. At the time, the ANC had more representatives in foreign countries than the apartheid government, and its growing influence in international circles couldn't be underestimated. Already in 1987, while I was awaiting trial, an official ANC delegation was received in Washington for the first time: that was a turning point. Once the United States had given our position its support instead of treating us as a terrorist organisation, we could move forward on a much bigger stage.

The elective conference was an exciting event because it stirred national revolutionary fervour. Most of the heroes of the movement who had been released from prison or who had returned from exile were there. It was an extraordinary occasion. Because the National Party had demonised us for decades and made laws to keep us out of the media, our people didn't yet know our faces, they hadn't heard us speak in public, though they knew us by our actions. And there we were – at the podium, on the floor, mingling, laughing, expressing ourselves in the ANC's customary way: with a fist in the air.

Comrade OR gave a soulful opening speech. He recounted his own dangerous escape into exile in 1960 and went on to pay tribute to the millions who had given the liberation movement their love and support.[15] 'One of the greatest historical failures of our times has been the inability of successive white regimes to halt our struggle,' he said. 'Even at the most difficult times our people never surrendered. Whether it was under the banner of Black Consciousness in the late 1960s and the 1970s, or with the Durban strikes of 1973, our people never ceased to struggle. As a result, despite all the schemes aimed at destroying our movement, we grew both in stature and effectiveness. Our survival and growth as a fighting force is the major victory that our people have scored.'

Fifty-six delegates were elected to the National Executive Committee at that conference. I was one of them, and I was honoured to be re-elected at every conference until 2017. At the first meeting of the NEC in 1991, I was elected to the National Working Committee (NWC), which met weekly with Mandela acting as chair. This was the first time I was able to participate in the leadership of my organisation while sitting face to face with the likes of Mandela, Tambo, Nzo and Slovo, discussing the future of our country. The challenges of the time were all-consuming. There were many renegades and enemies who did not want to see majority rule take place in the way we did. We were constantly addressing the issue of violence between members of the Inkatha Freedom Party and the ANC in Natal, as well as the violent extremism of the AWB.

All members of the NWC had to work full-time at Shell House, the ANC head office in Johannesburg. I was part of the organising committee, and my friend Sue Rabkin – who had given us so much support even while she was a hunted woman herself in Maputo – was committee secretary. It was a vibrant time at Shell House and we linked up with comrades we had known throughout the struggle and met young comrades who were pivotal to our efforts on the ground. One of the younger comrades I became friends with was Anne Vincent who was part of our intelligence structures, who later became Anne Sexwale. We remained friends for the next thirty years.

Mandela and Sisulu asked me to take responsibility for establishing the Patriotic Front, which was to be a broad alliance of liberation groups including the PAC to develop consensus and draw up a mandate for negotiations with the apartheid regime. I readily agreed to take up this major challenge at such a historic moment. My brother Gora was of course still very prominent within the PAC. Even though we in the ANC leadership had had our battles with the PAC, especially on Robben Island, we knew we had to set certain things aside in the interests of uniting our people.

I had to form a team and asked my good friend Thoraya Pandy to assist me. Phumla Williams – my contact in Maputo while I was underground in Durban in the early 1980s – approached the various organisations we wanted to bring together. In October 1991, more than four hundred delegates representing ninety-four organisations gathered at a hotel on the Durban beachfront to launch the Patriotic Front. Again, as with the elective conference, there were political parties, religious, cultural and community organisations, trade unions, youth and women's organisations and other movements from civil society present. Even the Democratic Party, the forerunner of the present-day Democratic Alliance, was there, but a 'presence' was as far as it would go. Its leader, Ken Andrew, explained that while the DP was 'not opposed' to the Patriotic Front, it was not prepared to participate in it. It was a liberal party, just as the DA is today, and the ANC's national revolutionary posture didn't fit its mandate. However, political organisations that were part of the bantustan system did take part. Our strategic objective was to win over as many organisations as possible.

Our task now was to support the main principles of the Harare Declaration, which was adopted by a subcommittee on southern Africa of the Organisation of African Unity at a summit in Zimbabwe on 21 August 1989. That declaration stated that only a constituent assembly, elected on the basis of universal suffrage, could draft a new constitution for a free South Africa. The adoption of the Harare Declaration was a most significant event. Without it, there wouldn't have been prisoner releases, or the unbanning of our organisations, or the kind of freedom we eventually achieved.

The Patriotic Front gave the ANC an advantage because it allowed us to take the initiative in defining the political agenda at that point of the struggle. It was frustrating when the PAC and the Azanian People's Organisation (AZAPO) withdrew, but their reasons were unfortunately in keeping with their modus operandi over the decades. They were not prepared to work with anyone who had been part of, or was still part of, the apartheid system.

The Convention for a Democratic South Africa (CODESA) was our next milestone. But just as we were getting started on these pivotal negotiations for a new, democratic country, the horror of the Boipatong massacre occurred in June 1992. At least forty-six residents of the township east of Johannesburg were massacred by local hostel dwellers, the attackers being supporters of the IFP. Shortly after the killings, the ANC made it known that the South African police had acted in collaboration with the IFP.

I suppose we were prepared for devastating incidents as a result of 'third force' activity – an umbrella term for covert activities by the security forces and its partners. This was already taking place, with the IFP – supported by the regime's intelligence, army and police – at war with the ANC, especially in Natal and the Transvaal. There were many deep-seated reasons for this, prominent among them a determination to disturb the ANC's determined path to victory at an election not far in the future. If the regime and the IFP could show that there was continued violence, and that this was 'black-on-black' violence, which apparently had nothing to do with white people, it could stall the whole process and relook at its 'generosity' to the liberation movements. If I say this was cynical, I would be light-hearted. It was barbaric. It showed that underneath many of those suits and ties making nice gestures towards us were devils whose hatred and racism were only then reaching their peak.

As a result of Boipatong, the ANC withdrew from CODESA.

Thirty-three
Lost opportunities

THESE WERE NOT THE ONLY issues on my mind. I was also concerned about how I could build a relationship with my daughter Cassia. Of all the challenges I was facing as a member of the ANC during that period, none could compare with learning to be a father, and showing my daughter that I loved her. But I felt I got it all wrong. Perhaps I was too rigid and distracted. Perhaps I should have made sure I was much more present in her life, and that she could rely on me to be there, in person, for her most special occasions.

The way it worked was that she and her mum Julie would sometimes visit me in Johannesburg, while Cassia would come and stay with me now and then during school holidays. But we couldn't strike a bond. I was fully aware that I didn't have the emotional skills to bridge the distance between us, and that it wasn't her fault that when she stayed with me, she would even cry at times and want to go back home. I was a stranger, and Cassia was a child who could have no understanding of the shortcomings I knew I had inside myself.

This was not uncommon among those of us who had been in the liberation movement all our lives. We hadn't had 'normal' relationships, and when you reach your fifties, your behaviour is so entrenched that to change your ways is like moving a mountain. The ANC, as a movement, had never assisted us in facing those challenges. We didn't even expect it to do so. On top of that, I had had no relationship with my own father. Ma was everything to me, and I had no example set to me for fatherhood. When Ma died when I was fourteen, I grew into a lonely teenager. I had a lot of difficulties relating to people emotionally, and this may also have affected my relationships.

I am sad to this day that I was not there for Cassia when she was growing up, and that she lacked a father figure. I wonder if my relationship with her somehow mirrored my own relationship with her mum. In the end, we were also strangers. By the early 1990s, as the political turmoil was barrelling around us, I was essentially still alone. I had to try and connect with people I loved in a different way. The opportunity came to go to France, and I planned to see Gora's children Yasir and Zareena who were living in Paris with their mother. But before we were even able to start a planned sight-seeing trip together, there was a transport strike which made it difficult to get around. I decided to take a train to Zurich in Switzerland instead, where I reconnected with Corinne Bischoff, the young Swiss woman who had been abducted with her husband from Swaziland by the apartheid security forces in 1986. That reunion included a journey on the iconic Glacier Express, which travels through the Alps. Perhaps this was the first time I had been able to sit in silence by myself and just gaze at the natural beauty around me while I thought properly about what I wanted for my life. I wished so much that I could have been sharing that trip with someone with whom I had a connection. I realised that what was missing completely in my life was a family of my own, into which Cassia would of course be welcomed. I promised myself that if I was ever so fortunate, I would take my family on the same train journey. The destination was Zermatt, a small mountain village at the foot of the Gornergrat ridge, which gives a perfect view of the Matterhorn. As I enjoyed its famous fondues and quaint culture, which were outside anything I had known, I resolved to make sure I would have that loving family.

The ANC rejoined CODESA in September 1992. The talks that ensued with the National Party took nearly two years, the main purpose being to address obstacles preventing multiparty negotiations. Here the Patriotic Front played a central role. Whenever there were problems at CODESA and the ANC was driven to make compromises, it consulted the Patriotic

Front for a fresh mandate. Our meetings were usually held under the chairmanship of Mandela. Once CODESA settled upon a declaration of intent, we were on a shining path forward. It agreed the parties would bring into being an undivided nation sharing a common citizenship; work to heal the divisions of the past; strive to improve the quality of life of the people; create a climate conducive to peaceful constitutional change by eliminating violence and promoting free political participation, and build a non-racial, non-sexist state reliant upon an independent judiciary.

CODESA established five working groups. I was deployed to the security group. Meanwhile, all of us at the ANC's head office were involved in campaigning for our party. Kathy and I canvassed in the northern Transvaal and I was also sent to northern Natal where I campaigned in Stanger with my friend and comrade Ashraf Suliman. Everywhere we went, we received a positive response for the ANC.

Everyone has a story to tell about where they were on 27 April 1994, election day. The world was transfixed by the footage of millions of people of all races standing patiently together for hours in snaking lines, waiting to cast their vote. I was deployed in the Newcastle and Ladysmith area in Natal as an observer. Although there were problems, I was engrossed by my duty. And I'm not only talking about my activities as an observer. I was so excited to vote for the first time in my life. The electricity in the atmosphere among the people can only be compared to that of Kliptown in 1955, when we ratified the Freedom Charter.

Forty years had gone by, and I was well aware of what those forty years had brought me. Yet I was experiencing the same sense of ownership of our destiny. My age, and all my experiences, desperate and triumphant, somehow melted away in the sheer thrill of having been witness to two such massive events in history, 1955 and 1994. That boy who had walked from the station back to Ma's house in Effingham was in my mind. While we walked, I liked to watch our shadows bouncing on the sand – hers tall, mine small – as the crickets buzzed and the train clattered away from us into the distance. She would unlock the door, and when we got inside, she'd make us some lunch and we'd sit at the table and tell stories.

I wasn't as aware then as I would be ten years later of how determined my country's leaders were to shut me out, send me 'back' to a land I didn't know, and decide that I wasn't worthy of representing my people in government one day. Little did they know.

I was on the ANC's list to stand for Parliament and was subsequently elected as an MP. I saw this as a new phase in our fight for liberation. I was appointed chairperson of the portfolio committee on foreign affairs and was also appointed by the president as a member of the joint committee on intelligence. That was the only committee which met behind closed doors, and we were all sworn to secrecy. The former apartheid minister of justice, Kobie Coetsee, became the deputy chair of the Senate in the new dispensation.

Coetsee took me by surprise after my swearing-in as an MP, saying he wanted to apologise for my abduction from Swaziland. That wasn't the only time a former senior member of the regime would apologise to me. Years later, a person who had once been part of the apartheid intelligence apparatus approached me at a formal dinner, took me aside, and echoed Coetsee's words. Another strange incident occurred when I met former foreign minister Pik Botha for the first time in 2000, at the end of an event on Robben Island. He approached me at the Cape Town docks and said that he had been opposed to my abduction from Swaziland. He claimed to have told his people that my abduction was illegal and a violation of international law. According to Pik, his officials wouldn't listen to him, but I had my doubts about his version. He seemed to know the finer details of my case, and even boasted that he knew my *nom de guerre* was Ahmed Zaheer, and that I had been travelling on an Indian passport.

As a new member of Parliament, I was assigned to the constituency of Chatsworth in Durban. I was offered accommodation there by Safura Khan, a blind woman with an amazing love of life. She travelled to work daily by bus and was a great motivational speaker. Sometimes when I returned to her home after a day's constituency work, I'd find the place in total darkness while Safura was busy at the stove cooking a curry for dinner. Her resilience inspires me to this day.

I met many people who had continued with their lives over the decades when I was in MK. Without those 'ordinary' people, holding the country together so courageously, believing in us, we would never have been able to carry on.

The ANC chief whip soon deployed me to a third committee, that of correctional services. Our job was to oversee the conditions in local prisons. We also visited numerous facilities in the United States to gain insight into how we could transform our own system. But that experience was deeply traumatic. It brought about a series of debilitating nightmares of cell grilles clanging open and shut, and I had no choice but to resign. I knew if I persevered there, my mental health would rapidly decline. I admire my colleagues who had similar histories to mine but who remained on the committee.

Once all my energies were focused on the foreign affairs committee, I began to find a new way in my life. There was a lot of travelling involved, but I was fortunate because my brother Gora, who was a PAC MP, was also on the committee, given his long history of diplomacy abroad. As members of the foreign affairs portfolio committee, Gora and I were part of a delegation that went on a trip to the UN in New York City and then to its offices in Geneva. At last we reconnected, meaningfully. One of my favourite memories is of going to Broadway with him to watch the *Phantom of the Opera* – and, again, we made every effort not to discuss politics. That had always been our way.

At the same time, I could see he was battling. His disillusionment with the PAC began shortly after it was unbanned. He disagreed with its refusal to give up the armed struggle and he couldn't come to terms with what he thought was its 'rabble-rousing' slogan of 'one settler, one bullet'. He was challenged by its refusal to commit to negotiations, and when it withdrew from the Patriotic Front, he really had to fight back. He believed in a broad, open-ended Africanism, and he felt the PAC was too narrow and nationalistic. He believed that ideology no longer served the country, and his attempts to change the PAC from within left him marginalised by more extremist elements. He nonetheless represented his party with fervour in Parliament.

Gora had a great sense of humour and made parliamentarians laugh often and hard. One day in Parliament, Gora made an unforgettable pan-Africanist speech in which he railed against South Africans buying Kentucky Fried Chicken when, as Africans, we were quite capable of frying our own chicken. This was met with rapturous applause.

Gora and I were accommodated during those early years in Acacia Park, the parliamentary village in Cape Town where the old white parliamentarians had once lived. It was a spartan place with simple houses, but since we lived near to each other, we would cook together at weekends. Gora had become an excellent chef in exile, and regularly spoiled me with home-cooked mutton and chicken curries. We took road trips together during our parliamentary breaks, and family reunions brought us both joy.

I also enjoyed the parliamentary sessions in Cape Town because it meant I got to see my daughter Cassia more often. Knowing that Cassia loved cricket, my good friend Zubeida Brey would take us to watch cricket at Newlands stadium. Julie wanted Cassia to attend the private school, Kingswood College, in Grahamstown, and I made that very worthwhile investment. Cassia excelled at everything she did and I was immensely proud of her. By the time she matriculated, she was the Dux scholar, scoring the highest marks in her grade. She went on to study her undergraduate degree at Stanford University, and obtained a master's degree in social psychology, before attending Stanford Medical School. She then did a second master's degree at Johns Hopkins in public health. Today, she works in New York among other global experts on HIV prevention, care and treatment projects being carried out in various countries internationally.

There was a lot of pressure on me to 'find a girlfriend' and settle down. I had many friends whom I socialised with, especially in Wynberg, and at one stage I developed a relationship with one of my comrades, the journalist Zubeida Jaffer, whom I have already mentioned. We had met for the first time after I was released from Robben Island and spent time together around the time of the 1994 elections. We began a romantic relationship, but then Zubeida had the opportunity to do her master's in journalism at Columbia University in New York, and that meant we were separated.

Although we saw each other in New York during an official visit I made on behalf of the ANC, I later received a letter from her saying she wanted to end our relationship. There was an age difference of twenty-one years between us, and I put it down partly to that. But I also realised I was struggling more than I could admit in coming to terms with life beyond imprisonment.

I did forge many new friendships during this time, one with a BBC radio journalist Arjum Wajid who had come to South Africa to cover the 1994 elections. I had taken her to meet many of our struggle stalwarts and she developed a keen interest in our struggle history. Arjum has remained one of my best friends.

I enjoyed my trips away tremendously. One of my favourite visits was to Vietnam with comrades Kgalema Motlanthe and Mendi Msimang. We visited the home of the great revolutionary Ho Chi Minh, whose fortitude had bolstered us in our years in MK. He had lived very simply, with only a single bed, a desk and a chair in his room. I was also honoured to be part of the first ANC delegation to the People's Republic of China in 1997, when South Africa established full diplomatic relations with that country. Comrades Blade Nzimande and Cheryl Carolus led the delegation as we charted new bonds with the Chinese Communist Party (CPC). Much like Ho Chi Minh, Mao Tse-tung had lived with no luxuries. I could understand how complicated it is to alter one's consciousness after decades of being at war.

In 1999, the ANC sent Thandi Modise and me to East Timor to meet Xanana Gusmão, the leader of the East Timorese independence movement, who had been imprisoned in Indonesia. He was leading the resistance from within prison. Gusmão was another example of a tireless freedom fighter who had lived without frills or special treatment. He was known to have walked from village to village to build support and recruit soldiers for the liberation movement he supported. He was instrumental in alerting the world to the massacre by the occupying Indonesians of two hundred and fifty of his people in the capital, Dili, in November 1991, whereupon he became a prime target of the Indonesian government.

Thandi and I travelled to Dili and could feel the tension as Indonesian-backed groups paraded through the streets threatening those people calling for their rights. We were appalled by what we saw, and we reported to the ANC that we feared there would be violence during the forthcoming referendum to decide East Timor's future. Indeed, it was a time of bloodshed, and that outcome affected us. Ultimately, Gusmão was released in 1999, and Mandela visited him in East Timor to express support for their freedom. When East Timor became independent, Gusmão was its first president from 2002 to 2007, and then prime minister until 2017.

Thirty-four
A great love story begins

I CAN MAP OUT MY most life-changing moments, and July 1998 was one of them. It's still vivid in my memory. I was invited to attend a workshop in Cape Town hosted by the Institute for Global Dialogue and the Institute for Democracy in South Africa (IDASA). We were preparing for a meeting of the Non-Aligned Movement (NAM), which is the forum of developing world states not aligned to any major power bloc. The workshop in Cape Town was meant to discuss our priorities for the NAM meeting later that year, in particular the need for a common approach to the reform of the UN Security Council.

I certainly was not expecting that event to change the course of my personal life. I have often reflected on how a few minutes can change you completely, such that you are not the same person anymore. This is what happened to me.

I had received a phone call a few days before the workshop from a young woman who would be presenting a paper on UN reform. I was to be the discussant of her paper, and she wanted to send it to my office ahead of time. That was my first interaction with Shannon Field, the woman who would become my true and only life partner.

I joined the workshop, flustered as usual and run off my feet, but looking forward to the intellectual exchange. I sat attentively listening to the presentation to which I had to respond, but I felt my mind drifting off into many different directions when Shannon took the floor, and found my gaze fixed on her. She smiled shyly.

After all the formalities, as we retired for refreshments, I made a beeline for her. It was a relief to find she was open to chatting. One of the first questions she asked me was which university I had attended. I was quick to respond: 'The university of Robben Island.' And I flashed a grin. She was immediately intrigued, and her questions and enthusiasm lit me up, too. Her interest in my struggle history stemmed from the fact that she had grown up in Durban at the same time as I was living in exile. But her family had later moved to Canada during the 1986 state of emergency. After a while, we saw that we were alone in the meeting hall, and despite having been prodded to join the other participants for snacks and drinks in an adjoining room, we were rooted to the spot and engrossed in conversation.

I got to learn that she had just finished a work contract with the UN Staff College in Turin, Italy, where she had specialised in issues relating to UN reform. But I was disappointed to hear that she would soon be returning to Canada.

I was keen to get to know more about Shannon, even though she was clearly much younger than me. I had missed out so much on love and relationships that I decided to throw caution to the wind. I offered to take her on a visit to Robben Island before she left South Africa and show her the cell in which I had been incarcerated. As I lay in bed later that night, I knew this would not be the last time I would be seeing her. I calculated how many days I should wait before calling her, so as not to seem too eager. I dragged out five more days before I finally placed the call. Shannon was in Johannesburg staying with her childhood friend Lauren, but would only be there for another ten days before she went back to Canada.

I don't know what exactly took over me at that moment, but I found myself inviting her to stay with me for her last week in the country, insisting she come back to Cape Town so that I could show her the sights. I noticed a hesitancy in her voice, and realised she was unable to change her plans. Shannon left for Canada as planned, but she did call me just before her departure to say goodbye and promised to keep in touch. I realised my chance to get to know this wonderful woman was evaporating, and I had done little to stop it. But I determined that I would write to her in the hope of keeping enough of a communication going to enable us to meet again.

I have been told many times that I am unrelenting, and I delivered on the promise I made to myself. She replied to every one of my letters or cards. In one of her letters she mentioned to me that a close friend had written to Mandela in 1993, telling him about her background and asking if he would consider sending her a note in honour of her twenty-first birthday. My old comrade Madiba replied a month later with belated birthday wishes in a letter that Shannon later framed. 'I understand that you are a South African who left with your parents when just 13 years old. So much has happened in South Africa in the last seven years that I wonder whether one day soon your parents and yourself might consider returning home. Although I can fully understand your parent's motivation in leaving, as South Africa moves into a new and very exciting period of our history, the birth of democracy, leading the way to a lengthy period of reconstruction and reconciliation, we will require all our youth and associated energy.'

This call to return home from the icon of the liberation struggle had become Shannon's driving mission, and it kept my hope alive that she would come back to South Africa. But sometimes we lose touch even with those we most want to communicate with, and for some time I never heard from her. That was until I received a call from her while I was attending the Commonwealth Heads of Government meeting in Durban. She was also there for the meeting and staying at the Elangeni Hotel. I was just around the corner and felt overcome with emotion at the thought of seeing her again. I rushed over to meet her without giving a thought to my attire or appearance. I must have looked a dreadful sight in my plain white, button-down work shirt that had a slight curry stain on it, no tie, and a hairstyle that long needed grooming. But she was overjoyed to see me and gave me a warm embrace.

We sat talking until we couldn't drink any more tea, and then went out to eat at my favourite Indian restaurant. She knew far more about Indian cuisine than I had anticipated, and regularly cooked curries for herself. We also spoke about her previous work trip with Doctors Without Borders in Southern Sudan. I thought this was very adventurous and admired her commitment to help vulnerable people.

As I proceeded to pay the bill after our feast, the waitress brought me a takeaway for home. Shannon asked why I wanted to eat a second dinner, and without thinking I said: 'This is for the woman I live with.' I saw a look of shock come over her face and I quickly caught myself. I was at pains to explain that I was lodging with my landlady Safura Khan, who wouldn't take a dime for the accommodation. We chuckled and I dropped her back at the Elangeni Hotel, promising to see her in the morning, as she was due to leave the following night.

We talked for hours the next day, all about my childhood, her childhood, and the things that inspired us. Shannon and I could have talked the whole day, but out of the blue my brother Essop called. It was very sad news: my mother had passed away. I had to race to take care of preparations for her funeral, as in the Muslim tradition we are obligated to bury the deceased before the sun goes down on the same day. Shannon looked on as I sped away in my little Toyota Corolla. Once again, Shannon went one way and I the other, for later that day she boarded a plane to visit Nigeria and Senegal. The parting was painful for me, even though Shannon vowed to call me as soon as she could.

Fourteen days after my mother died, another major tragedy befell our family – my beloved brother Gora passed away from what we believed was a heart attack. That flattened me. It was only eight years since we had been able to start rebuilding our relationship. He met his end far too early in life, at the age of sixty-three, and left us all in a terrible state. More than anyone else, it was Gora who would bring the extended family together, remember birthdays and entrench our bonds.

Shannon could sense that I was breaking under the strain of my grief, and she contacted me regularly to console me. That went on for many months and this was how our love story began. She eventually came to live with me in South Africa in December 2000, and so began a new life for me, with a woman thirty-five years younger than I was. I had never been happier.

For sixty-three years of my life, I had been beholden to no one but my organisation, the ANC, and I had never had to consider anyone in making my personal decisions. Now, I had a serious life partner, who had moved

A great love story begins

continents and given up her career to be with me. When I introduced Shannon to Madiba, he warmly welcomed her back home, and jokingly said, as he had often done in the past, 'If Ebie is to ever marry, the woman will have to ask him!'

My relationship with Shannon was quickly put under strain by the fact that I moved constantly between Cape Town, where I resided during parliamentary sittings, and Durban, where I had to do constituency work, in addition to a gruelling international travel schedule. This did not leave us much time to be together, which was particularly hard for someone who had left her family, friends and professional life behind. She must have really loved me to stick it out, despite all the bumps in the road.

Six months into our new life together, Shannon accompanied me on a multiparty parliamentary delegation to Israel and Palestine. It was an eye-opening experience as we witnessed first-hand the daily oppression meted out against the Palestinians at check points, in refugee camps, and we saw families sitting in the rubble of their demolished homes where they had lost everything. Our multi-party delegation met with Chairman Yasser Arafat at his compound in Ramallah, although he was noticeably unwell at the time. On our visit to Israel, we had met with Shimon Peres who was Minister of Foreign Affairs at the time, and also visited the Yad Vashem holocaust museum which was deeply emotional.

It was not my first visit to the Holy Land as I had travelled there in the late 1990s with my good friend Mohammed Dangor when we had been sent by the ANC on a fact-finding mission. Mohammed went on to become our ambassador in Syria and Libya, and we remained close friends. I have great respect for the Dangor family, and have also been close to Mohammed's sister Jessie Duarte, who later became the deputy secretary-general of the ANC.

At the end of our first year together, Shannon and I went on an adventure in the land of my forefathers. I had been to India before on an official visit and had been escorted around and stayed in good hotels as an official guest, but this time I wanted to experience the way ordinary people lived. I don't know if third-class travel was exactly what Shannon had in mind, but we traversed the state of Rajasthan by bus, on third-class trains and by car.

Udaipur was very romantic with its hotels in the style of the maharajas.

We would sit on the rooftop and listen to local musicians playing the sitar and tabla, the most beloved music of my life drifting into the night air. This was a very happy time for me. We then embarked on a three-day camel safari in the great Thar desert. The quietness of the desert was magnificent to experience. Our ninety-year-old camel driver could only motion to us as he spoke no English.

That night, we enjoyed a traditional Indian meal with chapati cooked over an open fire on the dunes. All was well until we began to feel the winter wind picking up. We signalled to the camel driver that we wanted to set up our tent as darkness had descended and the cold was beginning to bite. He took out two dirty green sleeping bags and threw them down on a sand dune, indicating to us that we must go and sleep. Dismayed, we insisted he take out a tent, only to discover that there were no tents. All we had was the sand with no protection from the night wind.

To this day, I can attest that this was the longest night of my life: longer than any night spent on the cold cement floor on Robben Island. The wind howled all around us, and I began to worry that there was no way I would survive. Shannon started panicking and took out every bit of clothing she had packed for the three days and wrapped them around me – woollen socks on my hands, extra sweatshirts wrapped around my head – but still we shivered uncontrollably within our awful sleeping bags. Then, I looked up at the night sky. I had never seen such a sight. There were literally millions of dazzling stars in the overwhelming galaxy hanging above our heads. To experience the Milky Way in this way was the closest I had ever felt to heaven.

Unfortunately, the night got worse. I saw huge dune beetles emerging out of the desert sand as the darkness deepened and watched in horror as the creatures started crawling all over our sleeping bags. I placed my sock-covered hands over my face and prayed that somehow the night would be over. I still don't quite know how we survived, but the next morning I could hardly move my limbs. It was as if they had been frozen solid. As the sun came up over the desert and warmed us, we defrosted. I made it quite clear that I would be going no further and insisted on riding back to our 4x4. The only problem was that I was so stiff that I simply could not get my leg over the camel. Frustrated and exhausted, I had no choice but to walk my camel all the way back to our vehicles.

Thirty-five
Making a home

AS MUCH AS SHANNON AND I were committed to each other, our careers were such that we became like ships passing in the night. Shannon had taken on the position of deputy director of the Institute for Global Dialogue (the organisation through which we initially met) and she developed an equally demanding international travel schedule of her own. I was always running between parliamentary sessions, attending to the demands of my constituency, and representing the ANC and parliament abroad. Something had to give.

Just as we were beginning to wonder how we were going to manage, Deputy President Jacob Zuma asked me to become his political and economic adviser. This paved a way for us to finally think of developing a real family life together in Gauteng. We first stayed in a small thatched house in Sunninghill, north of Sandton in Johannesburg. Ironically, it was in close proximity to Leeuwkop Prison, where I had first been so brutalised after my arrest for sabotage in 1963.

After a burglary in which our lives were put at risk, we decided to relocate to Pretoria. The move made sense as I was then working at the Union Buildings. We sought out the most protective environment possible, and settled in a security estate in Pretoria East. There was something uncomfortable about living among the wealthy with their luxury cars, boats and golf carts. But we found a cosy Mexican-style home with a front wall painted in Ndebele design in bright primary colours. Shortly after we moved in, a woman walking by remarked to me that she always called our place the 'Madiba house'. It seemed we had found our home.

Six months before we moved in, I asked Shannon to marry me and so proved Madiba wrong in his prediction that a woman would have to propose to me! The wedding was set for September 2004 at Gallagher Estate in Midrand, and we were finally married at a very emotional ceremony presided over by my Robben Island comrade, Reverend Stanley Magoba. He was a member of the PAC, but we had always been great friends, and I knew he would do me this great honour. Family and friends came to celebrate with us from many parts of the world. Also in attendance were Mama Winnie Mandela and her daughter Zindzi, as well as a number of revolutionaries from our movement, including Ronnie, Kathy, Squire, Albie, Sunny, the Pahad brothers, and comrades from the various chapters of my life. It was a day of days. One of my friends remarked that I was 'Mr Colgate' that night, as I never stopped smiling.

We decided to postpone our honeymoon for a few months until December, as Shannon had just started a new job as the director of international relations and trade in the Presidency. My old friend and comrade Eleanor Kasrils strongly recommended that we go to Phuket in Thailand for our honeymoon, specifically to the resort called the Chedi, which she and Ronnie had stayed at and enjoyed. So we made reservations and booked air tickets for that Christmas.

It must have been by God's grace, for at the last minute we were persuaded by Mumtaz, a Ugandan friend on a diplomatic posting in South Africa, to change our plans and visit her in Kampala before she was re-posted to London. Mumtaz organised for us to go gorilla trekking, which was very fortunate as it was difficult to secure tickets, and usually one had to book six months in advance. We figured the beach in Phuket would always be there for a holiday at another time.

On 26 December, as we were relaxing in Kampala, having had the experience of a lifetime in the jungles on the border between Uganda and the Congo on Christmas Day, we turned on the TV to see the shocking scenes of the tsunami engulfing the beach resorts in Phuket. Friends called us in a panic from Johannesburg to tell us that *The Star* had a front-page picture of a wall of water crashing into the Chedi, the very resort we had planned to stay at. One cannot help reflecting on how fortunate we were not to have gone there.

I do have to note, though, that gorilla trekking at the age of sixty-seven is not recommended. I had been to the gym to prepare and bought proper hiking boots, but it was a torturous eight-hour hike. We travelled twelve hours by car from Kampala on treacherous roads to get to the starting point, from where we would trek in groups of six, given the vulnerability of the endangered gorillas to human colds and flu. The arrangement was that we would walk until we found a family of gorillas, spend an hour with them, and then trek back. It was a truly memorable trip, though I hadn't expected the terrain to be quite so rugged. Our guides had to cut through thick virgin jungle with panga knives. As we had to cross rivers and mossy bridges, we hired two porters each to assist us.

As it turned out, the group of gorillas we were supposed to be tracking had crossed over into the Congo. Since there was no kind of border marking or fence, we could cross into Congo to look for them. We had a photographer from *National Geographic* in our group who had been on countless such treks, but the group of gorillas we ended up finding had his jaw dropping. He said it was the best sighting he had had in ten years. Shannon thought it might have something to do with the magic of Christmas Day. We managed to catch an entire family in a sunny clearing; the silverback was lying down and his youngsters were playing and swinging from branch to branch around him. It was a truly serene scene, and we were able to stand and watch them for an hour before we had to turn back.

The trek was hazardous. At one point the porters were holding both my arms and helping me cross a river by moving from one giant boulder to the next. The river was flowing fast, and before I knew it I had fallen in, despite the support of the porters. I was drenched – and we still had another five or six hours of hiking to go. Wet and exhausted, I jokingly told Shannon that it was time to get a divorce.

Thirty-six
Revolutionaries never retire

ONE OF THE MOST VALUABLE experiences in my professional life has been my foray into the world of conflict resolution. I had been working as Deputy President Jacob Zuma's political and economic adviser since 2002, and we had been deeply involved for a few years in mediating in the Burundi peace process.

As president, Nelson Mandela had succeeded in brokering a power-sharing agreement between the Hutu and Tutsi political parties in August 2000. The rebels, however, did not take part in the peace process and fighting had continued. It was now up to the new administration of President Thabo Mbeki to ensure that Mandela's legacy in Burundi would remain intact. Mbeki delegated the responsibility of mediating between the various antagonists in Burundi to his deputy president, who had proven himself an adept mediator in the political violence in KwaZulu-Natal during the negotiation process. Zuma was a people's person and related well to all the parties involved in Burundi, who believed he had the political gravitas and respect to negotiate a compromise between themselves.

What impressed me immensely was the way in which Zuma would mediate throughout the night without any sleep, in order to bring the parties to a common agreement. This would be replicated in one trip after another to Bujumbura, and I ended up being as exhausted as he was, as I was always expected to be at his side during these ongoing sessions. Even though Zuma had no formal education, he succeeded in bringing peace between the Burundian factions after seventeen international peace processes had failed. That was no small feat. Zuma brokered a number of ceasefire deals between the rebels and the government and managed to get the parties to agree to the Pretoria Accord in July 2004. This success entrenched Zuma's reputation as an effective mediator on the African continent.

It was during those years that I developed an understanding of what makes mediation successful. I learnt a great deal from the strategy and tactics of my former cellmate. These experiences stood me in good stead when I participated in mediation efforts in other conflicts around the world, alongside Roelf Meyer. Roelf had been the deputy minister of law and order in 1986 during the state of emergency, at the time I had been abducted from Swaziland. This made us natural enemies in the eyes of many South Africans, but our ability to move past our difficult history and collaborate in conflict resolution proved inspiring to many.

In 2002 the South African government sent Roelf Meyer and me to Palestine on a scoping visit to understand the situation on the ground. Roelf and I met President Yasser Arafat and other Palestinian leaders. The words of Shimon Peres that I recalled from my meeting with him on my previous visit were uppermost in my mind. Peres had said that the Palestinian issue was for him a moral dilemma, as never in the history of the Jewish people had they ever ruled over or oppressed another people. Such honesty from an Israeli leader surprised me at the time, and during every subsequent visit to the region those words echoed in my head. The Israeli–Palestinian conflict may never be satisfactorily resolved, but as peace-makers we have always been willing to try to bring the sides together and see if they can find a common and just approach to the way forward.

It was on our mission to Palestine that Roelf mentioned to me that he was involved in peace negotiations in Sri Lanka and requested that I join him on his next visit, which I readily agreed to do. That was the first of many visits I was to make to Sri Lanka with Roelf to share with the various parties there the South African experience of negotiations, transitional justice, and reconciliation, in the hope of bringing peace to that troubled island nation.

My first visit with Roelf to Sri Lanka took place one year after the signing of a ceasefire between the Sri Lankan government and the Liberation Tigers of Tamil Eelam (LTTE). We met with the government and civil society groups but were unable to meet the LTTE.

On a subsequent visit we ventured into the unknown to meet the LTTE in their stronghold. From Colombo we flew to Jaffna, the capital city of the country's most northern province, and from there we travelled by road to Kilinochchi, an area controlled by the minority Tamils, who had been fighting for an independent homeland since 1983. We were entering an area that few foreigners had ever seen.

In entering the Tamil-controlled area, we had to go through a border gate controlled by the Sri Lankan government, then through no man's land, and finally through another border gate controlled by the LTTE. On the other side was Kilinochchi, a vibrant Tamil city with shops, restaurants and temples. The founder and leader of the LTTE was Velupillai Prabhakaran, whose whereabouts were shrouded in secrecy. He lived in an underground bunker in the jungle, as the army had pursued him throughout the jungles of the north and east for decades. He and his fellow Tamil Tiger fighters each wore a cyanide capsule around their neck in case they were ever captured by the Sri Lankan army. The conflict had been long and bloody, with the Tamils using guerrilla tactics in their struggle for independence.

We were not able to see Prabhakaran for security reasons, but we did meet the political head of the LTTE, Suppayya Paramu Thamilselvan, who gave us a briefing about the recent ceasefire and an assessment of the political dynamics on the ground. We were warmly welcomed and fed a sumptuous lunch, which I thoroughly enjoyed, as I grew up eating Tamil curries in Durban. Thamilselvan held the view that South Africa could play a role in bringing about a peaceful resolution to the conflict. During this meeting, the LTTE made a formal request that the ANC assist in paving the way to peace in Sri Lanka. "The ANC has managed to transform from a military organisation into a political one, and we require such assistance as we move forward in the negotiation process. We have studied the South African model of governance and feel we can utilise such a federal model in our own country,' the secretary-general of the LTTE's Peace Secretariat said at the time.

Roelf and I were optimistic that a resolution to the conflict was possible, and we spent the next twelve years shuttling back and forth between South Africa and Sri Lanka in ongoing efforts to bring the two sides in the conflict closer together. We even invited the Tamil Tigers to South Africa in 2009 to impress upon them the need for peace and compromise.

After all those years invested in conflict resolution, when war broke out in 2015, the government massacred the entire upper echelon of the LTTE leadership on a beach after they had already surrendered. We were bitterly disappointed. Prabhakaran was killed with eighteen of his top leaders on 18 May in what everyone characterised as a cold-blooded massacre.

What followed was an even darker period in the history of the country. Thousands of Tamils were pushed into camps, many were severely tortured and killed. The horrendous details of what unfolded were later exposed by Yasmin Sooka, a former commissioner of the South African Truth and Reconciliation Commission, who served on the Panel of Experts advising the UN secretary-general on accountability for war crimes in Sri Lanka. As a result, she became a prime target of the Sri Lankan government.

My view is that the LTTE failed to use the ceasefire period to their advantage and that there was also a lack of commitment by the Sri Lankan government to seeking a solution to the Tamil question. Eventually the government sought a military solution and wiped out the resistance of the Tamil Tigers, in the process committing terrible crimes.

Roelf and I worked in other parts of the world. One of the most interesting and unusual places was Bolivia. The capital, La Paz, is situated on a high plateau and, because of the altitude, at times it is difficult to breathe. People in Bolivia have a natural remedy for altitude sickness, which is to drink coca tea made from the coca plant. From the airport we drove down into a deep valley and admired the homes built along the steep slopes of the valley. The indigenous people of Bolivia are particularly colourful in their traditional outfits, and they display an amazing range of arts and crafts.

We visited Bolivia in the middle of the most historic election campaign in the country's history. The leading candidate was Evo Morales, a charismatic indigenous leader. Morales was facing off against a formidable and well-resourced incumbent whose allegiance was to the wealthy and to the Americans. Morales represented a chance for real change in the country that would serve the people, and thus he presented a threat to the white elite. Roelf and I immediately hit it off with Morales when we met him. He struck us as an incredibly down-to-earth and genuine man of the people. He always wore his trademark blue, white and red jersey, even when he made trips abroad. He presented both of us with a similar jersey as souvenirs.

Our role in Bolivia was to share the South African experience of reconciliation and nation-building. We invited Morales to South Africa and he honoured the invitation soon after he won the presidential election in 2005. His election was a watershed moment for the region, as it marked the first electoral victory of an indigenous president in Latin America. Morales's supporters lauded him as a champion of indigenous rights, anti-imperialism and environmentalism, and while in office he stayed true to his left-wing agenda. Morales was credited with overseeing significant economic growth and poverty reduction, and his government was widely praised for increasing investment in schools, hospitals and infrastructure.

In the early part of his presidency, I led a delegation of the ANC alliance partners to Bolivia. Kgalema Motlanthe, secretary-general of the ANC, Blade Nzimande, general secretary of the Communist Party, and Zwelinzima Vavi, general secretary of COSATU, accompanied me on what was one of my most memorable trips abroad. When we arrived at the airport, we were greeted with garlands of fresh flowers, and Morales gave us an incredibly warm reception. As veterans of the left, we had certainly met our political soulmate.

Nepal was a place Shannon and I had dreamed of visiting, and we did in fact fulfil that dream at the end of our India tour in December 2001. Kathmandu has a magic all of its own, with its temples and famous white stupa in the centre of the city surrounded by multi-coloured prayer flags. We saw before us an enchanting scene as the Buddhist faithful walked round and round the stupa, spinning the ancient prayer wheels as they went. We also travelled by bus through the countryside to the lakeside town of Pokhara with its pristine lakes and snow-capped mountains. The town serves as a base for hikers setting off on their perilous journeys into the Himalayan mountains.

I never thought that seven years later I would be called upon to travel again to Nepal, but on a far more serious mission – to meet with seven opposition parties that were seeking the overthrow of the monarchy. Nepal was the only remaining Hindu kingdom in the world, with a king whom I considered particularly foolish. He involved himself in politics by disbanding parliament and the executive, and concentrated power in his hands.

Clandestinely, we held a three-day workshop in which I shared with the various parties how we in the ANC had been able to mobilise mass protests against the apartheid regime. On the third day, I was told that the palace had got to know of my presence and I had to leave immediately. But it seems the powers that be confused me with Lakhdar Brahimi, the former foreign minister of Algeria, who had also become involved in international conflict resolution efforts. Little did the palace know that the information I shared with the king's opposition ended up contributing to his subsequent demise. Within six months of my visit, King Gyanendra was deposed, and a republic established. I found myself once again being invited to Nepal to meet various political parties, including the ruling Nepalese Congress Party, the Communist Party, and the Maoists, among others. I shared with them our experience of transitioning to democracy.

To carry forward the conflict resolution work that Roelf and I had been involved in, we established a non-government organisation which we called In Transformation Initiative (ITI), of which I became the first patron and then one of the directors. Our team included Ivor Jenkins, who was formerly at IDASA, and Mohammed Bhabha, who had been with me in Parliament and then became a provincial minister in Mpumalanga. Together we formed a dynamic group. Later, Patience Zonge-Hwenha joined us. We carried out exciting missions, one of which was to travel to Bogota in Colombia and to Cuba to meet and discuss peace and reconciliation with the FARC rebels of Colombia. Our foray into the world of peace work on the African continent also took us to Madagascar, Zimbabwe, the Central African Republic, South Sudan and the Democratic Republic of the Congo.

Thirty-seven
Life starts at 70

I WANTED TO HAVE MORE children, even though age had caught up with me. Shannon was thirty-four and longed to have children of her own. I was somewhat concerned about how I would handle babies, but Shannon assured me that it would be the best thing that ever happened to me. It certainly was.

Shannon and I have always been very close friends with Albie Sachs and his wife Vanessa. When Albie, who was then about seventy, announced that Vanessa had fallen pregnant – beaming as he did so with excitement at the prospect of becoming a new dad – his good fortune gave me hope that there was still a chance for me to become a parent again.

Our daughter Sarah was born on 13 November 2006. Soon after she emerged into this world, the nurse handed her to me swaddled in blankets. I had never seen anything as exquisite as our tiny miracle. Nothing else measured up to that moment. The choice of her name was not only a way of honouring my Ma. Sarah is the name of the biblical wife of Abraham; the Hebrew word means 'princess'. In all three Abrahamic religions – Islam, Christianity and Judaism – Sarah is the 'mother of the nations'. We asked our close friend Devon Curtis, who is a lecturer in African politics at Cambridge University in the UK, to be Sarah's godmother. She is a fine example of the kind of person we would want our children to emulate.

When I turned seventy, not many months after Sarah's birth, Nelson Mandela invited us to tea with him at his office. He hugged our eight-month-old daughter, and was amazed that I had started a whole new life at that age. That warmth I knew so well made me almost believe this was a regular visit, even though it would be the last time that I was to sit down with him alone. He was just the same, joking about some of our comrades, commenting on those who had gained weight, and sharing affectionate stories about those who had been particularly close to his heart. He signed a photo album we had brought along with a gold pen. That is a cherished final memory of Comrade Mandela.

Not long after Sarah was born, having brought us everything we could have dreamed of, we decided that we very much wanted another child. It almost seemed too much to hope for at my age, but we had already managed to defeat the odds. The fact that I was seventy-one years old didn't faze me in the least, and when we finally got the news that a son was on the way, I looked forward to his arrival with all my heart. Never in my life did I ever think I would have a son. I was beaming with pride and imagining all the things my son and I would do together.

While Shannon was pregnant, we decided to do something quite untraditional and travel to Syria with little Sarah. As chair of the ANC's International Relations subcommittee, I was asked to accompany Secretary General Kgalema Motlanthe on a visit there. Our ambassador in Damascus Mohammed Dangor was thrilled to have us and went out of his way to take us to the ancient city of Maaloula where the inhabitants still speak Aramaic – the language Jesus Christ spoke. He also took us to see the ancient ruins in Palmyra which is near the border with Iraq and on a day trip to Beirut. The historical sites were fascinating.

A few months after our return, our son was born three weeks premature and had to be delivered by a Caesarean section. I donned a blue gown and head covering and entered the operating theatre to watch my son come into this world. I prayed hard until we saw our beautiful boy. We decided to name him Kadin, which in Arabic means 'friend' or 'companion'. Our house was again filled with fresh flowers and a stream of visitors. I was very protective of Kadin, as he was small and fragile, but he had a wonderful temperament and he kept me on my toes.

When Kadin was just a few months old, I was thrown into the 2009 election campaign, which involved criss-crossing the country on the campaign trail. As predicted, the ANC won a decisive victory and Jacob Zuma became president of the country. At that time, there were high hopes that he would prove to be a man of the people and ensure service delivery to the poorest of the poor. Zuma appointed me deputy minister of international relations and cooperation. Shannon was very happy for me to take on this position, but she was also worried about how I would manage to spend enough time with our two young children.

While most other members of Cabinet moved into houses provided by the state, we decided to stay in our own home and did not allow the state to pay for our utilities and security, as provided for in the ministerial handbook. It was a great benefit, though, to be given a driver by the state, as, at the age of seventy-two, it was becoming exhausting for me to drive to the many meetings and functions that my hectic schedule included. We were expected to be in Parliament from Tuesday to Friday, and with the constant overseas official visits on top of that, I never felt I had enough time to spend with my family.

But the experience of representing our country overseas and defending our foreign policy was deeply rewarding. In my first year as deputy minister in 2009 I had the opportunity of delivering a statement on behalf of South Africa at the UN Security Council on post-conflict peacebuilding. It was exciting being involved in diplomacy at that level. One of the highlights of my term was in 2012 when I presided over the UN Security Council meeting in New York on the situation in the Middle East when South Africa held the presidency of the Security Council. The meeting focused on the occupied Palestinian territories and attempts to resuscitate peace talks, which was a subject that mattered a great deal to me.

At the end of my term as deputy minister, I was appointed as parliamentary counsellor to the president, and so I went back to Parliament for a final stint of five years in 2014 at the age of seventy-six. Most people felt I should have retired long before and taken the opportunity to relax, but my constant refrain was that 'revolutionaries never retire'. I didn't relish the idea of sitting at home and watching TV every day to pass the time, and there was still so much work to be done in the country. But the weekly flights up and down to Cape Town were certainly tiring, and by the end of that term, I decided not to stand for Parliament again and to rather focus on conflict resolution work. That gave me a great sense of purpose: to try to make peace in troubled places.

The one place I had always wanted to take my children was to visit my father's village in Gujarat, India. I am fortunate to have had the opportunity to visit the village of Chasa in 2008. It was one of those 'hard to forget' moments when the chief counsellor and magistrate received me on my arrival with garlands of fresh flowers as if the 'village boy' was returning home. That was a very special moment for me. I was taken to the house where my father was born and was struck by its simplicity with a large cow standing outside the front door. I was hosted for lunch by our extended family whom I had never met before.

The reason why I had never attempted to make the journey before was the complicated instructions from my family as to how to get there. My brother had told me that I would have to take a train from Mumbai to Billamoria station in the state of Gujarat, and from there take a bus to Chasa. Once in Chasa, I would have to contact the postmaster who knew all the people in the village, and he would direct me to the home of my relatives. I doubted I would ever arrive at my destination!

In 2013, I was invited by the Government of India to visit Kochi in the state of Kerala to receive the prestigious Pravasi Bharatiya Samman Award, which was conferred on me by the President of India, Shri Pranab Mukherjee, on 9 January. The award is presented annually to persons of Indian origin living outside India who have contributed to its growth and prestige. The 9th of January was chosen as symbolic, to commemorate the return of Mahatma Gandhi from South Africa to India in 1915. My comrades Kathy Kathrada and Billy Nair had received the award in years before me, and my close friend and comrade, Ela Gandhi, the granddaughter of the Mahatma, received it the year after me. Ela and I worked closely together in Durban to promote the peaceful resolution of conflicts. Shannon went with me to India to receive the award. We especially loved floating down the interconnecting canals throughout Kerala on a house boat. The waterways have a gentle magic of their own.

Just over two years later, I was greatly honoured with yet another award from a foreign country, this time from Spain's King Felipe VI, who bestowed a knighthood on me when awarding me one of Spain's highest honours, the Order of Civil Merit. Kadin, who was six years old at the time, tried to convince me that knights didn't exist anymore, and that the king of Spain couldn't possibly make me a knight commander. 'I will only believe it if you have a sword,' he told me.

This was an unexpected honour, and I was humbled by the recognition. I had always operated as part of a collective and saw myself as a foot soldier of the ANC. Being knighted by a foreign country for my role in our struggle caught me by surprise. But the most important of the awards that I have received and cherish are the three medals given to me by the South African National Defence Force and the Umkhonto we Sizwe Military Veterans Association. Behind those medals and awards lie the struggle and the sacrifice of many of our people.

Thirty-eight
Celebrating life at a time of loss

WHILE WE WERE ON a visit to Myanmar in December 2013, Shannon was awoken by the incessant ringing of the telephone in our hotel room, only to receive the heart-breaking news that our beloved Madiba had passed away. It was a difficult moment to bear. We watched on the international news channels the outpouring of grief around the world. It was strange to be so far away from the mourning at home. We knew that every great person has to face their end, but somehow Nelson Mandela had seemed invincible. With his passing, it was now up to us, Madiba's foot soldiers, to carry the torch of reconciliation and nation-building in his absence. It would not be an easy task, as economic liberation is a monumental challenge that will take decades to realise.

Madiba's memorial service at the soccer stadium in Soweto was one of the largest gatherings of world leaders ever. It was also the largest memorial service in the history of South Africa, and of the African continent itself. It brought together a host of dignitaries, including two UN secretary-generals, both presidents of the European Union, two French presidents, four US presidents (Barack Obama, Bill Clinton, George W Bush and Jimmy Carter) and four British prime ministers (David Cameron, Gordon Brown, Tony Blair and John Major). We travelled to Madiba's rural home in Qunu in the Eastern Cape for his funeral. It was a grand send-off for a man who epitomised the triumph of the human spirit.

We didn't anticipate that over the next seven years we would lose so many stalwarts, including Ahmed Kathrada, Denis Goldberg, John Nkadimeng, Winnie Mandela, George Bizos and Andrew Mlangeni among many others.

Kathy had been a close friend of mine, and I was devastated by the loss. Just months before his passing he had insisted on being involved in choosing the venue for my eightieth birthday party which the Kathrada Foundation was hosting, but sadly he passed away just weeks before the event. It was a wonderful occasion which brought together so many of my struggle comrades with Hélène Passtoors even flying in from Belgium. Anant Singh had produced a surprise 12-minute video of my life, which carried wonderful footage taken by Liz Fish after my release from Robben Island in 1991. I greatly enjoyed the special dance performance performed by the Tribhangi dance troupe, which was a fusion of Indian and African dance routines. But best of all was the rap which my children performed about my life which will forever live on Youtube. Comrade Winnie Mandela had sat next to me that evening, but little did I know that it would be the last time I would see her as she passed away nine months later.

In 2020 the Covid-19 pandemic also took its toll on us. We lost many of our freedom fighters and activists along the way. It pained me that my two children, Sarah and Kadin, sacrificed so much so that I would stay safe from the virus. Sarah refused to go to school in person for 22 months, even when the rest of her classmates had gone back physically. Kadin spent endless hours in conversation with me at home about world events, and watching cricket and rugby. Both children, as well as Shannon gave up a lot to protect me. This I accept as testimony of their love for me.

It was to my great sorrow that in August 2020 my beloved younger brother Essop succumbed to complications associated with the virus and passed away at Morningside Hospital in Johannesburg. He fought hard for eleven weeks on a ventilator, but in the end blood clots in the brain caused a series of strokes. His death broke our family, and we have never been the same since. His passing left our beloved Fatima alone, and she suffered with great sorrow. Essop was our light. He was my rock.

At the age of fourteen, he had to leave school and go out to work to support our parents. My mother took the view that the education of her two older sons had only led to their involvement in politics, which had resulted in their leaving the family and going into prison or exile. So Essop was to keep out of politics, leave school and go to work. He did so willingly, and often held down two jobs in the early years. He and Fatima struggled financially as a young married couple, but their love was stronger than their circumstances, and in the end Essop became the most financially successful of all of us brothers.

Thirty-nine
Closing the circle

THE YEAR 2021 TURNED out to be agonising. When I was first diagnosed with lung cancer, I couldn't believe it. None of us could believe it. A number of oncologists asked me if I had ever smoked, as Adeno Carcinoma is usually a disease that befalls smokers, but I had never smoked in my life. But the more I pondered the matter, I remembered how during those fifteen years on Robben Island when I had to share a cell with over sixty other inmates, a number of them smoked and it was always a battle to get them to open the windows due to the cold Cape wind. There had also been the hazardous conditions in the quarry where we constantly inhaled dust while breaking stones.

The surgery I underwent in April, when half of my right lung had to be removed, was the most physically painful ordeal I have ever experienced. Many ribs were broken accidentally during the course of the surgery, and the recovery was slow and long. The doctors were against giving me either chemotherapy or radiation given my age.

I was looked after over many months by a very caring pulmonologist, Dr Ismail Hassan, the grandson of Comrade Molvi Cachalia, who is based at the Heart Hospital in Pretoria. This is the same hospital where Mandela had spent many weeks towards the end of his life. I am also grateful for the constant care of our helper Angela who has been an angel to our family over the past eleven years.

Shannon and my two children have been there for me every day, and I could never have endured this ordeal without them. One of them accompanied me for a daily walk in our complex, until I was no longer able to walk due to a lack of oxygen. The family has sat with me while I watched the news and worked hard to finish this book, which is my gift to all those I leave behind. These simple things that were done for me in the twilight of my life have meant the most to me. Thank you for making my life complete, for giving me the family that I had always yearned for, and for closing the circle.

I am so grateful that we have had so many wonderful memories as a family, and that my dream of taking my own family on the Glacier express train to the snowy mountain village of Zermatt was realised just after my eightieth birthday. Watching you toboggan down the snowy slopes, slipping our way through an ice palace, and sharing fondue together in the alps were unforgettable memories.

I have no regrets and I remain an optimist. I believe that South Africa will emerge stronger and more resilient from its present crisis, as it has done before. We have been through far worse and triumphed over adversity. Now is the time that we need to pull together and unite as a nation.

I often remember Louis Armstrong's song 'What a Wonderful World'. It is, indeed, a wonderful world. Sarah and Kadin, you are fortunate that you live in a free and democratic country, with a great deal of diversity. I have always told you that the world is a beautiful place because of the diversity within it. It's a world of different racial groups and people of different colours. There are many different languages and customs, ways of dressing, and a great variety of music and dancing. People enjoy different types of cuisine and have different forms of celebration. This is what makes our world such a beautiful place. South Africa is a microcosm of the world. Diversity brings richness to our country, and we need to enjoy living in such a country.

On Robben Island, we envisioned a 'new' South Africa. We were going to be the servants of the people. We were steadfastly against corruption, factionalism and ill-discipline. We condemned greed and the accumulation of wealth as we imbibed the values of comrades like Ahmed Kathrada, Harry Gwala, Stephen Dlamini, Zola Nqini, Reggie Vandeyar and others.

These values have become eroded, but we must struggle to return to our core principles and the reasons why we took up the greatest fight of all.

One of my favourite quotes is from the great writer Nikolai Ostrovsky. I have tried to live my life by this creed. 'Man's dearest possession is life. It is given to him but once, and he must live it so as to feel no torturing regrets for wasted years, never know the burning shame of a mean and petty past; so live that, dying, he might say: all my strength was given to the finest cause in all the world – the fight for the liberation of mankind.'

To succeed, we can never allow fear to get the better of us. We must essentially be 'beyond fear'.

Notes

1 https://www.sahistory.org.za/sites/default/files/RakometsiMS.pdf.
2 From Vinay Lal, 'Mandela, Luthuli and Mandela, Luthuli, and Nonviolence in the South African Freedom Struggle', *Ufahamu: A Journal of African Studies*, 2014, https://escholarship.org/content/qt5r64v5qg/qt5r64v5qg.pdf?t=ngmi79.
3 Read further about Jean Amery's philosophy here: https://www.dissentmagazine.org/article/what-the-holocaust-meant-the-thinking-of-primo-levy-and-jean-amery.
4 https://www.theguardian.com/world/2017/aug/10/robben-island-prison-south-africa.
5 You can read the whole transcript here: justice.gov.za/trc/hrvtrans/submit/anc2.htm.
6 Read more in Mac's paper at https://www.tandfonline.com/doi/full/10.1080/02582473.2018.1435732 and https://www.marxists.org/subject/africa/anc/1979/green-book.htm.
7 Vladimir Shubin, *ANC: A View from Moscow* (Cape Town, 2008).
8 Edwin T Smith, a Rutgers graduate schooled at SOMAFCO, recalls: 'By 1989, [it] was a complete settlement with a hospital, factories, a farm, maternity settlement, a creche, primary and secondary schools and an adult education programme. 'Suburbs' housing volunteers, teachers and the community surrounded [it]. In 1984, the Tanzanian government provided the ANC with [more] land in Dakawa.' Today, SOMAFCO is a College of Science and Technology. See https://www.news24.com/news24/SouthAfrica/News/or-tambo-dreamt-big-20171021.
9 Mohamed Cassim wrote in 'Detention and torture without trial: Section 29 of the Internal Security Act', *National Black Law Journal*, 1987: 'Section 29 ... grants broad discretion to make warrantless arrests and detain persons for interrogation who are suspected of terrorist activity. [It] does not prescribe any

time [and the prisoner remains] incommunicado.' See https://escholarship.org/content/qt9n14b6wb/qt9n14b6wb.pdf?t=nrwrbb.
10 Carmel Rickard, 'Back inside: The man in the hospital ward', *Weekly Mail*, 26 June 1987.
11 https://www.aljazeera.com/features/2020/4/20/death-on-the-10th-floor-the-search-for-truth-in-south-africa.
12 'Between 1961 and 1989, about 134 political prisoners were executed by the apartheid government at Pretoria Central Prison ... Two decades in particular – the 1960s and the 1980s – witnessed many political executions. While Pretoria Central prison was the main site for executions, it was not the only facility in the country to enact these murderous acts. See https://www.sahistory.org.za/article/political-executions-south-africa-apartheid-government-1961-1989.
13 David Beresford, 'South Africa's reluctant "terrorist" awaits sentence in Treason Trial', *Weekly Mail*, 16 January 1988.
14 https://www.washingtonpost.com/archive/politics/1989/01/17/s-africa-sentences-3-guerrillas/36f4d308-a4b4-454b-a8c1-8b0cc66b6c75/.
15 https://www.sahistory.org.za/archive/opening-address-ancs-48th-national-conference-o-r-tambo-durban-2-july-1991.

Index

90-day law *see* General Law Amendment Act, 1963
AbaseMakolweni 48
Aboobaker, Rashid 143, 144, 167
Abrahams, Archie (Billy Whitehead) 163
Acacia Park, Cape Town 253
Advance 45
African Bathing Beach 18 *see also* Laguna Beach
African Communist 53, 139
African National Congress (ANC) 2, 8, 9, 18, 27, 31–33, 35, 37, 39–42, 46–51, 54, 55, 57–59, 61, 63, 68, 73, 75, 88, 93, 99, 119–124, 130–133, 138–145, 147–148, 151–156, 159, 161, 162, 164–165, 167, 170, 172, 173–174, 177, 181–182, 183–185, 187, 196, 210, 213, 217–220, 224, 230, 232–237, 243–247, 249–255, 260, 261, 263, 269, 271, 272, 274, 275, 277
African People's Organisation (APO) 37
African Resistance Movement (ARM) 71
Afrikaner Weerstandsbeweging (AWB) 219, 226, 245
Afro-Asian Journalists Association 158
Agra 24

AI Kajee Hall 40
Akashvani 157
Alexander, Neville 85
Alexander, Ray 153
Alexander, Ray 153, 236
Algeria 1, 61, 73
Algerian National Liberation Front 61
Alipore 25
All India Radio 157
All-African Convention 37
All-India Peace and Solidarity Organisation 174
American Committee on Africa 174
Amery, Jean 78
ANC Women's League 244
ANC Youth League 32, 244
Angola 25, 145, 148, 154, 155, 157, 184, 215
Appellate Division, Supreme Court 239
Arafat, President Yasser 158, 261, 268
Area Political Military Councils (APMCs) 140
Arenstein, Jacqueline 58
Arenstein, Rowley 50, 57–58, 62, 82, 101
Askari: A Story of Collaboration and Betrayal in the Anti-Apartheid Struggle 162
Asmal, Kader 10, 236

Asmal, Louise 236
Asoka Hotel, Reservoir Hills 137
At the Mind's Limits 78
Avalon, The 3, 19
Azad, Maulana Kalam 28
Azanian People's Organisation (AZAPO) 247
Babenia, Natvarlal 'Natoo' 64, 66, 68, 85
Back Beach 18 *see also* Ocean Beach
Badsha, Naseema 10, 236
Badsha, Omar 10, 236
Baiju Bawra 3, 20
Bareen *see* Ebrahim, Moosa
Barnard, Niël 191, 233, 240
Battle of Cato Manor 31
Bay, the *see* Swaziland
BBC 157, 254
Beijing 158
Beirut 274
Bengal 24
Berea 3, 20, 39, 81
Berea Road Station, Durban 39
Berlin Wall 237
Bernstein, Lionel 'Rusty' 74
Bethal, Transvaal 46
Beyond Fear: Ebrahim Ismael Ebrahim versus the Apartheid State 239
Bhabha, Mohammed 202, 272
Bhana, Surendra 31
Bhushan, Bharat 3, 20
Big Daddy 19
Bischoff, Corinne 188, 219, 250, 189
Bizos, George 280
Black Consciousness 130, 131, 136, 147, 164, 245
Black Pimpernel *see* Mandela, Nelson
Blair, Tony 279
Bluff, Durban 65, 80
Bolivia 270–271
Bolshevik Revolution, The 115
Bon Chance club 3, 20
Boon, Rudi 219, 220
Bose, Subhas Chandra 28
Botha, Pik 188, 210, 252

Botha, President PW 138, 174, 175, 181, 201, 209, 234
Botswana 151, 161, 174
Boxer (warder) 102
Braam, Conny 183–185, 236
Brand, Christo 226
Brey, Zubeida 24, 235–236, 254
Britain 28, 29, 175
British Council of Churches 174
British Empire 54
British Labour Party 174
Brown, Gordon 279
Bryntirion, Pretoria 7
Bujumbura 267
Burger, Die 130
Burundi 267–268
Bush, George W 219, 279
Buthelezi, Chief Mangosuthu 58
Cachalia, Molvi 283
Calcutta 24
Cambridge University 273
Cameron, David 279
Camp Viana, Angola 145, 154, 156
Carlisle Street, Durban 54
Carolus, Cheryl 255
Carter, Jimmy 279
Cassim, Ahmed 199
Cato Manor 30, 31, 55 *see also* Umkhumbane
Caxito 156
Cele, Grace 139, 140, 188
Central African Republic 272
Central Political Education Committee 232
Chasa 25, 276
Chaskalson, Arthur 234
Chief *see* Luthuli, Chief Albert
Chikane, Moses 'Moss' 220, 230
China 57, 88, 255
Chinese Communist Party (CCP) 57, 255
Chirwa, James 128
Chongella Farm, Zambia 81
Church Square 222
Clairwood Indian High School 69

Clairwood, Durban 67
Clinton, Bill 279
Coetsee, Kobie 233, 252
Colombia 272
Colombo 269
Coloured House of Representatives 138
Columbia University, New York 107
Commonwealth Heads of Government 259
Communist Party of South Africa (CPSA) 29
Communist Party of the Soviet Union (CPSU) 59
Community Agency for Social Enquiry 224
Companion of OR Tambo Award 210
Comrade MD *see* Naicker, MD
Comrade T-Man 156 *see also* Pule, Ernest
Congress Alliance 120
Congress of Democrats 42, 93
Congress of the People 41
Convention for a Democratic South Africa (CODESA) 247, 250–251
Cornforth, Maurice 124
Cowley House, Woodstock 10
CR Swart, Durban 178–179
Crimson League 3, 19–21
Cronje, Jack 192–193
Cry, the Beloved Country 40
Cuba 62, 68, 142, 155, 272
Curries Fountain 46
Curtis, Devon 273
Curtis, Jeanette *see* Schoon, Jeanette
Czechoslovakia 88, 184
Dadoo, Dr Yusuf 29, 32, 61, 138, 153
Dakawa, Tanzania 218
Daliet (no surname) 24
Dangor, Mohammed 261, 274
Daniels, Justice Hekkie 215, 241
Dar es Salaam 157–158
Das Kapital 125
Davids, Cynthia 236
Day of the Covenant, The 63
De Jonge, Klaas 167, 181, 183, 205–206
De Kock, Eugene 164, 191, 217
Deadly Ethnic Riot, The 30
Deetlefs, Nicolas 13, 195–199, 206–208, 210–211, 219, 224, 226
Defend Free Speech Convention 32
Defiance Campaign, 1952 29, 35, 41, 161
Delmas 215
Delmas Treason Trial 220, 221, 230
Democratic Republic of the Congo 167, 264, 265, 272
Dhlomo, Mapiki 230
Dhlomo, Sibongiseni 230
Dialectical Materialism 124
Dikeledi, Paul 141, 187, 220
Dingane, King 63
Dittrich, Boris 219
Dladla, Simon 163, 202, 213–216, 225, 229
Dlamini, Jacob 162
Dlamini, Stephen 4, 61, 81, 120, 121, 122, 123, 284
Dlamini-Zuma, Nkosazana 169, 171
Dlangamandla, Raymond 145
Doctors Without Borders 259
Doctors' Pact 32
Documentary History of Indian South Africans 31
Dolny, Helena 184
Drum magazine 20
Du Plessis, Sergeant 101–102
Duarte, Jessie (Dangor) 261
Duma, Bafana 75
Duma, Tsarist Russia 57
Durban Central Prison 64, 84, 136
Durban, South Africa 2, 3, 8, 18, 19, 21, 23, 24, 25, 28, 29, 30, 32, 36, 39, 40, 41, 45, 46, 47, 48, 49, 50, 53, 54, 55, 63, 64, 65, 66, 67, 68, 69, 74, 75, 76, 80, 82, 84, 91, 101, 107, 109, 110, 111, 112, 113, 129, 131, 135, 136, 138, 145, 156, 163, 171–172, 175, 177, 178, 202, 223, 230, 236, 244, 245, 246, 252, 258, 259, 261, 276

Dutch Anti-Apartheid Movement 174, 183, 219
Dutcheens 3, 20
Dutt, Geeta 157
East Germany 216
East Timor 255
Eastern Transvaal 191, 213
Ebrahim, Enver 178
Ebrahim, Essop 36, 111, 158, 169, 178, 200, 202, 243, 260, 280–281
Ebrahim, Fatima 169, 178
Ebrahim, Gora 36, 47, 48, 49, 51, 90, 157, 158, 223, 246, 254, 260
Ebrahim, Kadin 5, 7, 274, 277, 280, 284
Ebrahim, Nazeem 178
Ebrahim, Saleem 178
Ebrahim, Sarah 5, 7, 25, 273–274, 280, 284
Ebrahim, Shannon 5, 210, 257–252, 263–265, 271, 273–276, 279, 280, 284
Ebrahim, Yasir 158, 169, 250
Ebrahim, Zareena 169, 250
Eduardo Mondlane University 167, 184
Effingham 14, 23–25, 251
Effingham's quarry 23
Erasmus, Paul 209
Essack, Karrim 158
Essop, Salim 196
Ethiopia 73
Extension of University Education Act, 1959 69
Farquhar, Warrant Officer JC 195, 198
Fear (recruit) 164–165
Felipe VI, King 276
Fighting Talk 51
First, Ruth 46, 142, 162, 167, 184
Fischer, Bram 88
Fish, Liz 243, 280*39*
Flash 39
FLN (Nigeria) 1
Forbes, Ashley 229, 230, 233, 235, 237, 238
Fort Hare University College 69, 93
Franas, Jude 230
France 105, 151, 250
Freedom Charter 40–43, 45, 48, 105, 124, 131, 251
Frelimo 131, 142, 144, 161
French Anti-Apartheid Movement 174
Gallagher Estate, Midrand 264
Gandhi, Mahatma 3, 28–29, 46, 51, 61, 276
Gangat, Comrade Ismail 40–42
Gebuza 140, 141, 164, 181, 187 *see also* Nyanda, Siphiwe
General Assembly, United Nations 87
General Law Amendment Act, 1963 (90-day law) 73, 78, 119
German Invasion Plan 149
Ghetto Act 23
Giovanni's Room 8
Goldberg, Denis 74, 280
Goldreich, Arthur 80
Gordhan, Pravin 137, 138, 163, 177, 181
Government Gazette 50
Gqabi, Joe 120, 121, 152
Great Patriotic War 148
Green Book, The 152, 161
Grey Street, Durban 3, 18, 19, 36
Greyville, Durban 3, 17, 18, 36, 56, 136
Griggs Bookstore 55
Grobler, Colonel 77, 80, 197, 198
Group Areas Act, 1950 3, 17, 21, 22, 32, 180, 223
Groutville 48
Guardian, The 45, 92, 174
Gujarat, India 19, 24, 25, 64, 179
Gusmão, Xanana 255
Gwala, Harry 4, 120–123, 189, 284
Gyanendra, King 272
Hadhramaut, Yemen 25
Halimeh, Ali 158
Hammarsdale, Natal 83
Hanekom, Trish 209
Hani, Chris 69, 147, 152, 182
Harare Declaration, 1989 246
Harris, John 71
Hassan, Dr Ismail 283
Hatia Flats, Prince Edward Street 36

Hazrat Soofie Saheb 138
Heart Hospital, Pretoria 283
Henochsberg, Judge Edgar 50
Hertzog, JBM 27, 30
Hill, Ken 40
Hillbrow, Johannesburg 170
Himalaya Hotel 3, 20
Ho Chi Minh 255
Hogan, Barbara 209
Hoosen, Ayesha 36, 109, 169
Hoosen, Goolam 24
Hoosen, Shaenaaz 109–110
Horowitz, Donald L 30
House of Assembly 138
In Transformation Initiative (ITI) 272
India 24, 2830, 36, 64, 110, 157, 214, 220, 252, 261, 271, 276
Indian House of Delegates 138
Indian University College, Salisbury Island 69–70
Industrial and Commercial Workers' Union 32
Inkatha Freedom Party 58, 245
Institute for Global Dialogue 257, 263
Institute of the Non-Aligned Movement (IDASA) 257, 272
International Red Cross 128
International Relations subcommittee, ANC 274
Irish Anti-Apartheid Movement 236
Island Students Association (ISA) 70
Israel 261, 268
Jaffer, Kay 236
Jaffer, Mansoor 236
Jaffer, Mrs 235, 236
Jaffer, Zubeida 254
Jaffna 269
Jana, Priscilla 199–203, 218
Jardez, Xaviere 158
Jassat, Abdulhay 80
Jassat, Essop 42
Jenkins, Ivor 272
Jinnah, Muhammad Ali 28
Jobodwana, ZN 219
Johannesburg General Hospital 198

John Vorster Square 13, 14, 143, 195–203, 206, 208, 209, 224
John, Michael 20–21
Kabwe, Zambia 172–174, 182
Kajee, AS (Kohsaan) 66
Kallenbach, Hermann 46
Kamdar, Mahomed 137
Kamdar, Shaida 137
Kampala 264–265
Kapoor, Raj 3, 20
Kasrils, Eleanor 54–57, 74–76, 80, 264
Kasrils, Ronnie 55, 58, 61, 63–67, 74–77, 79, 88, 142, 144, 169, 184, 218–219, 264
Kathrada, Ahmad 'Kathy' 4, 74, 113, 226, 229, 243, 251, 264, 276, 280, 284
Kati, James 123
Kellerman, Major PA 95, 101, 104–105
Khama, Seretse 69
Khan, Abdul Majid 25
Khan, Cassim 23, 199
Khan, Habiba 20
Khan, Hafiza Bibi 25, 223
Khan, Mary 24, 92
Khan, Saffura 252, 260
Khan, Sam 32
Khan, Sarah Bibi 14
Khan, Zubeida 24
Khatri, Uma Devi 110
Khumalo, Vusi 218
Kilinochchi 269
King Edward VII Hospital, Durban 230
King, Martin Luther Jr 29
Kingswood College, Grahamstown 254
Kliptown, Soweto 41–42, 45, 105, 251
Kloof, Durban 74–77, 79
Kongwa, Tanzania 88
Kotane, Moses 57
Kriel, Ashley 234
Kroonstad Prison 208–209
Kruger, Jimmy 129–130
Kumar, Kishore 157
Kumari, Meena 3, 20

KwaDukuza 48
KwaZulu 58
KwaZulu-Natal 267
Laguna Beach 18 *see also* African Bathing Beach
Lakhani Chambers 18, 32
Lasich, Dr Angelo 179
Leader, The 223
Leeuwkop Prison 89, 92, 135, 263
'Left-wing' Childishness and the Petty-Bourgeois Mentality 62
Leftwich, Adrian 70–71, 217
Lekota, Mosiuoa 'Terror' 132, 220, 230–231, 233
Lenasia, Johannesburg 243
Lenin, Vladimir 57–58, 62, 147–151
Leninism 57, 58, 120, 124, 131
Leprosy Repression Act, 1891 91
Lesotho 54, 151, 162
Lewin, Hugh 71
Liberal Party 40, 71
Liberation Tigers of Tamil Eelam (LTTE) 269
Liberia 73
Lilliesleaf, Rivonia 73
Limpopo 168
Little Rivonia Trial 78
Long Journey of Clement Zulu, The 243
Long Walk to Freedom 62
Los Angeles Times 221
Lourens, Jansie 209
Lumumba, Patrice 148
Lusaka 8, 139–142, 145, 147–148, 151, 152, 153, 157, 161, 164, 172, 181, 182, 183–185, 214, 219, 232
Luthuli, Chief Albert 48–50, 62, 84, 152
Maaloula 274
Mabhida, Moses 50, 141, 152, 161
Machel, President Samora 161, 181
Macmillan, Harold 87
Madagascar 272
Madiba *see* Mandela, Nelson
Madikizela-Mandela, Winnie 234, 264, 280
Madras 24

Maduna, Penuell 136
Magano, Peter 120, 123
Maharaj, Mac 152, 161, 181, 261
Mahlangu, Solomon 159, 234
Mahlobe, Vusumuzi 230
Mahomed, Advocate Ismail 201, 214
Majola, Malusi 230
Major, John 279
Makana FA 127
Make, Cassius 141, 220
Makgothi, Henry 'Squire' 120–121, 123, 159
Makwetu, Clarence 121
Malan, DF 29–30
Malanazi *see* Malan, DF
Malkerns, Swaziland 165
Mandela, Nelson 1, 2, 8, 9, 32–33, 47, 51, 58, 61, 62, 69, 73, 74, 75, 93, 92, 95, 113, 131, 133, 138, 153, 184, 213, 229–235, 243, 245, 246, 251, 255, 259, 267, 274, 279–280, 283
Mandela, Zindzi 264
Mandla Judson Kuzwayo (MJK) unit 163, 170–171, 177
Mange, James 243–244
Mangena, Mosibudi 130, 133
Mangeshkar, Lata 157
Manning Rangers 3, 20
Manthata, Tom 230
Manzini 107, 140, 141, 142, 164–165, 1681, 181, 182, 188, 189, 190
Manzini Teacher Training College 188
Mao Tse-tung 255
Maoism 57, 272
Maphumulo, Khumbuzile 219
Maphumulo, Shadrack 2, 8, 91, 140, 163, 189, 190, 219–220
Marley, Bob 157
Marx, Karl 128
Marxism and the National Question 81
Marxist-Leninism 58, 120, 124, 131
Maseko, Mandla 163, 202, 213, 215, 216, 225, 229
Masemola, Jeff 106, 113
Masondo, Amos 131

Masondo, Andrew 93, 119–120
Mass Democratic Movement 133, 163
Matthews, Joe 50
Matthews, ZK 40
May Day protests 33
Mazimbu Liberation Camp 159
Mbabane 2, 8, 107, 168–169, 171, 187, 190, 240
Mbanjwa, Solomon 78, 82–83
Mbeki, Govan 74, 133, 229
Mbele, George 81
Mbokodo 141
McDougall, Gay 219
McFadden, Gavin 165
McFadden, Keith 165
McFadden, Percival 165
Mdingi, Leonard 57
Mdingi, Mzwandile Mcgloria 119, 123
Meer, Fatima 40
Meer, Ismail 40
Melbourne, New Zealand 240
Memela, Totsie 181, 218
Merebank, Durban 65
Meyer, Roelf 268–272
Meyiwa, Matthews 83, 232
Mgabela, Douglas 120
Mgcina, Ralph 164
Midmar Dam 77, 81
Military Intelligence (MI) 171–172
MK Durban Central Unit 64
Mkhwanazi, Johannes 'Joe' 218
Mlangeni, Andrew 74, 280
Mlokoti, Christopher 121
Modan, Mohamed Adam (Ebie's father) 24
Modise, Joe 152
Modise, Thandi 208, 255
Mogotsi, Mrs 200
Mohamed, Elaine 163
Mohamed, Jennifer 163
Mohamed, Julie 11
Mohamed, Professor Ismail 163, 201, 214
Mohamed, Yunus 93
Mohammed, Pine 19

Molefe, Popo 220, 230
Molobi, Eric 133
Moodley, Poomoney 54–55, 137
Moola, Max 19
Moolla, Mosie 80
Moonsamy, Kay 50, 153
Moonsamy, Kisten 67, 81, 130, 140
Morales, Evo 270–271
Morningside Hospital, Johannesburg 280
Morocco 1
Morogoro conference 35, 153
Morogoro, Tanzania 88, 159
Morris Seabelo Rehabilitation Centre (Quatro) 145
Moseneke, Dikgang 116, 127
Mothopeng, Zeph 121
Motlanthe, Kgalema 255, 271, 274
Motsepe, Godfrey 210
Motsoaledi, Elias 74, 213, 231, 237
Movement for the Liberation of Angola (MPLA) 155
Mozambique 8, 131, 139, 142–144, 145, 151, 161, 163, 167, 181–182, 184, 210, 215, 216
Mr X1 *see* September, Reggie
Msimang, Mendi 255
Msomi, Ordway 230
Mswati III, King 141, 142
Mthembi, Sankie 148
Mtolo, Bruno 74–78, 79, 8, 82, 217
Mtshali, Steven 74
Mugabe, Robert 69
Murray Bay 9, 91
Mustapha, Muhamad 145
Mxenge, Griffiths 88, 192–193
Myanmar 279
Naicker, Dr Gangathura Mohambry 'Monty' 29, 90
Naicker, George 87, 94, 111, 139–140, 145, 147–148, 152, 153, 188
Naicker, MD 64, 77
Naicker, MP 45, 47, 48, 51, 67
Naidoo, Indres 101–102, 119, 143, 145
Naidoo, MD 62, 64

Naidoo, Phyllis 49, 54–55, 80, 113, 162, 219–220, 236
Naidoo, Sadhan 81
Naidoo, Sha 81
Naidu, Kessie 224
Nair, Billy 67, 74, 81, 82, 85, 89, 91, 276
Nanabhai, Shirish 119, 127, 145
Natal Indian Congress (NIC) 18, 20, 26, 35, 37, 39, 66, 153
Natal Indian Youth Congress 85
Natal Provincial Notice 206, 1930 18
Natal Regional Command, MK 74, 80
Natal Urban Machinery 140–141
Nataller, Die 66
National Democratic Revolution (NDR) 59
National Executive Committee (NEC) 33, 147, 153, 174, 182, 218, 232, 245
National Geographic 265
National Party 27, 29, 30, 32, 35, 40, 42, 66, 130, 138, 233, 244, 250
National Socialist German Workers' Party (the Nazis) 30
National Union for the Total Independence of Angola (UNITA) 155, 157
National Union of South African Students (NUSAS) 70–71
Naude, Captain 97, 104, 193
Ndawonde, David 75–77
Ndlanzi, Sibusiso 230
Ndlovu, Curnick 61, 74
Nehru, Jawaharla 28–29
Nepal 271–272
Nepalese Communist Party 272
New Age 41, 45, 47, 48, 51, 63, 64, 65, 67, 68, 75
New Zealand Court of Appeal 240
Ngcobo, AB 48–49
Ngendane, Selby 116, 120–121
Ngudle, Looksmart 81
Nguqu, Bafo 230
Ngwenya, Muziwakhe 140 *see also* Zulu, Thami
Nhlanhla, Joe 148, 157
NIC Youth Congress 64
Nigeria 73, 260
Nkadimeng, John 142, 218, 280
Nkobi, Thomas (Comrade TG) 153
Nkomati Accord, 1984 181, 220
Nkrumah, Kwame 120
Nofomela, Almond 241
Non-European Unity Movement (NEUM) 51
Novo Catengue 154
Nqini, Zola 4, 105, 121, 123, 162, 284
NUSAS Loan Fund 70 *see also* Political Freedom Fund
Nyanda, Siphiwe 140–141, 164 *see also* Gebuza
Nyanda, Zweli 'Douglas' 141, 164
Nyerere, Julius 69, 159
Nzimande, Blade 255, 271
Nzo, Comrade Alfred 147–148, 152, 245
OAU Secretariat 174
Obama, Barack 279
Ocean Beach 18 *see also* Back Beach
Odessa, Soviet Union 88
Old Man Salot *see* Ebrahim, Moosa
Olivier, Professor SP 70
Operation Barbarossa 149
Operation Vula 182, 183, 185
Operation Vula 184, 237
Orange Free State 41
Organisation of African Unity (OAU) 47, 87, 158, 246
Orkin, Mark 224
Ostrovsky, Nikolai 4, 285
Oudh 24
Overport 19, 171, 177
Pachai, Bridglal 31
Pahad, Essop 10
Pakistan 24, 28, 36
Palace of Justice, Church Square 222
Palestine 158, 261, 268
Palestine Liberation Organisation (PLO) 158
Palmyra 274

Pan Africanist Congress (PAC) 9,
    46–50, 61, 63, 93, 102, 116, 119–
    123, 132–133, 147, 153, 158, 174,
    199–201, 220, 233, 241, 246–247,
    253, 264
Pandy, Begum 236
Pandy, Fatima 236
Pandy, Rabia 236
Pandy, Thoraya 236, 246
Pandy, Yasmina 235
Park Station, Johannesburg 71
Passtoors, Hélène 167–182, 183, 195,
    205–211, 236, 280
Paton, Alan 40
Patrice Lumumba University 148
Patriotic Front 246, 250, 253
Peer, Badsha 68
People's Republic of China 57, 255
People's United Democratic Movement
    (PUDEMO), Swaziland 165
People's World, The 45
Peres, Shimon 261, 268
Perumal, David 64, 68, 80
Phala, Alfred 232
Phantom of the Opera 253
Pietermaritzburg 51, 76, 83, 84, 89,
    91, 178
Piliso, Mzwai 152
Pillay, Booby (Sunny Singh) 220
Pillay, Ivan 140, 144, 145, 210
Pillay, Rajuluxmi 'Rajes' 140, 144, 145
Pillay, Siva 64, 113
Pillay, Thumba 82, 113
Pillay, TVR 140
Pine Street Post Office, Durban 111
Pine Valley, Mbabane, Swaziland 2, 8,
    187, 215
Pinetown, Durban 8
Pinochet, Augusto 209
Pokela, John 121
Pokhara 271
Political Freedom Fund 70 *see also*
    NUSAS Loan Fund
Political Military Committee,
    Swaziland 140

Politico-Military Council (PMC) 140
Pollsmoor Prison 74, 226, 229, 235
Poqo 63
Prabhakaran 269–270
Pretoria Central Prison 74, 173, 208,
    220
Pretoria East 263
Prinsloo, Harry 214–215
Prisoners' Association 127
Psychology Book on Sex 115
Public Safety Act, 1956 93
Pule, Ernest 156 *see also* Comrade
    T-Man
Quatro *see* Morris Seabelo
    Rehabilitation Centre
Qunu, Eastern Cape 279
Rabkin, Sue 143, 245
Radio Moscow 157
Rafi, Mohammed 157
Raj cinema 3, 19
Rajbansi, Amichand 230
Ramlakan, Vejay 230
Randeree, Dr 153–154
Rasool, Kaye 180
Rasool, Lambie 171
Raymonds, Cyril 164
Red Square 18, 37, 39–43, 148
Regional Political Military Councils
    (RPMCs) 140, 182
Renamo 142, 161, 168, 181, 182
Reservation of Separate Amenities
    Act, 1953 18
Reservoir Hills 8, 136, 137, 139, 177,
    178, 201
Riotous Assemblies Act, 1956 93
Rivonia Trial 78, 80, 83, 85, 95, 131,
    213, 231
Robben Island 2, 4, 8–10, 13, 64, 74,
    85, 86, 87–97, 102, 103, 105, 106,
    107, 109, 111, 112, 116, 119–125,
    129–133, 135–137, 143–144, 147,
    152–153, 173, 189, 199, 201, 219,
    220, 226–227, 229–238, 243, 246,
    252, 254, 258, 262, 264, 280, 283,
    284

Roef, Moulana 138
Roef, Shanaaz 138
Rossburgh 68
Royal Picture Palace 3, 19
Royal Swazi Police 162
Russian Revolution 148
SABC 157
Sachs, Albie 143, 162, 264, 273
Saloojee, Babla 81
Salot, Dawood 19–20
Salot, Eunice 20
Salot, Gloves 19–20
Salot, Lighty 19–20
Salot, Mascot 19–20
Sandton, Johannesburg 263
Sanjay, Kumar 220
Sanjee, Bobby 220
Sastri College 21, 45, 69
Sastri, Honourable VS Srinivasa 45
Satchwell, Kathy 206
Savage, Warrant Officer 193
Saville Street 18
Sayyed, Naeem 110
Scala cinema 3, 19
Schneider, Daniel 188, 219
Schoon, Brigadier Willem 192–193, 195, 241
Schoon, Jeanette (Curtis) 192
Sechaba 139, 153
Security Branch 136, 162, 172, 177–180, 191, 192, 215, 217
Sedibe, Glory Lefoshie 162, 216
Seedat, Dawood 41, 45
Sello, Kalakhi 54, 57
Separate Red Banner Kremlin Regiment 148
September, Dulcie 85, 151, 210
September, Reggie 119, 183
September, Vanessa 273
Sexwale, Anne 245 *see also* Vincent, Anne
Shah Jehan movie house 3, 19
Shaik, Moe 163, 171, 210, 220
Shaik, Shamim 171, 210, 220
Shaik, Yunis 170, 171, 210, 220

Shaka Zulu 24, 48, 140
Shankar, Ravi 2, 128
Sharpeville massacre 49, 53, 54, 63–64
Shell House 245
Shongwe, Queen Dzeliwe 141
Shree 420 3
Shubin, Vladimir 154
Sigwela, Ezra 130, 243
Silver Lakes, Pretoria 7
Simelane, Stalwart 40
Simons, Jack 153, 236
Singh, Anant 280
Singh, Jaydew Nasib 50
Singh, Sunny 64, 129, 143, 144, 220
Sisulu, Albertina 188, 221
Sisulu, Lindiwe 188, 202, 221
Sisulu, Walter 50, 58, 74, 133, 188, 229, 246
Sizani, Stone 131
Slovo, Joe 140, 142, 144, 152, 167, 182, 184, 245
Smuts, Prime Minister Jan 29, 66
Smyth, Lauren 258
Sobhuza II, King 141
Sobukwe, Robert 47, 69, 119
Socialist Republic of Vietnam 152, 255
Socialist Unity Party, New Zealand 174
Solomon Mahlangu Freedom College (SOMAFCO) 159
Soni, Shirish 171, 210
South African Coloured People's Organisation 37, 42
South African Communist Party (SACP) 46, 53–54, 57, 58, 63, 73, 75, 88, 139, 153, 174, 201, 210, 233, 236
South African Congress of Trade Unions (SACTU) 67, 122, 123
South African Council of Trade Unions 218
South African Defence Force (SADF) 141, 154, 174, 188, 214, 216
South African Indian Congress (SAIC) 29, 51, 53, 62
South African Non-Racial Olympic

Committee (SANROC) 90
South African Students Movement 130
South Sudan 272
Soviet Foreign Policy 115
Soweto, Johannesburg 41, 130, 132, 133, 154, 170, 171, 174, 181, 190, 279
Sparg, Marion 209
Sparks, Douglas 94, 120
Special Branch 164, 209
Sri Lanka 268–270
Stanger 48, 251
Star, The 173, 264
State and Revolution, The 62
State of Emergency 50, 54, 61, 258, 268
Steenkamp, Mr 77, 114
Stiles gang 3, 20
Street with No Name, The 20
Strijdom Square 222
Strydom, Barend 197, 222
Suliman, Ashraf 251
Sunninghill, Johannesburg 263
Suppression of Communism Act, 1950 37, 53, 93, 131, 240
Susan Kruger ferry 9, 91
Suttner, Raymond 198
Suzman, Helen 102
Swanepoel, Lieutenant Theunis 'Rooi Rus' 1, 196
Swaziland 2, 8, 107, 108, 139–142, 144–145, 147, 151, 161–165, 168–173, 175, 178–179, 181–182, 183–184, 187–190, 193, 195, 199–202, 210, 213–221, 233, 239–241, 243, 250, 252, 268
Sweden 143
Swedish Social Democratic Party 174
Syria 261, 274
Tambo, OR 61, 69, 140, 147, 152, 164, 167, 182, 185, 187, 216, 232, 234, 245
Tamil Tigers 270
Tfwala, Queen Ntombi 141
Thamilselvan, Suppayya Paramu 269
Thatcher, Prime Minister Margaret 219
Timol, Ahmed 143–144, 195–196
Timol, Mohammed 143–144
Transkei 57
Transvaal 25, 36, 43, 69, 120, 140, 191, 213, 215–216, 223, 247, 251
Transvaal Indian Congress 42
Transvaal Urban Machinery 140
Treason Trial, 1956 58, 220, 222, 230, 241
Tricameral Parliament 138, 230
Truth and Reconciliation Commission 164, 210, 270
Tsanine, Elise Augusto 142
Tshabalala, Dr Manto 159
Tshwete, Steve 10, 94, 120, 123, 133, 243
Tunisia 73
Uganda 73, 264
Umfana Kanina 24
Umgeni River 177
Umgeni Road, Durban 20, 55
Umgugu Reserve 187
Umkhonto we Sizwe (MK) 25, 48, 56, 62–65, 71, 75, 77, 82, 84, 88, 93, 124, 129, 131, 140, 152–159, 163–165, 167, 168, 171, 172, 173, 188, 190, 191, 206, 210, 213, 215, 216, 217, 224, 229, 234, 244, 252, 255, 277
Umkhonto we Sizwe Military Veterans Association 279
Umkhumbane 55 *see also* Cato Manor
UN Security Council 257, 275
UN Staff College, Turin, Italy 258
Uncle Charlie's Junction, Johannesburg 191
Union Buildings 263
Union of South Africa 25, 70
United Democratic Front 139, 163, 165
United Nations 28, 49, 87, 158
University of Cape Town 69

University of Durban-Westville 163
University of Lesotho 163
University of London 163
University of Natal 54, 69, 179
University of South Africa (Unisa) 113
University of the Western Cape 69, 163
University of the Witwatersrand, The 69, 90
University of Zambia 163
Unlawful Organisations Act, 1960 93
USSR 57, 215–216
Vahed, Akie 19
Valjee, Dr Ashwin 180
Valley of a Thousand Hills 76
Van der Walt, Louise 226
Van Leynseele, Brigitte 168–169, 177, 206
Van Leynseele, Fabrice 168
Van Leynseele, Philippe 168
Van Leynseele, Yves 168
Van Riebeeck, Jan 35
Vandeyar, Reggie 4, 43, 105, 284
Vetch's Pier 18
Victor Verster Prison 74, 229, 232–234
Victory Lounge 3, 20
Vincent, Anne 245 *see also* Sexwale, Anne
Vlakplaas 164, 191, 192, 217
Voice of America 157
Voortrekkers 63
Wajid, Arjum 255
Washington DC 203, 244
Waterford Kamhlaba United World College, Mbabane 168–169
Wattville, Benoni 145
Weekly Mail 179, 213
Wells, Cassia 107–108, 202, 203, 249, 250, 254
Wells, Julie 167
West German Anti-Apartheid Movement 174
Westville 8, 137, 163
Wethli, Ed 184
What Is to Be Done? 62
White Lady 9
Williams, Phumla 171, 246
Witness X *see* Mtolo, Bruno
Wolpe, Harold 80
Wynberg 10, 235, 254
Xuma, AB 27, 32–33
Yalta, Crimea 149
Yu Chin Chan Club 85
Yunus Mohamed and Associates 193
Zambia 8, 81, 139, 151, 163, 172, 173, 182, 184, 190
Zermatt 250, 284
Zimbabwe 151, 181, 205, 206, 246, 272
Zonge-Hwenha, Patience 272
Zulu, Clement 243244
Zulu, Joshua 83, 88
Zulu, Thami 140 *see also* Ngwenya, Muziwakhe
Zulu, Thami 140–141, 187
Zuma, Jacob 91, 123, 128, 142, 144, 161, 189, 217, 235, 263, 267, 275
Zwane, Dumisane 189